Economics,
Accounting,
and Property
Theory

Economics, Accounting, and Property Theory

David P. Ellerman
Boston College
and Industrial
Cooperative Association

LexingtonBooks
D.C. Heath and Company
Lexington, Massachusetts
Toronto

Library of Congress Cataloging in Publication Data

Ellerman, David P.
  Economics, accounting, and property theory.

  Bibliography: p.
  Includes index.
  1. Accounting. 2. Economics. 3. Property. I. Title.
HF5657.E54   1982   657'.73   82–47648
ISBN 0–669–05552–2

Copyright © 1982 by D.C. Heath and Company

Published simultaneously in Canada

Printed in the United States of America

International Standard Book Number: 0–669–05552–2

Library of Congress Catalog Card Number: 82–47648

Dedicated to my father and mother

Contents

Preface

This book has four primary goals:

1. to present the first modern *mathematical formulation of double-entry bookkeeping,*
2. to present a model of value accounting in accordance with the *Generally Understood Principles of Economics* (GUPE) as opposed to the *Generally Accepted Accounting Principles* (GAAP),
3. to use the mathematical double-entry formalism to develop the first successful model of *property accounting,* an objective accounting model that eschews all valuation by accounting directly in terms of property rights, and
4. to use the property-accounting machinery to show that a *fundamental logical gap* in neoclassical economic theory is the *neglect of appropriation* in production.

This book serves as an introduction to a new, or revived, type of economic theory, *property theory.* It cuts across a number of conventional disciplines such as economics, accounting, and jurisprudence. Only positive or descriptive property theory is considered here. The subject matter is the stocks and flows of property rights and obligations that change by transactions and by appropriations in production.

Some of the rudiments of descriptive property theory have been informally presented elsewhere (Ellerman 1980a). A more complete and rigorous development of the theory awaited the proper mathematical framework. The proper framework arose quite naturally out of the mathematical formulation of double-entry bookkeeping (see appendix). This formulation, using the *group of differences* from modern abstract algebra, is apparently the first complete modern mathematical treatment of double-entry bookkeeping. Since double-entry bookkeeping can thus be seen as the first presentation of the group-of-differences construction, the group is renamed the *Pacioli group* after the mathematician, Luca Pacioli, who first published the double-entry system in 1494. There are several generalizations that arise out of the mathematics such as double-entry vector accounting and double-entry multiplicative accounting.

Value accounting deals with the economic values of the stocks and flows of property rights and obligations. By developing double-entry value accounting in a rigorous mathematical fashion, it becomes clear how the formalism can be generalized to deal directly with the underlying property rights rather than just the value of the property rights. *Vector accounting* is the formal machinery for accounting for different types of quantities that cannot be meaningfully added together (like apples and oranges). Prices or other valuations are conventionally used to collapse the disparate quantities together to form accounting values. Vector accounting allows accounting to proceed without prices or other valuations. The *monetary unit* is not needed.

Vector accounting is the form and property theory is the content; the combination is *property accounting*. It is the formalization of property theory within a vector-accounting framework. Property accounting is the realization of an old idea that many accountants have thought to be impossible, namely, *accounting without valuation*. In one fell swoop, property accounting undercuts the valuation controversies of value accounting by keeping accounts directly in terms of the physical stocks and flows of property rights in a productive enterprise. Property accounting is also the foundation for a theory of the firm that deals with the institutional aspects of the firm that are neglected in price theory, such as the structure of rights involved in production.

A property-accounting model deals with the objective underlying physical skeleton of an economic enterprise. Cash-flow accounting, which deals objectively with stocks and flows of cash, is a fragment (the cash component) of the property-accounting model. Property accounting extends that objectivity to all types of property involved in an economic enterprise. Given a set of prices or values for the various types of commodities, a value-accounting model can be derived from a property accounting model by evaluating the property rights at the prices.

Our methodology derives from carrying over the general methods and techniques of mathematical model building from mathematical economics to accounting. The aim of *mathematical accounting* is not immediate practicality; the aim is the clear and distinct presentation of the first principles of the science of accounting.

A standard example of a simplified manufacturing enterprise is used throughout most of the exposition. The employees of a corporation produce one type of output by using raw materials and one type of machinery. In chapters 1, 2, and 3, the example is used to develop a market-value-accounting model. This model is intended as a model of value accounting from the viewpoint of economic theory. It is accounting in accordance with the Generally Understood Principles of Economics (GUPE), as opposed to the Generally Accepted Accounting Principles (GAAP). There are notable differences. Under GUPE, all assets are evaluated at their current market values. Input inventories are evaluated at current replacement costs, and output inventories are valued at selling price (or selling price minus selling costs, but there are no selling costs in the model). Thus revenues are recognized on a production basis rather than a sales basis in the market-value-accounting model.

A particularly difficult and controversial aspect of accounting (and economics) is the treatment of time and the interest rate. There are two equivalent ways to account for interest. In general, there are two ways to account for the use of a durable asset: (1) a flow treatment and (2) a stock treatment. In the flow treatment, using the asset is treated as using up the services (for example, machine-hours) of the asset. In the stock treatment, using the asset is treated as using up an asset of a given vintage and producing an asset with a one-time-period-older vintage. The two equivalent treatments of interest arise from taking the asset to be *capital value* itself. Models of value accounting according to economic theory (GUPE) will be presented using both treatments. Modern general equilibrium theory is in the spirit of the stock treatment since that theory considers the same commodity during different time periods are distinct commodities. Hence that treatment of interest will be employed in chapters 1, 2, and 3. In chapter 10, value accounting according to GUPE is derived using the simpler flow treatment.

In chapter 4, a conventional value-accounting model is developed for the sake of comparison. Final-goods inventories are valued or carried on the books at direct cost, and revenue is recognized on a sales basis. The effect of time is ignored except for debt capital.

The first four chapters do not use the mathematical treatment of double-entry bookkeeping. In chapters 5 and 6, that treatment is developed informally. A more rigorous development is contained in the appendix. The framework of double-entry vector accounting is presented in chapter 5. The double-entry method is applied in chapter 6 to perform additive algebraic operations on equations. Simple examples of scalar balance-sheet accounting and of vector accounting are presented. One consequence of the mathematical formulation of double-entry bookkeeping is the observation that the additive algebra of T-accounts is completely analogous to the ordinary multiplicative algebra of fractions. Multiplication replaces addition, and the numerator (top) and denominator (bottom) of fractions replace the left-hand side (debit) and right-hand side (credit) of T-accounts. Hence a complete multiplicative double-entry bookkeeping system can be developed. An example of this system is also presented in chapter 6 to see the double-entry principles at work in a new context.

In chapter 7, the formal development is halted temporarily so that the basic content of descriptive property theory can be summarized. An introductory model of property accounting is presented in chapter 7 just to give the flavor of the subject matter. The full-blown property-accounting model, which articulates descriptive property theory within a vector-accounting framework, is given in chapter 8. The model is somewhat complicated and impractical due to the treatment of commodities in different time periods as distinct commodities.

The treatment of time-differentiated commodities as distinct commodities is relaxed in chapter 9 where a simplified model of property accounting is worked out. Chapter 10 carries out the derivation of a value-accounting model from a property-accounting model by evaluating the property accounts at a given set of prices. The simplified property-accounting model is evaluated at the market prices to obtain the simplified market-value-accounting model. It is the treatment of value accounting according to GUPE that uses the simpler flow method of accounting for interest as the cost of the services of capital value. The simplified property and value models are more practical than the earlier models. A property-accounting model processes much more information than a value-accounting model, but, with sufficiently broad categories of property, it should be well within the capabilities of modern computers.

Chapter 11 gives some comments on selected topics in the accounting literature such as the meaning of *double-entry*—as opposed to *single-entry—bookkeeping* and *transactions matrices*. An analysis is also presented of the previous work in the direction of property accounting. Essentially the only significant work in this direction in the accounting literature is Professor Yuji Ijiri's pioneering work (1965, 1966, 1967) on *multidimensional physical accounting*. The analysis of his model (1966, 1967) shows that Ijiri clearly envisioned the idea of property accounting, but that the idea could not be developed successfully without the mathematical machinery of the Pacioli group.

The last two chapters, chapters 12 and 13, are devoted to applications of some of the insights gained through the development of property accounting. The major insight is the *discovery of appropriation*—as a phenomenon involved in normal production. Appropriation has been neglected and ignored in modern economic theory so that significant portions of neoclassical theory are vitiated by the "discovery" of appropriation. Indeed, the *neglect of appropriation* could be characterized as the *fundamental logical gap* in neoclassical economic theory. The last two chapters informally analyze some of the many errors that result from attempts to describe production while neglecting appropriation. From the property-theoretic viewpoint, production is appropriation.

The discovery of appropriation undermines some basic notions of capital theory and corporate-finance theory. It is shown that such notions as *capitalized value of an asset,* the *net productivity* or *marginal efficiency of a capital asset,* and the *capitalized value of a corporation* typically involve the assumption of present property rights to future commodities that only can be appropriated in the future. Future-produced goods have a present value, but it is quite another matter to claim the existence of present property rights to commodities produced in the future. Property to be appropriated in the future cannot be already owned now.

The difficulties surrounding appropriation emerge in accounting under the topic of *goodwill*. Goodwill, as defined in a standard model of corporate valuation under competitive conditions (Miller and Modigliani 1961), is shown to be the value of property that is appropriated in the future—so there is no present property right to (unpurchased or purchased) goodwill.

In the last chapter, the impact of the discovery of appropriation on neo-classical price theory is outlined. The neglect of appropriation is fatal whenever price theory strays from the special case of universal constant returns to scale. One major casualty is the attempt to show the existence of a competitive equilibrium with decreasing returns to scale and positive pure profits in a private-enterprise capitalist economy, for example, the *Arrow-Debreu model* of general equilibrium. Indeed, the machinery of competitive general equilibrium only works under uniform constant returns to scale in the marketable inputs and zero pure profits—because in that case appropriation can be ignored for the purposes of price theory. A competitive capitalist economy exhibiting decreasing returns to scale in the marketable inputs has a game-theoretically indeterminate outcome. As noted elsewhere (Ellerman 1980a), the very notions of supply-and-demand schedules will tend to dissolve in the acid of production arbitrage.

1 Economic Theory

Economic Theory and Accounting Theory

This book is an essay in accounting and economic theory. Accounting has been largely a practical art, not a theoretical science (while economics has tended to be just the opposite). As in so many fields, such as physics and economics, the mathematical formulation of the discipline is key to the development of the discipline as a science. The first full-blown mathematical formulation of double-entry bookkeeping is presented here (see appendix)—almost five centuries after another mathematician, Luca Pacioli (1494), first published the double-entry-bookkeeping method as a system. Accordingly, we shall present models that contribute to accounting as a theoretical science, not as an applied practice. In analogy with mathematical physics or mathematical economics, these models are part of *mathematical accounting.*

Mathematical accounting, like mathematical economics, aims at the construction of models that clearly and distinctly display the first principles of the science. The aim is not immediate practicality. Idealized assumptions are used whenever these will simplify and clarify the models. This approach always will beg some practical questions but we hope it will not beg the fundamental theoretical questions. For instance, our models in theoretical or mathematical accounting will assume perfect frictionless markets in which commodities may be bought or sold at the same uniform price, just as a model in physics might assume a frictionless inclined plane. Given the power and efficacy of mathematical model building in the other sciences, we need not justify or apologize for using these methods in accounting theory.

Ordinary double-entry accounting is *value accounting,* since it utilizes numbers representing the economic value of property rights and obligations. We shall first present a theoretical model of value accounting based on economic theory. Conventional value accounting is based on the *Generally Accepted Accounting Principles* (GAAP). These accounting principles are derived from an admixture of precedent, practical considerations, agreed upon conventions, tax and securities laws, and judicial rulings. In contrast, we will present a theoretical value-accounting model based on the *Generally Understood Principles of Economics* (GUPE).

1

Ours is not the first accounting model that presumes to be based on or to utilize *the* principles of economics (for example, Canning 1929; Edwards and Bell 1961; Alexander 1962). But, economics is not a settled and static discipline. For instance, S.S. Alexander (1962) and many other economists have argued that accountants should follow the lead of capital theory and value assets at the present capitalized value of the *future earnings of the asset.* This approach would imply adding (unpurchased) *goodwill* to balance sheets and recognizing changes in goodwill on income statements. Accountants, for a variety of reasons, have resisted these economists' suggestions about goodwill. In our opinion, the accountants are right. The economists' suggested treatment of goodwill and the aspects of capital theory behind the suggestions are incorrect, as will be explained in chapters 12 and 13. Given these controversies in economic theory (particularly, capital theory), it must be pointed out that our model or any other model of accounting based on the Generally Understood Principles of Economics is really based on the particular author's view of those principles.

Our model of value accounting according to economics is informed by the new type of accounting presented in later chapters. Property accounting or physical accounting, as opposed to value accounting, directly accounts for the underlying stocks and flows of property rights. There is no valuation in property accounting. When a valuation is *realized* by a market transaction, property accounting records the physical amounts of money (or equivalent credit) paid or received.

The aim of value accounting is to account for value. The accounting entity is provided with prices at which the entity's inputs and outputs may be bought and sold. The external institutions or agencies providing these prices could be, for example, competitive or noncompetitive markets, government agencies, or a larger entity containing the accounting unit as a segment. In any case, the prices will be called *market prices.* Market prices provide the ultimate standard for valuation in value accounting.

Conventional value accounting also tries to obey the *realization principle,* the principle that only realized market valuations should be recognized. Thus conventional accounting focuses on the historical entry costs for inputs and does not recognize the value of outputs until sold. Those transactions are the entry and exit market transactions that realize or verify the input and output valuations.

Conventional value accounting thus tries to satisfy at least two principles: (1) market valuation is the standard of valuation and (2) only realized market valuation is recognized. The problem is that the two principles cannot be simultaneously satisfied. By definition, there can be no realized market valuations *between* entry to and exit from the firm. Hence in any one accounting system, the description of the internal activities of the enterprise must sacrifice either market valuation or the realization principle.

Conventional value accounting has not clearly recognized the impossibility of simultaneously satisfying the two principles so it has utilized a confusing mixture of valuation and realization standards.

Property accounting provides the way out of the impasse. It is the natural domain for the realization principle since it deals exclusively with objective physical quantities. Hence there is a natural division of labor between value accounting and property accounting. Value accounting should deal with market valuation regardless of realization, and property accounting should deal with objectively verifiable physical quantities regardless of their valuation.

> In view of the confusion, emotionalism, and even mysticism that have surrounded the realization concept, this author suggests that accountants abandon the term. In its place, emphasis should be placed on the reporting of valuation changes of all types, although the nature of the change and the reliability of the measurement should also be disclosed. (Hendriksen 1977, pp. 183–184)

The realization principle should have no role in value accounting, and market valuations should have no role in property accounting.

Market-Value Accounting

The value-accounting model based on economic theory will rigorously follow the:

> *Market-Value Principle:* all the entity's assets and liabilities are valued according to their current market values regardless of whether the valuations are realized or not.

All changes in valuation are recognized when they occur. All inventories are carried at their current market value. Input inventories are carried at current costs as recommended by Edwards and Bell (1961), Sprouse and Moonitz (1962), American Accounting Association (1966), Chambers (1966), Sterling (1970), and many others. Output inventories are carried at selling price (or, in the presence of selling costs, at net selling price).

In the accounting literature, *cost* is often juxtaposed to value. That juxtaposition is a false dichotomy. The economically and managerially relevant cost is the current market value of the inputs. Any historical cost that differs from current market value is an irrelevant bygone. Managerial decisions based on outdated costs are apt to be erroneous. The verifiability of historical cost is beside the point. Irrelevant data are not made relevant by being verified.

It will be argued that a firm does not know unrealized market values.

This objection seems overstated. If a going concern is in the business of buying certain inputs to produce and sell certain outputs, then it should have a fair idea of the current input and output prices. Indeed, the measurement requirements for the market-value rule are the same as for the lower of cost or market rule. The objection has more weight for inventories or intermediate goods or goods in process—where estimates of market value should be used in place of the verified but irrelevant historical costs of the primary goods and services.

These measurement questions are, in any case, only of concern to accounting as an applied discipline, not as a theoretical science. Engineering is not theoretical physics. Engineering is based ultimately on physics, but engineers often apply rules of thumb and shortcut calculations rather than exact laws and employ estimates and approximations when precise measurements are too costly or are unavailable. These practices do not disprove or invalidate theoretical physics. There is a similar relationship between theoretical and applied accounting. The question of the theoretical definition of an accounting variable is distinct from the practical question of measuring or estimating the variable.

If all inventories are carried at current market value, then changes in value must be recognized when they occur—not when they are realized or verified by market transactions. Value changes occur in two ways: (1) price changes and (2) quantity changes. Price changes result in capital gains or losses such as inventory revaluations. Quantity changes occur in production: the inputs are used up and outputs are produced.

> The basic concept of revenue is that it is a flow process—the creation of goods and services by an enterprise during a specific interval of time. Paton and Littleton called it the product of the enterprise (Hendriksen 1977, p. 178)
>
> By definition, an expense is incurred when goods or services are consumed or used in the process of obtaining revenue. (Hendriksen 1977, p. 197)

The value of the inputs expires when the inputs are consumed in production, and the value of the outputs is created in production. Hence revenues and expenses should both be recognized on the same symmetrical basis, production.

Accounting for Interest

Time puts a difference on commodities. The *same* commodities at different times are economically distinct (but related) commodities. Apples today and apples tomorrow are like "apples and oranges." They cannot be meaningfully added together as if they were the same commodity.

Apples and oranges are physically incommensurate. Market prices provide a way that apples can be transformed into oranges by market exchange. Dollars (or any other good) now and dollars (or the same good) at the end of the year are distinct commodities like apples and oranges. A credit or loan transaction is an ordinary market exchange between commodities that are differentiated by delivery date rather than by other characteristics. Lending is the exchange of present value in return for future value and borrowing is the reverse. The market interest rate provides the intertemporal market exchange rate between present dollars and future dollars.

Our theoretical model of market-value accounting uses the highly simplified assumption that there is one risk-free interest rate r at which money may be borrowed or lent. The interest rate r is a decimal so $100r$ is the corresponding percent. The present amount of PV now-dollars trades on the market for $FV = PV(1 + r)^n$ dollars n years from now. This is the *law of discounting:*

$$FV = PV(1 + r)^n.$$

The reverse transformation is given by the *law of compounding:*

$$PV = FV/(1 + r)^n.$$

Conventional accounting (GAAP) treats credit or loan transactions unlike any other market transactions and treats interest unlike any other market price. Accounting according to economic theory (GUPE) systematically applies the precepts that intertemporal market exchange is an ordinary transaction between time-differentiated commodities and that the interest rate is an ordinary market exchange rate. Hence loan transactions should be accounted for like any other market transaction, as a simple value swap. A market exchange is, by definition, a trade in equal market values. Being a value swap, a market exchange should not itself generate any revenue or expense entries, although it might trigger the recognition of revenue on the basis of sales or trigger the expiration of the costs of inputs not charged to any inventories (for example, fixed overhead cash costs).

The basis of the problem is the conventional accounting practice of not compounding past-dollar amounts, such as beginning-of-the-year balance-sheet totals, into present terms for accounting calculations. Consider a loan with principal PV at the interest rate r to be paid off in one year with $(1 + r)PV$ year-end dollars. The loan balance would be carried on the books as PV beginning-of-the-year dollars prior to recording the loan payment of $(1 + r)PV$. If all of $(1 + r)PV$ were subtracted from PV, it would show a negative balance. Hence only $PV(1 + r) - rPV = PV$ is applied as a principal reduction and the remaining rPV is charged as an interest expense. The mistake is to carry the loan balance at PV beginning-of-the-year dollars on the year-end books. All year-beginning dollar amounts should be compounded by $(1 + r)$ into the market equivalent year-end dollar amounts for the year-end calculations. Then the year-end balance would be $(1 + r)PV$ year-end dollars and it would be exactly canceled with the loan payment of $(1 + r)PV$ year-end dollars, without any expense entry being generated.

Consider another loan in the amount PV at the annual interest rate r to be amortized in n equal annual payments of PMT. The market exchange is PV now-dollars in return for the series of n payments PMT. Hence they have the same market value, so in terms of now-dollars:

$$PV = PMT/(1 + r) + PMT/(1 + r)^2 + \ldots + PMT/(1 + r)^n.$$

Suppose the loan is made at time $t = 0$. Let $B(t)$ be the postpayment balance due on the loan at time t in time t dollars for $t = 0, 1, \ldots, n$. Prior to the time t payment, the amount due is $(1 + r)B(t - 1)$, so the balance due after the t-th payment is:

$$B(t) = (1 + r)B(t - 1) - PMT.$$

At the boundaries of $t = 0$ and $t = n$, we have the conditions $B(0) = PV$ and $B(n) = 0$.

The usual convention for arriving at the principal and interest portions of the t-th payment PMT is obtained by rearranging the last equation as follows:

$$PMT = (1 + r)B(t - 1) - B(t)$$
$$= rB(t - 1) + [B(t - 1) - B(t)]$$
$$= \text{Interest} \quad + \text{Principal}.$$

If time is correctly accounted for then it is not necessary to divide loan payments into principal and interest portions in the first place. In the loan example, the time 0 loan balance PV is not conventionally reexpressed at time 1 as $(1 + r)PV$ time 1 dollars. It is expressed on the balance sheet as simply PV dollars prior to the first payment PMT. If the first payment PMT and the subsequent payments PMT were all subtracted from PV as the loan was paid off, then the amount due on the loan would be driven to zero long before the payments were finished. Hence there is the conventional need to treat only a portion of each payment as a principal reduction with the remainder being expensed as interest.

Accountants are accustomed to discounting future-dollar amounts into present terms, but the symmetrical compounding of past values into present values has been largely neglected. Yet accounting is largely concerned with relating the past to the present. The key to the proper treatment of interest is the systematic compounding of past-dollar amounts into present terms for accounting calculations. Both sides of the beginning-of-the-year balance-sheet equation:

$$\text{Assets} = \text{Liabilities} + \text{Net Worth}$$

must be compounded by $(1 + r)$ to maintain it as an equation prior to the year-end calculations. All the asset, debt, and net-worth values must be reexpressed in year-end dollars so the year-end accounting will deal only with oranges rather than apples and oranges. The compounding does not represent a transaction. It only expresses the same beginning-of-the-year balance sheet in a new unit of account, year-end dollars instead of beginning-of-the-year dollars.

With compounding in the loan example, the prepayment time 1 amount of the loan *on the balance sheet* is $(1 + r)PV = (1 + r)B(0)$. Then the payment *PMT* can be subtracted to yield the postpayment balance-sheet amount of the loan as $B(1) = (1 + r)B(0) - PMT$. Similarly at time t, the prepayment balance of the loan on the balance sheet is $(1 + r)B(t - 1)$, and the postpayment balance is $B(t) = (1 + r)B(t - 1) - PMT$. The last payment exactly reduces the balance to zero; that is, $(1 + r)B(n - 1) - PMT = B(n) = 0$. The practice of always compounding past balance-sheet amounts into present terms eliminates the need to treat part of the payments as interest expense. Each payment is all loan repayment (that is, all balance reduction) and there are no interest expenses generated by the loan payments—as one would expect from a quid pro quo market transaction.

A firm might be a creditor as well as a debtor. Proper accounting does not require that loan payments by or to the firm be split into principal reductions and interest portions with the latter treated as either interest expense or interest revenue. The treatment of loans to the firm should be mirrored in the treatment of loans by the firm. If an account or note receivable in the amount PV now-dollars at the interest rate r is paid off in $(1 + r)PV$ year-end dollars, that is a straight asset swap that should have no effect on net income. The beginning-of-the-year balance-sheet asset value PV is compounded to $(1 + r)PV$ for the year-end calculations and then it is canceled by the $(1 + r)PV$ payments. Correct interest accounting involves no interest expense in loan payments by the firm and no interest income or revenue in loan payments to the firm. A market exchange is a value swap that should not generate any effect on net income.

It is often convenient to consider the right-hand side of the balance sheet (Liabilities and Net Worth) as the *sources* of capital, while the left-hand side (Assets) represents the *uses* of capital. Conventional accounting treats interest as an expense associated with a particular source of capital, debt capital. From the economic viewpoint, a debt transaction is a market exchange that itself generates no expense entries. A debt transaction can be construed as the purchase of capital services, and the purchase of capital services or the purchase of any other input is not itself an expense. It is the use of the capital; that is, the using up of capital services, that should generate the expense entry, and that use is independent of the source of the capital in debt or equity. Hence interest expenses are associated with the uses of capital, the left-hand side of the balance sheet, not with the sources of capital on the right-hand side, such as debt or equity.

The conventional wisdom is that interest is the cost of using debt capital. It is held that, according to economic theory, interest is the implicit opportunity cost of using equity capital, so equity interest should be expensed like debt interest even though the equity-interest expense is not *realized* in a market transaction. Strictly speaking, both views are incorrect since debt and equity are not uses of capital. One does not *use* debt or equity capital. One uses cash or other embodiments of capital that had their source in debt or equity financing. Interest is the cost of using capital—regardless of its source. Hence interest expenses will be associated with the uses of capital, the assets listed on the left-hand side of the balance sheet, that are being used by the firm.

In the development of the market-value model, we shall see how an interest-expense term emerges in the accounting treatment of all the present assets the firm is using—such as cash, the inventories, and the fixed assets. If instead of using some capital, it is loaned out to others in interest-bearing notes, then the loan payback completes a market transaction that generates no interest-expense or interest-revenue entries. Total asset value can be represented as the sum of: (1) the value of the present assets being used by the firm, plus (2) the value of the capital loaned to others, the notes receivable, and other debts owed to the firm. The total interest expense will be the interest on the first part, the value of the present assets being used by the firm. Hence the net reduction to net income due to interest could be represented as the interest on all the assets minus the interest on the notes receivable; that is:

Assets Interest − Notes-Receivable Interest.

Robert N. Anthony (1975, 1978) has obtained the same results concerning accounting for interest by following a different line of reasoning. Anthony uses the conventional treatment of debt interest as an expense but argues that interest on equity should also be treated as an expense. Moreover, he uses the conventional accounting of interest on notes receivable as revenue. By his reasoning, the net reduction to net income due to interest is therefore:

Debt Interest + Equity Interest − Notes-Receivable Interest.

Since Assets equals Debt plus Equity, our results about accounting for interest coincide with Anthony's results.

There are two equivalent ways to account for interest. In general there are two equivalent ways to account for the use of a capital asset: (1) the flow treatment and (2) the stock treatment. In the flow treatment, using the asset is treated as using up the services of the asset (for example, machine-hours or dollar-years). In the stock treatment, using the asset is treated as converting the asset from a given vintage to a one-time-period-older vintage. The two equivalent treatments of interest arise by taking the asset to be the most general asset, capital value itself. In the stock treatment, now-dollars (present capital values) are differentiated from year-from-now dollars (future capital values), and the interest rate determines the rate of exchange between these two commodities. In the flow treatment, the interest rate is the cost of the flow of the capital services, dollar-years.

Michio Morishima has noted the two alternative methods of accounting for capital assets. He calls the flow and stock treatments, respectively, *neoclassical accounting* and *von Neumann accounting* (1973, p. 164 footnote 2). David Gale (1973) uses a similar principle regarding the equivalence of two ways of treating interest.

Modern general-equilibrium theory (for example, Debreu 1959) treats the same type of commodities at distinct times as distinct commodities, which is in the spirit of the stock treatment. This stock treatment, with time-differentiated commodities, will be used in the market-value-accounting model developed in chapters 1, 2, and 3, and in the full-blown property-accounting model of chapter 8. The simplified property- and market-value-accounting models of chapters 9 and 10 are obtained by switching to the simpler flow treatment, which does not utilize time-differentiated commodities. The conventional accounting treatment of interest, extended by Anthony to include equity interest, is a flow treatment.

Capital Theory and Accounting

In this section, we consider the role of interest and depreciation in accounting for fixed assets. The economics of time in general and the economic theory of durable assets in particular is known as *capital theory*. Capital-theoretic notions are used in managerial finance analysis, for example, capital-budgeting techniques (for instance, Bierman and Smidt 1960 or

Weston and Brigham 1971), but these concepts have not been consistently integrated into conventional accounting practice.

A sequence of n annual one-dollar payments beginning at the end of the year would exchange on the market for the present value:

$$a(n,r) = 1/(1 + r) + 1/(1 + r)^2 + \ldots + 1/(1 + r)^n.$$

In financial arithmetic, this quantity $a(n,r)$ is called the *present value of an ordinary annuity of one*. For nonzero r, it can be expressed as:

$$a(n,r) = (1 - 1/(1 + r)^n)/r.$$

A loan with the principal value PV could be paid off with the sequence of n annual payments of:

$$PMT = PV/a(n,r)$$

since the present value of those payments is $PMTa(n,r) = PV$.

Consider a machine or other capital asset that has a market price when new of C, that yields K units of capital services (for example, machine-hours) per year for n years, and has a resale or scrap value of S after n years. With the assumption of no maintenance costs, let R be the rental-per-unit capital services so it can be rented or leased for RK a year (paid at the end of the year).

The same real stream of capital services, K units per year for n years, can be obtained in two ways: (1) by purchasing, using, and reselling the asset or (2) by renting the asset. The discounted present value of the financial outlay for the buy option is:

$$C - S/(1 + r)^n.$$

The discounted present value of the financial outlay for the lease option is:

$$RK/(1 + r) + RK/(1 + r)^2 + \ldots + RK/(1 + r)^n = RKa(n,r).$$

Any rational system of valuation would not assign different values to the same commodities in different legal packages. In particular, competitive arbitrage between buy and lease markets would enforce equality between the two outlays that purchase the same real stream of capital services:

$$C - S/(1 + r)^n = RKa(n,r).$$

Hence, the new machine price C can be expressed as the discounted present value of the rentals and the scrap value: $RKa(n,r) + S/(1 + r)^n$.

After m years of use, a new depreciable asset is transformed into a vintage m asset. More equations relating the buy and lease outlays can be obtained for assets of each vintage. Let $C(m)$ be the market price of a vintage m machine so $C(0) = C$ and $C(n) = S$. The remaining stream of $n - m$ years of capital services can be obtained with the outlay of the present value $C(m) - S/(1 + r)^{(n - m)}$ or the outlay with the present value RKa $(n - m,r)$. Hence competitive valuation would enforce the equation:

$$C(m) = RKa(n - m,r) + S/(1 + r)^{(n - m)}.$$

To obtain the machine's services for a single year, the firm could rent it for RK (no maintenance) or the firm could borrow money to buy a machine of vintage $m - 1$, use it, sell it as a vintage m machine, and pay back the loan with interest. The resale obtains $C(m)$ while $(1 + r)C(m - 1)$ is needed to pay off the loan so the net cost of the machine's services for the year is:

$$(1 + r)C(m - 1) - C(m) = [C(m - 1) - C(m)] + rC(m - 1).$$

Again competitive arbitrage would enforce the equality of the two valuations of a year's services:

$$RK = [C(m - 1) - C(m)] + rC(m - 1).$$

Economic depreciation is the opposite of appreciation. It is the decrease in the market value of an asset as it is used and thus as it increases in vintage. For a vintage $m - 1$ machine, the *economic depreciation* for a year's use is $C(m - 1) - C(m)$. The interest-carrying charge on the value of the asset is $rC(m - 1)$. Hence the previous equation is:

$$\text{Rental} = \text{Depreciation} + \text{Interest}.$$

In the presence of maintenance costs, a maintenance term could be added to the right-hand side or the rental could be interpreted as net of maintenance costs.

A rational accounting system, like any rational system of valuation, should not account differently for the same commodities obtained in different ways. Yet conventional accounting treats the use of capital services differently depending on whether the asset yielding the services is purchased or leased. If the machine is rented, the rental RK is expensed. If the machine is owned, the depreciation is expensed. However, instead of treating the interest as the cost of a *use* of capital value, present accounting practice treats interest as an expense associated with a certain *source* of capital, namely, debt capital. Interest can be expensed only for debt capital. Thus interest on the machine's capital value would be expensed if the machine were purchased with debt financing but not with equity financing. However, the source of the capital value in debt or equity should be quite irrelevant to the interest expense. It is the use of the capital value $C(m - 1)$ for a year's time that requires the interest expense $rC(m - 1)$.

Depreciation accounting has wandered far afield from the basic idea of depreciation as reflecting the fall in the value of a durable asset over a time period. The use of a variety of economically ad hoc depreciation procedures and accelerated-depreciation tax gimmicks has undermined the interpretation of book amounts as serious appraisals of asset values. The book amounts are seen more as mere reservoirs of future tax deductions.

There is one method of depreciation that, when properly applied, yields the correct economic depreciation. That method is the *annuity method* of depreciation (for example, Gordon and Shillinglaw 1969, pp. 333–335; Edwards and Bell 1970, pp. 176–179). The annuity method is sometimes applied to a capital asset by using a *quasi rent* as the asset's annual yield and by using an internal rate of return as a measure of the asset's percentage yield. However, we shall see in chapter 12 that the concepts of an asset's quasi rent and internal rate of return (the so-called marginal efficiency of capital) impute certain future property rights to the asset that in fact are not a part of the ownership rights of the asset. The annual market yield is the rental RK (or net rental with maintenance costs) and the market percent rate of return is the interest rate r.

Starting with the original cost $C(0)$ of the machine in the previous example, the annuity method subtracts the interest term $rC(0)$ from the rental RK to yield the depreciation $RK - rC(0)$. Hence the new book value of the asset is:

$$C(0) - [RK - rC(0)] = (1 + r)C(0) - RK = C(1),$$

which is the market value of a one-year-old machine by the previous arbitrage enforced equation relating machine-rental and purchase markets. Starting with a machine with the value $C(m - 1)$, the depreciation is $RK - rC(m - 1)$ so the new value is:

$$C(m - 1) - [RK - rC(m - 1)] = (1 + r)C(m - 1) - RK = C(m),$$

the market value of a vintage m machine. Thus if the annuity method is properly used to compute the depreciation and asset's book value, then:

$$\text{Book Value} = \text{Market Value}$$
$$C(m - 1) - [RK - rC(m - 1)] = C(m),$$

and

$$\text{Annuity-Method Depreciation} = \text{Economic Depreciation}$$
$$[RK - rC(m - 1)] = C(m - 1) - C(m).$$

2 The Market-Value-Accounting Model

General Description

The principle of evaluating all assets and liabilities at market value will be used to construct a theoretical model of value accounting. To keep the model uncomplicated, we assume the corporation manufactures one type of output using as inputs raw materials, the services of fixed equipment or machinery, and, of course, labor. The fixed equipment is assumed to be one machine of vintage $m - 1$ (as considered in chapter 1). All other assets, such as cash, final goods, and raw materials, will be inventoried. No goods-in-process inventory will be used. The accounting time period under consideration goes from time T to time $T + 1$. The time period could be a month, a quarter, a year, or any other convenient period, but we will call it a *year*. Except for occasional remarks about the effect of price changes, we will simplify the model by assuming constant prices.

All assets, such as the current-asset inventories and the fixed assets, are carried on the books at market value.

> There is a difference here between accounting and economics. In economics (and in fact), the manufacturing process is regarded as creating value, and this value includes an allowance for profit, but in financial accounting only the *costs* of manufacture are recognized as adding to the value of the product during the manufacturing cycle; all the profit (that is, the increase in the owners' equity) is recorded at the time of sale. (Anthony 1970, pp. 62–63)

Thus final-goods inventories are carried at market value instead of cost. On the input side, the raw-materials inventories are carried at current market cost, which is called *replacement cost* (see, for example, Revsine 1973). Except in the treatment of interest, the difference between replacement- and historical-cost methods will not show in our model due to the assumption of constant prices.

If value is both used up and created in the production process, then both expenses and revenues should be recognized on a production basis. By recognizing revenues on a production as opposed to a sales basis (see, for example, Burns and Hendrickson 1972, pp. 384–387), the accounting model establishes symmetry between revenues and expenses, between inputs and outputs. The expenses and revenues are, respectively, the values of the inputs used up and the outputs produced by the internal operations of the firm. The external transactions of purchasing inputs and selling outputs do not generate expense or revenue entries, but the correct amounts of raw-material expense and revenues can be obtained from the raw-material purchases and final-goods sales figures by correcting for inventory investment or disinvestment.

In the previous section on capital theory, it was emphasized that the trade of one dollar now for $1 + r$ dollars a year from now is an ordinary market exchange. Capital value is being rented or, equivalently, the use of the services of capital value (abstractly, the command over resources) is being bought and sold. If financial capital is viewed as a capital good, then, since it has no depreciation or maintenance, we have: Rental equals Interest. When revenues and expenses are being recognized on a production basis, the purchase or sale of commodities does not itself generate expense or revenue entries. In particular, this rule applies when the commodity bought or sold is the use of the services of financial capital. Thus, when the firm borrows capital and pays it back with interest, that interest payment is just the market price for those capital services. That purchase does not generate an expense entry any more than the mere purchase of any other input. It is the use of capital services over the time period that creates the interest expense, and that use is independent of the source of the capital in debt or equity.

Similar conclusions hold concerning revenues. When the firm loans out financial capital by depositing its cash reserves, making short-term investments, or extending credit, the interest payments received are simply the market price of those capital services. Since revenues are being recognized on a production basis, not a sales basis, those interest payments do not generate revenue entries. However, when there is a change in the interest rate, then any balance-sheet item showing the present value of future receipts or payments would be revalued leading to a capital gain or loss. Such capital gains or losses will not appear in this model since we are assuming constant prices.

The Revenue and Expense Definitions

Since we are explicitly accounting for the passage of time, assumptions must be made about the timing of transactions. We will account for all transactions within the time period from time T to $T + 1$ as if they occurred at the end of the period. The debits and credits from the transactions and adjusting entries change the accounts in the balance-sheet equation at time T

to yield the balance-sheet equation at time $T + 1$. But the transactions are timed at time $T + 1$ while the accounts in the time T balance-sheet equation are in terms of time T dollars. By multiplying all balance-sheet accounts at time T by $1 + r$, the same equation is expressed in terms of time $T + 1$ dollars. Then the debits and credits stated in terms of $T + 1$ dollars can be applied meaningfully to yield the new balance-sheet equation at time $T + 1$.

The inventory calculations will utilize a mathematical identity called the *stock-flow equation:*

Beginning Stock + Inflow = Outflow + Ending Stock.

The stock-flow equation always has two versions, as an equation of physical quantities and as an equation of value quantities. Both versions will be used.

As raw-material expenses are being recognized on a production basis (that is, as the materials are being used up in production), those expenses can be computed from raw-material purchases by correcting for inventory investment. The raw materials, like any other commodities, at different times will be treated as distinct but related commodities. The payment upon delivery-price-per-unit raw material is assumed constant at P'. However, if delivery is one time period before payment, the price is $(1 + r)P'$. Raw materials a period ago and raw materials now are distinct commodities with the respective prices $(1 + r)P'$ and P' in year-end dollars. The holding of raw-materials inventory for a time period converts the one commodity into the other.

Let $RM(T)$ be the number of physical units of raw materials in the inventory at time T. It has the value $P'RM(T)$ at time T and the value $(1 + r)P'RM(T)$ at time $T + 1$. Let X' be the raw-material purchases during the period (inflow) so $X = RM(T) + X' - RM(T + 1)$ is the physical amount used up in production during the period (outflow). The raw-material expense is computed as:

Outflow = Inflow + Beginning Stock − Ending Stock,

(that is, the inflow corrected for net-stock investment) when all quantities are valued in year-end dollars.

Raw-Materials Purchases	=	$P'X'$
Beginning Raw-Materials Inventory	=	$(1 + r)P'RM(T)$
− Ending Raw-Materials Inventory	=	$- P'RM(T + 1)$
Raw-Materials Expense	=	$rP'RM(T) + P'X.$

Thus the raw-material expense to be charged to the period's operations is $P'X = P'[RM(T) + X' - RM(T + 1)]$, the value of the raw materials used up in production plus $rP'RM(T)$, the interest-carrying charge on the capital value of the beginning raw-materials inventory. A similar interest term will appear in the other inventory calculations.

Cash, like all the current assets, is treated formally as an inventory. Since cash is neither produced nor used up in production, the only expense item generated by the cash inventory is the interest-carrying charge on the capital value embodied in the cash inventory. Let $CASH(T)$ be the balance at time T. Let $NCF(T)$ be the net cash flow (inflow minus outflow) during the time period from T to $T + 1$ (with all transactions timed at the end of the period). Thus $CASH(T + 1) = CASH(T) + NCF(T)$. The cash price of cash is one, but the price at the end of the period of a dollar at the period's beginning is $1 + r$. The cash expense is the value that went into the cash inventory but never exited in the cash expenditures or ending cash inventory:

Beginning Cash Inventory	$=$	$(1 + r)CASH(T)$
Net Cash Flow	$=$	$NCF(T)$
$-$ Ending Cash Inventory	$=$	$-CASH(T + 1)$
Cash Expense	$=$	$rCASH(T).$

Since revenue is being recognized on a production basis, the revenue (and the expense item associated with final goods) can be computed from the sales of final goods by correcting for inventory disinvestment. Let P be the unit price of final goods and let Q' be the number of units sold during the time period. Let $FG(T)$ be the number of physical units in the final-goods inventory at time T. Hence $Q = FG(T + 1) + Q' - FG(T)$ is the number of physical units of output produced during the period. The revenue and final-goods inventory interest-carrying charge for the period's operations can be computed as follows:

Sales	$=$	PQ'
Ending Final-Goods Inventory	$=$	$PFG(T + 1)$
$-$ Beginning Final-Goods Inventory	$=$	$-(1 + r)PFG(T)$
Revenue $-$ Final-Goods Interest Charge	$=$	$PQ - rPFG(T).$

The expense and revenue items so far considered are associated with the current assets. We are assuming that the only fixed asset is a machine that is of vintage $m - 1$ at time T. The operations of the time period convert the vintage $m - 1$ machine worth $C(m - 1)$ in time T dollars into a vintage m machine worth $C(m)$ in time $T + 1$ dollars. Hence the expense associated with it, computed in time $T + 1$ dollars, is:

Fixed Equipment Purchases	$=$	0
Beginning Fixed Equipment	$=$	$(1 + r)C(m - 1)$
$-$ Ending Fixed Equipment	$=$	$-C(m)$

Fixed Equipment Expense	$=$	$[C(m - 1) - C(m)] + rC(m - 1)$
	$=$	Depreciation + Interest.

We will group all labor together and assume L units of labor are performed during the period. The wage rate is W (paid at the period's end), so the labor expense is WL. Ordinarily any input that is not prepaid, inventoried, or purchased on credit, such as labor, would be expensed as it is purchased. However, to keep separate the purchase of such an input from its use in production, we will introduce an intermediate account, *Labor* in this case, to be debited when the input is purchased and credited when the input is used in production. It can be thought of as an inventory account that ordinarily would have a zero balance at the beginning and end of each period:

Labor Purchases	$=$	WL
Beginning Labor	$=$	0
$-$ Ending Labor	$=$	0

Labor Expense	$=$	$WL.$

Turning to the liabilities side of the balance sheet, we will assume a very simple debt structure. At time T, there is only one debt outstanding, which will be paid off with two equal payments of D dollars at times $T + 1$ and $T + 2$. Thus the discounted present value of the debt at time T is:

$$D(T) = D/(1 + r) + D/(1 + r)^2.$$

Leaving aside the debt payment D at $T + 1$ for the moment, the passage of time does not generate any expense entry at constant interest rates. As time passes from T to $T + 1$, the old debt $D(T)$, worth $(1 + r)D(T)$ in time $T + 1$ dollars, is replaced by the discounted present value of the remaining payments, $D + D/(1 + r)$, which equals $(1 + r)D(T)$. The current payment D is made so the new balance-sheet debt is: $D(T + 1) = D/(1 + r)$. The expense entry associated with the debts is computed in time $T + 1$ dollars as follows:

Debt Payment	$=$	D
Ending Debt Value	$=$	$D(T + 1)$
$-$ Beginning Debt Value	$=$	$-(1 + r)D(T)$

Debt Expense	$=$	$0.$

As noted before, there is no expense associated with paying off a debt with interest—at constant interest rates.

If the interest rate had decreased from r to r' at time $T + 1$, the discounted value $D(T + 1)$ would change to $D/(1 + r')$ and there would be a positive debt expense of $D[1/(1 + r') - 1/(1 + r)]$. The nature of that debt expense would be a capital loss not an interest expense. In the present model, all prices are constant so such a capital-loss term would not appear.

The Economic Profit

The *economic profits* $\pi(T)$ (also known as *pure profits*) of the firm for the time period from time T to $T + 1$ are the revenues minus the expenses:

$$\pi(T) = PQ - rPFG(T) - rCASH(T) - P'X - rP'RM(T)$$
$$- [C(m - 1) - C(m)] - rC(m - 1) - WL.$$

On the asset side of the balance sheet, there are the cash, final-goods, and raw-materials inventories and the fixed asset or machine. The gross book value of all the assets at time T is:

$$GBV(T) = CASH(T) + PFG(T) + P'RM(T) + C(m - 1).$$

At time $T + 1$, the gross book value is:

$$GBV(T + 1) = CASH(T + 1) + PFG(T + 1) + P'RM(T+1) + C(m).$$

Using the equation for $GBV(T)$, the economic profits can be rewritten as:

$$\pi(T) = PQ - rPFG(T) - rCASH(T) - P'X - rP'RM(T)$$
$$- [C(m - 1) - C(m)] - rC(m - 1) - WL$$

$$= PQ - P'X - WL - [C(m - 1) - C(m)] - r(CASH(T)$$
$$+ PFG(T) + P'RM(T) + C(m - 1))$$

$$= PQ - P'X - WL - [C(m - 1) - C(m)] - rGBV(T).$$

The economic profit is the net market value created in production, the value of the products produced minus the value of all the services and commodities consumed by the operations of the corporation for the time period. The interest charge $rGBV(T)$ is for consuming the services of the capital value $GBV(T)$, regardless of the source of that value in debt or equity. Since $rGBV(T) = rD(T) + rNBV(T)$, the total interest charge is equal to the conventional debt interest plus what Anthony (1975, 1978) calls *equity interest*. Our treatment of interest thus agrees with Anthony's conclusion that there should be an interest expense equal to debt interest and equity interest.

Let $DIV(T)$ be the dividends declared and paid out at time $T + 1$. Let $SUBS(T)$ be the net subscriptions (subscriptions minus redemptions) for shares during the time period. They are paid in at time $T + 1$. The net cash flow $NCF(T)$ for the time period can now be computed as:

$$NCF(T) = PQ' - P'X' - WL - D - DIV(T) + SUBS(T),$$

so $CASH(T + 1) = CASH(T) + NCF(T)$. The gross book value GBV $(T + 1)$ of all the assets at $T + 1$ can be expanded as follows:

$$
\begin{aligned}
GBV(T + 1) &= CASH(T + 1) + PFG(T + 1) + P'RM(T + 1) + C(m) \\
&= CASH(T) + NCF(T) + PFG(T) + P(Q - Q') \\
&\quad + P'RM(T) + P'(X' - X) + C(m) \\
&= [CASH(T) + PFG(T) + P'RM(T) + C(m - 1)] \\
&\quad + NCF(T) + P(Q - Q') + P'(X' - X) + C(m) \\
&\quad - C(m - 1) \\
&= GBV(T) + NCF(T) + P(Q - Q') + P'(X' - X) \\
&\quad - [C(m - 1) - C(m)] \\
&= \text{Gross Book Value at } T + \text{Gross Investment} \\
&\quad - \text{Depreciation} \\
&= \text{Gross Book Value at } T + \text{Net Investment} \\
&= \text{Gross Book Value at } T + 1.
\end{aligned}
$$

The gross investment is the increase in the three inventories:

$$\text{Gross Investment} = NCF(T) + P(Q - Q') + P'(X' - X).$$

The *net book value* at time T is:

$$NBV(T) = GBV(T) - D(T).$$

At time $T + 1$, the net book value $NBV(T + 1)$ can be computed as follows:

$$
\begin{aligned}
NBV(T + 1) &= GBV(T + 1) - [(1 + r)D(T) - D] \\
&= GBV(T) + NCF(T) + P(Q - Q') + P'(X' - X) \\
&\quad - [C(m - 1) - C(m)] - (1 + r)D(T) + D \\
&= NBV(T) + PQ' - P'X' - WL - D - DIV(T) \\
&\quad + SUBS(T) + P(Q - Q') + P'(X' - X) \\
&\quad - [C(m - 1) - C(m)] - rD(T) + D \\
&= NBV(T) + PQ - P'X - WL \\
&\quad - [C(m - 1) - C(m)] - rD(T) - DIV(T) \\
&\quad + SUBS(T) \\
&= NBV(T) + A(T) - DIV(T) + SUBS(T),
\end{aligned}
$$

where

$$
\begin{aligned}
A(T) &= PQ - P'X - WL - [C(m - 1) - C(m)] - rD(T) \\
&= \pi(T) + rNBV(T)
\end{aligned}
$$

are the *accounting profits* for the time period. The accounting profits are like the economic profits $\pi(T)$ except that only the interest on debt capital is deducted. Hence we have that the difference in equity between the two balance sheets, not correcting for the time difference and after dividends and net subscriptions, is:

$$NBV(T + 1) - NBV(T) = A(T) - DIV(T) + SUBS(T).$$

The owners and members of the corporation have two functional roles: (1) they supply the net capital value $NBV(T)$ to the corporation and (2) they are the residual claimants of the net market value created by the operations of the firm for the time period. The value of the services of the capital $NBV(T)$ for the time period is $rNBV(T)$, and the net value created by the operations is the economic profit $\pi(T)$. Hence the accounting profit:

$$A(T) = rNBV(T) + \pi(T)$$

is the sum of the returns to the owners in their two functional roles.

3 Market-Value-Accounting Statements

Initial Balance Sheet

The transactions will be presented in a simple summary form so, for example, all raw-material purchases or all sales will be treated as single transactions. The beginning balance sheet is:

Balance Sheet at Time T in Time T Dollars

Assets		Liabilities	
Cash	$CASH(T)$	Creditor 1	$D(T)$
Final-goods inventory	$PFG(T)$		
Raw-materials inventory	$P'RM(T)$		
Fixed equipment	$C(m - 1)$	Net worth	$NBV(T)$
Total Assets	$GBV(T)$	Total liabilities and net worth	$D(T) + NBV(T)$

All transactions are expressed in year-end dollars timed at time $T + 1$. Hence it is necessary to reexpress the initial balance sheet in time $T + 1$ dollars so that, in applying the debits and credits, one won't be adding apples and oranges.

Balance Sheet at Time T in Time $T + 1$ Dollars

Assets		Liabilities	
Cash	$(1 + r)CASH(T)$	Creditor 1	$(1 + r)D(T)$
Final-goods inventory	$(1 + r)PFG(T)$		
Raw-materials inventory	$(1 + r)P'RM(T)$		
Fixed equipment	$(1 + r)C(m - 1)$	Net worth	$(1 + r)NBV(T)$
Total assets	$(1 + r)GBV(T)$	Total liabilities and net worth	$(1 + r)(D(T) + NBV(T))$

Transactions can be divided into external and internal transactions. The internal transactions record the economic effects of the internal operations of the firm, the using up of the inputs, and the production of the outputs. These internal transactions are perfectly real, but they are not realized as external market transactions. All the internal operations will be represented as transactions with the temporary account, Production. In addition to the using up of the inputs such as raw materials X and labor L, and the production of the outputs Q, the internal operations turn the vintage $m - 1$ machine into a vintage m machine, and the operations turn all the inventories into a one-period-older inventories. To record the use of the machine, Production uses up the vintage $m - 1$ machine and produces the vintage m machine. To record the aging of the inventory stock, Production is represented as using up the initial stock and then reproducing the same initial stock at the end of the period. For example, the initial final-goods inventory is worth $(1 + r)PFG(T)$ in $T + 1$ dollars. The internal operation of just carrying that inventory turns the initial time T inventory worth $(1 + r)PFG(T)$ into the same $FG(T)$ physical units at time $T + 1$, which is worth $PFG(T)$ in time $T + 1$ dollars. Hence the expense associated with carrying the inventory is the difference, $rPFG(T)$, the interest-carrying charge on the value of the inventory. The same operations are applied to the raw-materials and cash inventories.

Journal

See journal on facing page ————————————————▶▶

All that remains are the closing transactions that close the temporary accounts into the summary temporary account, Change in Net Worth, which is then closed into Net Worth. The closing transactions are only marked with C.

Journal

Transaction	Description	Accounts	[Debit	//	Credit]
1.	Purchase raw materials	Raw-materials inventory Cash	$P'X'$		$P'X'$
2.	Purchase labor	Labor Cash	WL		WL
3.	Begin aging final-goods inventory	Production Final-goods inventory	$(1+r)PFG(T)$		$(1+r)PFG(T)$
4.	End aging final-goods inventory	Final-goods inventory Production	$PFG(T)$		$PFG(T)$
5.	Begin aging cash inventory	Production Cash	$(1+r)CASH(T)$		$(1+r)CASH(T)$
6.	End aging cash inventory	Cash Production	$CASH(T)$		$CASH(T)$
7.	Begin aging raw-materials inventory	Production Raw-materials inventory	$(1+r)P'RM(T)$		$(1+r)P'RM(T)$
8.	End aging raw-materials inventory	Raw-materials inventory Production	$P'RM(T)$		$P'RM(T)$
9.	Use of raw-materials in production	Production Raw-materials inventory	$P'X$		$P'X$
10.	Use of labor in production	Production Labor	WL		WL
11.	Begin use of the machine	Production Fixed equipment	$(1+r)C(m-1)$		$(1+r)C(m-1)$

Journal continued

Transaction	Description	Accounts	//	[Debit	//	Credit]
12.	End use of the machine	Fixed equipment Production		$C(m)$		$C(m)$
13.	Production of the final goods	Final-goods inventory Production		PQ		PQ
14.	Sale of the final goods	Cash Final-goods inventory		PQ'		PQ'
15.	Debt payment of D	Creditor 1 Cash		D		D
16.	Dividend payment	Dividends Cash		$DIV(T)$		$DIV(T)$
17.	Receipt of net sub-scriptions	Cash Subscriptions		$SUBS(T)$		$SUBS(T)$

C.	Close Production into
	   Change in Net Worth
		Production
		   Change in Net Worth
				$\pi(T)$		$\pi(T)$

C.	Close Dividends into
	   Change in Net Worth
		Change in Net Worth
		   Dividends
				$DIV(T)$		$DIV(T)$

C.	Close Subscriptions into
	   Change in Net Worth
		Subscriptions
		   Change in Net Worth
				$SUBS(T)$		$SUBS(T)$

C.	Close Change in Net Worth into Net Worth	Change in Net Worth Net Worth		$NBV(T+1) -$ $(1+r)NBV(T)$		$NBV(T+1) -$ $(1+r)NBV(T)$

Ledger

The initial entries in the ledger balance sheet T-accounts are the account balances after the unit of value has been readjusted to the end of the year (time $T + 1$) dollars. They are the entries from the balance sheet at time T in time $T + 1$ dollars. Totaling entries are marked by ($<$).

See ledger next page

Ledger

Cash
Ref	Debit	Credit	Ref
(6)	$(1+r)CASH(T)$	$P'X'$	(1)
(14)	$CASH(T)$	WL	(2)
(17)	PQ'	$(1+r)CASH(T)$	(5)
	$SUBS(T)$	D	(15)
		$DIV(T)$	(16)
(<)	$CASH(T+1)$	$CASH(T+1)$	(<)

Final-Goods Inventory
Ref	Debit	Credit	Ref
(4)	$(1+r)PFG(T)$	$(1+r)PFG(T)$	(3)
(13)	$PFG(T)$	PQ'	(14)
	PQ	$PFG(T+1)$	(<)
(<)	$PFG(T+1)$		

Raw-Materials Inventory
Ref	Debit	Credit	Ref
(1)	$(1+r)P'RM(T)$	$(1+r)P'RM(T)$	(7)
(8)	$P'RM(T)$	$P'X$	(9)
(<)	$P'RM(T+1)$	$P'RM(T+1)$	(<)

Labor
Ref	Debit	Credit	Ref
(2)	WL	WL	(10)
	0		

Creditor 1
Ref	Debit	Credit	Ref
(15)	D	$(1+r)D(T)$	
(<)	$D(T+1)$	$D(T+1)$	(<)

Fixed Equipment
Ref	Debit	Credit	Ref
(12)	$(1+r)C(m-1)$	$(1+r)C(m-1)$	(11)
	$C(m)$	$C(m)$	(<)
(<)	$C(m)$		

Production
Ref	Debit	Credit	Ref
(3)	$(1+r)PFG(T)$	$PFG(T)$	(4)
(5)	$(1+r)CASH(T)$	$CASH(T)$	(6)
(7)	$(1+r)P'RM(T)$	$P'RM(T)$	(8)
(9)	$P'X$	$C(m)$	(12)
(10)	WL	PQ	(13)
(11)	$(1+r)C(m-1)$		
(C)	$\pi(t)$		

Net Worth
Ref	Debit	Credit	Ref
		$(1+r)NBV(T)$	
		$NBV(T+1) -$	
(<)	$NBV(T+1)$	$(1+r)NBV(T)$	(C)

Subscriptions
Ref	Debit	Credit	Ref
(C)	$SUBS(T)$	$SUBS(T)$	(17)

Change in Net Worth
Ref	Debit	Credit	Ref
(C)	$DIV(T)$	$\pi(T)$	(C)
(C)	$SUBS(T)$	$NBV(T+1) -$	(C)
		$(1+r)NBV(T)$	

Dividends
Ref	Debit	Credit	Ref
(16)	$DIV(T)$	$DIV(T)$	(C)

Income Statement

Sales $= PQ'$
Ending final-goods inventory $= PFG(T + 1)$
$-$ Beginning final-goods inventory $= -(1 + r)PFG(T)$

Revenue $-$ final-goods inventory charge $= PQ - rPFG(T)$

Labor expense $=$ WL

Net cash flow $= NCF(T)$
Beginning cash inventory $= (1 + r)CASH(T)$
$-$ Ending cash inventory $= -CASH(T + 1)$

Cash expense $=$ $rCASH(T)$

Raw-materials purchases $= P'X'$
Beginning raw-materials inventory $= (1 + r)P'RM(T)$
$-$ Ending raw-materials inventory $= -P'RM(T + 1)$

Raw-materials expense $=$ $rP'RM(T) + P'X$

Fixed equipment purchases $= 0$
Beginning fixed equipment $= (1 + r)C(m - 1)$
$-$ Ending fixed equipment $= -C(m)$

Fixed equipment expense $=$ $[C(m - 1) - C(m)] +$
$rC(m - 1)$

Debt payment $= D$
Ending debt value $= D(T + 1)$
$-$ Beginning debt value $= -(1 + r)D(T)$

Debt expense $=$ 0

Economic profits $= \pi(T)$

$-$ Dividends $= -DIV(T)$
Subscriptions $= SUBS(T)$

Change in net worth $= NBV(T + 1) - (1 + r)NBV(T)$

Ending Balance Sheet

Balance Sheet at Time $T + 1$ in Time $T + 1$ Dollars

Assets		Liabilities	
Cash	$CASH(T)$	*Creditor* 1	$D(T + 1)$
Final-goods inventory	$PFG(T + 1)$		
Raw-materials inventory	$P'RM(T + 1)$		
Fixed equipment	$C(m)$	Net worth	$NBV(T + 1)$
Total assets	$GBV(T + 1)$	Total liabilities and net worth	$D(T + 1) +$ $NBV(T + 1)$

4

A Conventional Value-Accounting Model

Initial Balance Sheet

For the sake of comparison, the economic activity recorded in the market-value-accounting model will be modeled here using more conventional value-accounting methods. There are numerous differences. In conventional value accounting, revenue is recognized on a sale basis instead of a production basis. The inventories for final goods and raw materials are valued at some measure of historical cost instead of market value. Dollar amounts from different time periods are added together without correcting for the effect of interest. The interest on debt capital is treated as an expense and the interest received on debts to the firm is treated as revenue (although there are no such debts in our example). However, since we have assumed the availability of market prices for machines of various vintages or the availability of machine-rental rates, we have used economic depreciation as the differential in used asset values or, equivalently, depreciation as calculated by the annuity method. The usual depreciation deductions have only a pragmatic appeal and have no role in a theoretical model of accounting.

The Production account will be replaced by the conventional Revenue and Expense accounts. Accumulated Depreciation will be used as a contra-account to Fixed Equipment. As we are not assuming a known past history to the firm, we will start the final-goods inventory off at zero; that is, $FG(T) = 0$.

Balance Sheet at Time T

Assets		Liabilities	
Cash	$CASH(T)$	Creditor 1	$D(T)$
Final-goods inventory	0		
Raw-materials inventory	$P'RM(T)$		
Fixed equipment	$C(0)$	Net worth	$NBV(T)$
− Accumulated depreciation	$C(0) - C(m - 1)$		
Net fixed equipment	$C(m - 1)$		
Total assets	$GBV(T)$	Total liabilities and net worth	$D(T) + NBV(T)$

Journal

Transaction	Description	Accounts	[Debit	//	Credit]
1.	Purchase raw materials	Raw-materials inventory	$P'X'$		
		Cash			$P'X'$
2.	Purchase labor	Final-goods inventory	WL		
		Cash			WL
3.	Use of raw-materials in production	Final-goods inventory	$P'X$		
		Raw materials inventory			$P'X$
4.	Sale of the final goods	Cash	PQ'		
		Revenue			PQ'
5.	Cost expiration of final goods	Cost of goods sold	$(P'X + WL)Q'/Q$		
		Final-goods inventory			$(P'X + WL)Q'/Q$
6.	Debt payment of D	Creditor 1	$D - rD(T)$		
		Cash			$D - rD(T)$
7.	Interest on Debt	Interest expense	$rD(T)$		
		Cash			$rD(T)$
8.	Depreciation on machinery	Depreciation	$C(m - 1) - C(m)$		
		Accumulated depreciation			$C(m - 1) - C(m)$

	Account	Debit	Credit
9.	Dividend payment		
	Dividends	$DIV(T)$	
	Cash		$DIV(T)$
10.	Receipt of net subscriptions		
	Cash	$SUBS(T)$	
	Subscriptions		$SUBS(T)$
C.	Close revenue		
	Revenue	PQ'	
	Change in net worth		PQ'
C.	Close COGS into change in net worth		
	Change in net worth	$(P'X + WL)Q'/Q$	
	Cost of goods sold		$(P'X + WL)Q'/Q$
C.	Close interest expense		
	Change in net worth	$rD(T)$	
	Interest expense		$rD(T)$
C.	Close depreciation expense		
	Change in net worth	$C(m-1) - C(m)$	
	Depreciation		$C(m-1) - C(m)$
C.	Close dividends		
	Change in net worth	$DIV(T)$	
	Dividends		$DIV(T)$
C.	Close subscriptions		
	Subscriptions	$SUBS(T)$	
	Change in net worth		$SUBS(T)$

The labor L uses the raw materials X to produce the outputs Q. Hence the direct cost-per-unit output is $(P'X + WL)/Q$ and the cost of goods sold is $(P'X + WL)Q'/Q$. The accounting profit, Revenue minus Expenses, in this conventional value-accounting model is:

$$A\#(T) = \text{Revenue} - COGS - \text{Depreciation Expense} - \text{Interest Expense}$$

$$= PQ' - (P'X + WL)Q'/Q - (C(m - 1) - C(m))$$

$$- rD(T),$$

where the sharp sign ($\#$) marks quantities that differ from the corresponding quantities in the previous market-value-accounting model. The final closing transaction is:

Transaction	Description	Accounts	[Debit // Credit]
C.	Close change in net worth into net worth	Change in net worth	$A\#(T) - DIV(T) + SUBS(T)$
		Net worth	$A\#(T) - DIV(T) + SUBS(T)$

In the previous market-value-accounting model, the accounting profit was:

$$A(T) = PQ - P'X - WL - (C(m - 1) - C(m)) - rD(T).$$

The difference between the two accounting profits is due to the different revenue recognitions and the different final-goods-inventory valuations:

$$A(T) - A\#(T) = (Q - Q')(P - (P'X + WL)/Q),$$

which is the physical increase in final-goods inventory times the gross margin per unit. The difference is the gross margin *lost* on the final goods used to increase the amount in inventory. This amount will also show up as the difference between the ending final-goods-inventory amounts in the market-value-accounting model and the conventional value-accounting model. The ending gross and net book values in the conventional model will therefore be reduced by that amount:

$$GBV\#(T + 1) = GBV(T + 1) - (A(T) - A\#(T)),$$

and

$$NBV\#(T + 1) = NBV(T + 1) - (A(T) - A\#(T)).$$

Ledger

Cash

(4)	$CASH(T)$	(1)	$P'X'$	
(10)	PQ'	(2)	WL	
	$SUBS(T)$	(6)	$D - rD(T)$	
		(7)	$rD(T)$	
		(9)	$DIV(T)$	
		$(<)$	$CASH(T + 1)$	
$(<)$	$CASH(T + 1)$			

Raw-Materials Inventory

(1)	$P'RM(T)$	(3)	$P'X$	
	$P'X'$	$(<)$	$P'RM(T + 1)$	
$(<)$	$P'RM(T + 1)$			

Fixed Equipment

	$C(0)$

Net Worth

	$NBV(T)$	
	$A\#(T) - DIV(T)$	
	$+ SUBS(T)$	(C)
	$(<)$ $NBV\#(T + 1)$	
$(<)$ $NBV\#(T + 1)$		

Final-Goods Inventory

(2)	0	(5)	$(P'X + WL)Q'/Q$
(3)	WL	$(<)$	$(P'X + WL)(Q - Q')/Q$
	$P'X$		
$(<)$	$(P'X + WL)(Q - Q')/Q$		

Accumulated Depreciation

		(8)	$C(0) - C(m - 1)$
			$C(m - 1) - C(m)$
$(<)$	$C(0) - C(m)$	$(<)$	$C(0) - C(m)$

Creditor 1

(6)	$D - rD(T)$		$D(T)$
$(<)$	$D(T + 1)$		
		$(<)$	$D(T + 1)$

Revenue

(C)	PQ'	(4)	PQ'

Cost of Goods Sold

(5)	$(P'X + WL)Q'/Q$	(C)	$(P'X + WL)Q'/Q$

Ledger continued

Depreciation

(8) $C(m-1) - C(m)$ | $C(m-1) - C(m)$ (C)

Interest Expense

(7) $rD(T)$ | $rD(T)$ (C)

Dividends

(9) $DIV(T)$ | $DIV(T)$ (C)

Subscriptions

(C) $SUBS(T)$ | $SUBS(T)$ (10)

Change in Net Worth

(C)	$C(m-1) - C(m)$	PQ'	(C)
(C)	$rD(T)$	$SUBS(T)$	(C)
(C)	$DIV(T)$		
(C)	$(P'X + WL)Q'/Q$		
(C)	$A\#(T) - DIV(T)$		
	$+SUBS(T)$		

Income Statement and Ending Balance Sheet

Income Statement

Revenue	PQ'
– Expenses:	
Cost of goods sold	$(P'X + WL)Q'/Q$
Depreciation	$C(m - 1) - C(m)$
Interest expense	$rD(T)$
Accounting profit	$A\#(T)$
– Dividends	$DIV(T)$
Subscriptions	$SUBS(T)$
Change in net worth	$A\#(T) - DIV(T) + SUBS(T)$

Balance Sheet at Time $T + 1$

Assets		Liabilities	
Cash	$CASH(T + 1)$	Creditor 1	$D(T + 1)$
Final-goods inventory	$(P'X + WL) \times$ $(Q - Q')/Q$		
Raw-materials inventory	$P'RM(T + 1)$		
Fixed equipment	$C(0)$	Net worth	$NBV\#(T + 1)$
– Accumulated depreciation	$C(0) - C(m)$		
Net fixed equipment	$C(m)$		
Total assets	$GBV\#(T + 1)$	Total liabilities and and net worth	$D(T + 1)$ $+ NBV\#(T + 1)$

Conventional value accounting and market-value accounting differ in their treatment of unrealized valuations (for example, the valuation of unsold final-goods inventory) and in the treatment of interest. Property accounting avoids unrealized valuations altogether so the same property accounting underlies both value-accounting models. Because property accounting deals with the *physical* amounts of property, it is unperturbed by the valuation controversies of normal accounting.

If a principle of valuation can be agreed upon, then a preferred model of value accounting is obtained from property accounting by applying the valuation principle to the underlying property rights. If the principle of valuation is that of valuing all property rights at their market value, then the market-value-accounting model results:

Market Prices × Property Accounting = Market-Value Accounting.

5 Vector Accounting

Vectors

Let R be the real numbers and let R^+ be the nonnegative reals (positive and zero). Single real numbers s are called *scalars*. Ordered lists of real numbers $(x, y, \ldots, z)$ are called *vectors*. Vectors with the same number of entries or components in the list can be added together by adding the corresponding components, for example: $(5,1,0) + (-2,3,6) = (3,4,6)$.

The set of all vectors with n real components (positive or negative including zero) is denoted R^n. The set of all vectors with n components and all components being nonnegative (positive or zero), is denoted R^{n+}. These vectors with all nonnegative components are called *nonnegative vectors*.

Vectors will be used either as *property vectors* or as *price vectors*. In either case, each component of the vector is associated with a type of commodity. In a property vector, each component represents a certain number of units of that type of commodity. In a price vector, each component represents the price per unit of that type of commodity. Given a property vector $Y = (y_1, \ldots, y_n)$ and the price vector $P = (p_1, \ldots, p_n)$, the *scalar product* of P and Y is the scalar:

$$P \times Y = p_1 y_1 + \ldots + p_n y_n.$$

Economically, the scalar product $P \times Y$ is the *value* of the property vector Y when evaluated at the price vector P.

Value accounting works with scalars representing economic values. Property accounting works with property vectors. Property-accounting statements are transformed into value-accounting statements by taking the scalar product of the price vector times all the property vectors to obtain the value of the property vectors. If accounting was viewed only from the mathematical perspective ignoring the economic interpretation, then value accounting would be called *scalar accounting* and property accounting would be called *vector accounting*. The use of property vectors or commodity vectors has long been commonplace in economics as a result of von Neumann's work (for example, 1935) and the development of linear programming, activity analysis, and game theory.

Single-entry accounting uses positive and negative numbers. Single-entry value accounting uses positive and negative scalars in R, while single-entry property accounting uses vectors in R^n with positive and negative components. Normal value accounting, however, uses the double-entry method. Negative numbers do not appear in double-entry accounting. The numbers used in double-entry value accounting are all nonnegative reals in R^+. The vectors used in double-entry property accounting are all nonnegative vectors in R^{n+}.

The Algebra of T-accounts

The modern algebraic treatment of double-entry accounting, the algebra of T-accounts, will be presented here and used in our development of double-entry property accounting. A more mathematical treatment of the algebra of T-accounts will be presented in the appendix together with some comments on the literature on the mathematical treatment of accounting. The algebraic machinery was not used in our development of value accounting so that the novelty of market-value accounting according to economic theory would not be compounded by a new algebraic formalism. Since the property accounting is essentially new in any case, the appropriate algebraic framework will be used from the beginning in property accounting.

The basic entities in the algebra of T-accounts are the *T-terms*, $[d // c]$. They are ordered pairs of elements d and c. The square brackets are used to enclose the two elements so that a T-term will not be confused with a vector whose components are enclosed by parentheses. The left-hand entry d is the *debit* and the right-hand entry c is the *credit*. The debit is separated from the credit by a double slash following a suggestion by Pacioli himself (see appendix). The double slash is also reminiscent of the single slash used to separate the numerator and denominator of a fraction. The algebraic laws governing the multiplication of fractions with positive whole numbers as numerators and denominators are precisely the multiplicative version of the algebraic laws governing the addition of T-terms. The equivalence between the multiplicative algebra of fractions and the additive algebra of T-terms will be used below for explanatory purposes.

In an algebraic formulation of double-entry value accounting, the elements d and c in the T-terms $[d // c]$ would be nonnegative scalars drawn from R^+. In double-entry property accounting, the elements d and c in the T-terms $[d // c]$ are vectors with n nonnegative components drawn from R^{n+}. The laws governing the addition of scalars s are the same as the addition laws for vectors (s) with $n = 1$ component. Hence we will develop the algebra of T-accounts using T-terms $[d // c]$ with d and c being nonnegative vectors in R^{n+}, and the algebra of T-terms used in value accounting will simply be the special case of $n = 1$. All vectors henceforth are from R^{n+} for some n; that is, are nonnegative vectors with n components, unless otherwise stated.

Vectors with the same number of components n are added together by adding the corresponding components; for example, $(3,7,2) + (0,5,3) = (3,12,5)$. The sum of two nonnegative vectors is nonnegative. One vector could be subtracted from another vector by subtracting the corresponding components. However, the difference between two nonnegative vectors is not necessarily nonnegative; for example, $(3,7,2) - (0,5,3) = (3,2,-1)$. Since all vectors appearing in double-entry accounting must be nonnegative, subtraction is *not* a permissible operation *between vectors* in the algebra of T-accounts. However, the effect of subtraction will be obtained by other means.

T-terms $[d // c]$ have two entries, the debit entry d and the credit entry c. The *sum* of two T-terms is obtained by adding the corresponding entries:

$$[d // c] + [d' // c'] = [d + d' // c + c'].$$

In the addition of scalars, the element zero, 0, is called the *additive identity* since when added to any scalar s, it yields the same scalar, $s + 0 = s$. The zero vector with n components, also denoted 0, is the vector in R^{n+} with all components equal to zero. It functions as the additive identity in the addition of vectors since for any vector Y with n components, $Y + 0 = Y$. The *zero T-term* $[0 // 0]$ is the T-term with each entry equal to zero (the zero vector or the zero scalar as the case may be). It functions as the additive identity in the addition of T-terms:

$$[d // c] + [0 // 0] = [d // c].$$

It must be defined as to when two T-terms are equal. Two vectors are equal only when the corresponding components are equal, but two T-terms can be equal under more general conditions. In the special case of value accounting, two T-accounts would be equal if they have the same balance. For example, suppose that the T-accounts $[d // c]$ and $[d' // c']$ have the same debit balance. This means that $d - c$ and $d' - c'$ are both nonnegative and equal. If the accounts had the same credit balance, then $c - d$ and $c' - d'$ would be nonnegative and equal. However, we are not "allowed" to use this definition of equality of T-accounts since it involves subtraction. If we move the negative terms to the other side of each equation $d - c = d' - c'$ and $c - d = c' - d'$, then in both cases we arrive at the same equation, $d + c' = d' + c$. This equation does not involve subtraction. Moreover, it makes sense when the debit and credit entries are vectors instead of just scalars. Hence the *equality of T-terms* is defined as follows:

$$[d // c] = [d' // c'] \text{ if } d + c' = d' + c.$$

There is a convenient way to state this definition. Given two T-terms, $[d \mathbin{//} c]$ and $[d' \mathbin{//} c']$, their *cross sums* are the two elements $d + c'$ and $d' + c$ obtained by adding the debit entry in one T-term to the credit entry in the other T-term. Then two T-terms are equal if and only if their cross sums are equal.

The subtraction of a scalar is really the addition of the negative of the scalar; for example; $7 - 5 = 7 + (-5) = 2$. The subtraction of a vector is the addition of the negative of the vector; for example: $(3,7,2) - (0,5,3) = (3,7,2) + (0,-5,-3) = (3,2,-1)$. Since double-entry accounting uses only nonnegative scalars or vectors, the operation of taking the negative of a scalar or vector is also not allowed. However, one can take the negative of a T-term. The *negative* or *reverse* of a T-term is obtained by *reversing* the debit and credit entries:

$$-[d \mathbin{//} c] = [c \mathbin{//} d].$$

Hence the *subtraction* of one T-term from another is allowed by adding the reverse of the subtracted T-term:

$$[d \mathbin{//} c] - [d' \mathbin{//} c'] = [d \mathbin{//} c] + [c' \mathbin{//} d'] = [d + c' \mathbin{//} c + d'].$$

It should be noted that this subtraction of T-terms never involves the subtraction of the vectors or scalars that appear as the entries in the T-term (since the entries are reversed and then added). As with numbers, the addition of a T-term and its negative is the additive identity:

$$[d \mathbin{//} c] + [c \mathbin{//} d] = [d + c \mathbin{//} c + d] = [0 \mathbin{//} 0].$$

The second T-term equation, $[d + c \mathbin{//} c + d] = [0 \mathbin{//} 0]$, follows from the definition of equality of T-terms and the vector or scalar equation, $d + c + 0 = c + d + 0$.

In modern algebra, this (additive) algebra of T-terms is called the *group of differences* (Bourbaki 1974, p. 20). Since the informal algebra of T-accounts was developed over six centuries ago by Italian merchants and published by the mathematician Luca Pacioli in 1494, it seems appropriate to name the group of differences, the *Pacioli group*. This name has not been previously used since the identity between the algebra of T-accounts and the group of differences has not been previously observed (see appendix).

The development so far of the additive algebra of T-terms is all paralleled in the multiplicative algebra of fractions d/c with positive whole number numerators and denominators (excluding zero). Just as T-terms add together by adding corresponding entries, so fractions multiply together by multiplying corresponding entries:

$$(d/c)(d'/c') = dd'/cc'.$$

The multiplicative analogies of taking-the-reverse and subtraction are taking-the-reciprocal and division, respectively. Just as subtracting x means adding on the negative or reverse of x, so dividing by x means multiplying by the reciprocal of x. The reverse of a T-term is obtained by reversing the debit and credit entries, and the reciprocal of a fraction is obtained by reversing the numerator and denominator. Thus just as:

$$[d \mathbin{//} c] - [d' \mathbin{//} c'] = [d \mathbin{//} c] + [c' \mathbin{//} d'] = [d + c' \mathbin{//} c + d']$$

in the additive algebra of T-terms, so we have

$$(d/c) \div (d'/c') = (d/c)(c'/d') = dc'/cd'$$

in the multiplicative algebra of fractions. Given two fractions d/c and d'/c', their *cross multiples* are the two numbers dc' and cd', obtained by multiplying the numerator in one fraction times the denominator in the other fraction. Then two fractions are defined as being equal if and only if their cross multiples are equal:

$$d/c = d'/c' \text{ if and only if } dc' = cd'.$$

In the multiplication of positive whole numbers, the number one, 1, functions as the multiplicative identity since $(d)(1) = d$. The fraction $1/1$ functions as the multiplicative identity in the multiplication of fractions (with positive nonzero numerators and denominators) since $(d/c)(1/1) = (d/c)$. The reciprocal of a fraction is the fraction such that, when multiplied times the original fraction, yields the multiplicative identity:

$$(d/c)(c/d) = dc/cd = 1/1.$$

Since a T-term, like a fraction, can be represented in many ways, we must be careful to distinguish between a T-term and its representations. If $[d \mathbin{//} c] = [d' \mathbin{//} c']$ but d is not equal to d' or c is not equal to c', then $[d \mathbin{//} c]$ and $[d' \mathbin{//} c']$ are said to be *distinct representations* of the same T-term.

The Reduced Representation of a T-term

In scalar accounting, each T-term $[d \mathbin{//} c]$ is equal to a T-term $[d - c \mathbin{//} 0]$ or $[0 \mathbin{//} c - d]$ where either the credit or debit entry is zero (depending on whether $d - c$ or $c - d$ is nonnegative). Let $min(d,c)$ be the scalar which is the *minimum* of d and c. Then $d - min(d,c)$ and $c - min(d,c)$ are both necessarily nonnegative if d and c are, and:

$$[d \mathbin{/\mkern-5mu/} c] = [d - min(d,c) \mathbin{/\mkern-5mu/} c - min(d,c)].$$

Moreover, $[d - min(d,c) \mathbin{/\mkern-5mu/} c - min(d,c)]$ is the T-term equal to $[d \mathbin{/\mkern-5mu/} c]$ where either the credit or debit entry is zero. In value accounting, when one *totals* and *takes the balance* of a T-account $[d \mathbin{/\mkern-5mu/} c]$, one obtains the T-account $[d - min(d,c) \mathbin{/\mkern-5mu/} c - min(d,c)]$ where one entry is zero and the other entry is the *balance* of the account. After an account has been balanced in this fashion, the minimum of the two entries is zero; that is:

$$min(d - min(d,c), c - min(d,c)) = 0.$$

Hence we will say that a representation $[d' \mathbin{/\mkern-5mu/} c']$ of a T-term is *reduced* if $min(d',c') = 0$.

In vector accounting, the debit and credit entries, d and c, in a T-term $[d \mathbin{/\mkern-5mu/} c]$ are nonnegative vectors. It is *not* true that either $d - c$ or $c - d$ is a nonnegative vector. For example:

$$(3,7,2) - (0,5,3) = (3,2,-1) \text{ and } (0,5,3) - (3,7,2) = (-3,-2,1).$$

Hence, in vector accounting, it is not true that any T-term $[d \mathbin{/\mkern-5mu/} c]$ can be expressed in a form $[d - c \mathbin{/\mkern-5mu/} 0]$ or $[0 \mathbin{/\mkern-5mu/} c - d]$. The reduced representation of any T-term found in scalar accounting generalizes, not to the entire debit or credit vectors, but to the *components* of the debit and credit vectors. In short, the reduced representation generalizes *component-wise* to vector accounting.

Given two vectors d and c with n components each, let $min(d,c)$ be the vector whose *i-th* component is the minimum of the *i-th* components of d and c for $i = 1, \ldots , n$. For example:

$$min((3,7,2),(0,5,3)) = (0,5,2).$$

If d and c are nonnegative, then $d - min(d,c)$ and $c - min(d,c)$ are both nonnegative, and:

$$[d \mathbin{/\mkern-5mu/} c] = [d - min(d,c) \mathbin{/\mkern-5mu/} c - min(d,c)].$$

For instance:

$$[(3,7,2) \mathbin{/\mkern-5mu/} (0,5,3)] = [(3,7,2) - (0,5,2) \mathbin{/\mkern-5mu/} (0,5,3) - (0,5,2)]$$
$$= [(3,2,0) \mathbin{/\mkern-5mu/} (0,0,1)].$$

In the representation $[d - min(d,c) // c - min(d,c)]$, for each component i with $i = 1, \ldots, n$, the i-th component of the debit vector $d - min(d,c)$ or the i-th component of the credit vector $c - min(d,c)$ is zero. Hence the minimum of those two vectors is the zero vector. Thus, in vector accounting, we can similarly define that a representation $[d' // c']$ of a T-term is *reduced* if $min(d',c') = 0$. It should be noted that *reducedness* is a property not of T-terms, but of their representations.

It has been shown that every T-term $[d // c]$ in vector accounting has at least one reduced representation, $[d - min(d,c) // c - min(d,c)]$. We will now show that it is unique. This is proved by showing that if $[d // c]$ and $[d' // c']$ represent the same T-term; that is, if $[d // c] = [d' // c']$, and if both are reduced, that is, $min(d,c) = 0 = min(d',c')$, then they are the same representation; that is, $d = d'$ and $c = c'$.

If the nonnegative vector c' is added to d and c in $min(d,c) = 0$, then it will increase the minimum by c'; that is, $min(d + c', c + c') = 0 + c' = c'$. But since $[d // c] = [d' // c']$, we have $d + c' = d' + c$, so substituting $d' + c$ for $d + c'$ yields $min(d' + c, c + c') = c'$. If the nonnegative vector c is subtracted from $d' + c$ and $c + c'$, then it will reduce the minimum by c:

$$min(d' + c - c, c + c' - c) = min(d',c') = c' - c.$$

But since $[d' // c']$ is also reduced, $0 = min(d',c') = c' - c$ so $c' = c$. By interchanging d' for c' and d for c in the above proof, one similarly proves that $d' = d$. Hence it has been shown that each T-term $[d // c]$ in vector accounting has a *unique* reduced representation:

$$[d - min(d,c) // c - min(d,c)].$$

In vector accounting, the process of totaling and taking the balance of a T-account means reducing it to its unique reduced representation.

There is another way to express the unique reduced representation of a T-term. For any vector Y with positive and/or negative components, the *positive part* of Y, $pos(Y)$, is the vector whose i-th component is $max(y_i,0)$, the maximum of y_i, the i-th component of Y, and zero. The *negative part* of Y, $neg(Y)$, can be defined as $pos(-Y)$. Then $pos(Y)$ and $neg(Y)$ are nonnegative vectors, $min(pos(Y),neg(Y)) = 0$, and $Y = pos(Y) - neg(Y)$. Moreover, for any nonnegative vectors d and c:

$$d - min(d,c) = neg(c - d) \text{ and } c - min(d,c) = pos(c - d).$$

Hence the unique reduced representation of a T-term $[d // c]$ can be expressed as:

$$[neg(c - d) // pos(c - d)].$$

These results about the reduced representation of a T-term all carry over to the multiplicative algebra of fractions of positive whole numbers. Given two nonnegative numbers d and c, the minimum $min(d,c)$ could be defined as the largest nonnegative number that could be subtracted from both d and c with a nonnegative result. Translating into multiplicative terms, given two positive whole numbers d and c, the *greatest common divisor* $gcd(d,c)$ is the largest whole number that could be divided into both d and c with whole number results. Given a fraction d/c, the result of dividing both the numerator and denominator by their greatest common divisor yields another representation of the same fraction:

$$d/c = (d \div gcd(d,c))/(c \div gcd(d,c)).$$

The multiplicative analogue of the definition of reduced, $min(d,c) = 0$, is the definition of d and c being *relatively prime*, $gcd(d,c) = 1$. If d and c are relatively prime, then the fraction d/c is said to be *reduced to lowest terms*. For example, 12/28 and 15/35 are distinct representations of the same fraction; that is, $12/28 = 15/35$, but neither is reduced to lowest terms since $gcd(12,28) = 4$ and $gcd(15,35) = 5$. In any representation of a fraction, if the numerator and denominator are divided by their greatest common divisor, the result is the *unique* representation of the fraction in lowest terms. In the example, it is 3/7. Thus reducing a fraction to its lowest terms corresponds to totaling and taking the balance of a T-account; that is, reducing the T-account to its reduced representation.

6 The Double-Entry Method

Additive Operations on Equations

The algebra of T-accounts developed in the previous chapter is a precise formulation and generalization of the algebraic machinery used implicitly in traditional double-entry bookkeeping. The specific use of the algebra of T-accounts in double-entry bookkeeping to perform valid algebraic operations on equations (such as the balance-sheet equation) is called the *double-entry method.*

A valid algebraic operation on equations is an operation that transforms (correct) equations into (correct) equations. In the algebra of T-accounts, a T-term $[m // m']$ equals the zero $[0 // 0]$ if and only if $m + 0 = m' + 0$; that is, $m = m'$. Hence any *equation,* such as $m = m'$ with nonnegative m and m', can be represented in the algebra of T-accounts as a *zero-term,* such as $[m // m']$ (a T-term equal to the zero $[0 // 0]$); that is:

$$\text{Equation} = \text{Zero-term.}$$

A zero-term obtained by representing an equation will be called an *equation zero-term* (or equational zero-term). Thus a valid algebraic operation of transforming equations into equations would be represented in the algebra of T-accounts as an operation that transforms zero-terms into zero-terms; that is, zero into zero. There is one such operation—*add zero:* Nothing plus nothing equals nothing.

The events that change accounting equations are the *transactions.* A transaction involves a debit d and a credit c that are equal; that is, $d = c$. Hence a transaction is also represented in the algebra of T-accounts by a zero-term $[d // c]$. A zero-term representing a transaction will be called a *transaction zero-term* (or transactional zero-term). The effect of the transaction involving d and c on the equation $m = m'$ is formulated in the algebra of T-accounts by adding the transaction zero-term $[d // c]$ to the equation zero-term $[m // m']$ to obtain the new zero-term $[m + d // m' + c]$ representing the new equation $m + d = m' + c$. The double-entry method is this technique of representing accounting equations and transactions as zero-terms in the algebra of T-accounts so that valid algebraic operations:

Original Equation + Transactions ⟶ Resultant Equation,

become the simple operation of adding zeroes to zero to get zero:

$$\text{Original Equation} \atop \text{Zero-Term} \quad + \quad {\text{Transaction} \atop \text{Zero-Terms}} \quad = \quad {\text{Resultant Equation} \atop \text{Zero-Term.}}$$

A Balance-Sheet Example

The double-entry method will now be developed in more detail by considering a simple example using conventional balance-sheet accounting. Using the widest accounting categories, the initial balance-sheet equation is:

Assets = Liabilities + Net Worth.

In terms of stock-flow distinction, the balance-sheet accounts are stock accounts (or permanent accounts). By the basic stock-flow equation, the ending stock can be obtained by adding the net inflow to the initial stock:

Beginning Stock + Inflow − Outflow = Ending Stock.

The flows may be represented by accounts called *flow accounts* (or temporary accounts), and the addition of the net inflow to the initial stock to obtain the ending stock is called *closing the summary temporary account into the permanent account.* With the Net Worth stock account, we associate the flow accounts: Revenue equals Inflow and Expense equals Outflow. Then the balance-sheet equation is:

Assets = Liabilities + Net Worth + Revenue − Expense.

To translate or encode an equation into an equational zero-term, we must first move all accounts preceded by negative signs to the other side of the equation so that all accounts occur positively. Such an equation is said to be in *positive form:*

Assets + Expenses = Liabilities + Net Worth + Revenue.

It is the position of an account in the equation in positive form that identifies the account as a Left-Hand Side (LHS) or debit-balance account, or as a Right-Hand Side (RHS) or credit-balance account.

Consider the following initial balance sheet:

$$\text{Assets} + \text{Expenses} = \text{Liabilities} + \text{Net Worth} + \text{Revenue}$$

$$6000 + 0 = 3500 + 2500 + 0.$$

The LHS accounts encode as debit-balance T-terms, the RHS accounts encode as credit-balance T-terms, and the sum of the T-terms thus obtained is the equation zero-term.

Assets	Expenses	Liabilities	Net Worth	Revenue
[6000 // 0] +	[0 // 0] +	[0 // 3500] +	[0 // 2500] +	[0 // 0].

There is no equality sign in the equation zero-term. The whole T-term (sum of five T-terms) is equal to [0 // 0]. The T-terms (five in this case) that make up the equation zero-term can only be added together; that is, there are only plus signs between them. Hence the plus signs can be deleted (that is, left implicit) leaving a set of labeled T-terms, and the accounts can be shuffled around in any order.

Assets	Liabilities	Net Worth	Revenue	Expenses
[6000 // 0]	[0 // 3500]	[0 // 2500]	[0 // 0]	[0 // 0]

Heretofore, we have only used the phrase *T-account* heuristically. Now a T-account can be formally defined as a labeled T-term in an equation zero-term where the label is taken to include the coding information as to whether the T-term was encoded from the left- or right-hand side of the original equation.

The *ledger* is then defined as the set of T-accounts (labeled T-terms) in an equation zero-term. Since the ledger is just an abbreviated form of the equational zero-term (without the plus signs), the sum of all the T-accounts in the ledger is a zero-term. That summation is usually called the *trial balance*.

A transaction is represented or encoded in the algebra of T-accounts as another zero-term, usually the sum of a T-term and its reverse. For a transaction to be recorded with an equal debit d and a credit c, the corresponding transaction zero-term is $[d // 0] + [0 // c]$. Debiting d to an account means adding the T-term $[d // 0]$ to the T-account, and crediting c to an account means adding the T-term $[0 // c]$ to the T-account. The list of transaction zero-terms added to the original equation zero-term (to obtain the resultant equation zero-term) is the *journal*. Thus we have:

Ledger = Equation Zero-term

and

Journal = List of Transaction Zero-terms.

Here, we consider a few simple transactions:

1. $1400 is expended on productive inputs
2. $1600 of output is produced and sold, and
3. $900 of principal is paid on a loan.

Journal

Transaction	Description	Accounts	[Debit	//	Credit]
1.	$1400 expended on inputs	Expense Assets	[1400 [0	// //	0] 1400]
2.	$1600 outputs produced and sold	Assets Revenue	[1600 [0	// //	0] 1600]
3.	$900 principal payment on loan	Liabilities Assets	[900 [0	// //	0] 900]

The debit and credit parts of the transaction zero-terms can then be added to the appropriate T-accounts in the ledger. In other words:

Posting to the Ledger = Adding the Transaction Zero-terms to the Equation Zero-term.

Assets	Liabilities	Net Worth	Revenue	Expenses
[6000 // 0]	[0 // 3500]	[0 // 2500]	[0 // 0]	[0 // 0]
[0 // 1400]	[900 // 0]		[0 // 1600]	[1400 // 0]
[1600 // 0]				
[0 // 900]				
[7600//2300]	[900//3500]	[0 // 2500]	[0 // 1600]	[1400 // 0]

The temporary or flow accounts are then closed by the closing transactions (marked by C).

Transaction	Description	Accounts	[Debit	//	Credit]
C.	Close revenue into net worth	Revenue Net worth	[1600 [0	// //	0] 1600]
C.	Close expense into net worth	Net worth Expense	[1400 [0	// //	0] 1400]

The T-terms from these closing transaction zero-terms can then be added to the appropriate T-accounts and the T-accounts can be put into reduced form to obtain the following ledger:

Assets	Liabilities	Net Worth	Revenue	Expenses
[5300 // 0]	[0 // 2600]	[0 // 2700]	[0 // 0]	[0 // 0]

The resulting T-terms under the T-account headings must be decoded properly to obtain the resultant equation. The T-accounts encoded from the LHS (or RHS) of the original equation would have their debit (or credit) balances decoded on the LHS (or RHS) of the resultant equation. Thus, the *final balance-sheet equation:*

Assets	+ Expenses =	Liabilities	+ Net Worth +	Revenue
5300	+ 0 =	2600	+ 2700 +	0

Vector Accounting with Apples and Oranges

The next example uses the formal machinery of vector accounting but is otherwise independent of the specific property-theoretic use of vector accounting that is called *property accounting*. In this example, bookkeeping with vectors is used to update a vector equation obtained by cross-classifying a multicommodity inventory as to source and location. A firm carries two commodities, apples and oranges, in inventory. The apples and oranges can come from either of two suppliers A and B. The suppliers A and B will be represented by *Row* 1 and *Row* 2 in the rectangular array given below. The fruit can be inventoried at any of three outlets X, Y, and Z. The outlets are represented by the three columns in the array. The commodity vectors have two components representing numbers of apples and oranges, respectively.

Whenever the same entities can be divided into categories under two different schemes of classification (for example, rows and columns), there is an equation stating that the sum of the entities under one scheme equals the sum under the other scheme—since they are the same objects doubly classified. We will derive our equation from a rectangular array of doubly classified vectors of apples and oranges. Each cell in the array can be conveniently thought of as a box containing the apples and oranges.

	Column 1	Column 2	Column 3
Row 1	(100,200)	(50,150)	(300,250)
Row 2	(150,100)	(250,100)	(200,50)

Equating the row and column sum yields the following initial vector equation:

Row 1   Row 2   Column 1   Column 2   Column 3

(450,600) + (600,250) =   (250,300)   +   (300,250) + (500,300).

To illustrate the use of flow accounts in this context, we arbitrarily pick an account such as *Row 2* and associate with it the flow accounts:

Row 2 Net Inflow = Row 2 In − Row 2 Out.

Adding the flow accounts to the previous equation and putting the equation into positive form yields:

Row 1   Row 2   Row 2 In

(450,600)   +   (600,250)   +   (0, 0)   =

Column 1   Column 2   Column 3   Row 2 Out

(250,300)   +   (300,250)   +   (500,300)   +   (0, 0).

To simplify notation, the zero vector (0,0) will whenever possible be written as just 0. The vector equation is then encoded as the following equation zero-term:

	Row 1		Row 2		Row 2 In	

$$[(450,600) \mathbin{//} 0] \; + \; [(600,250) \mathbin{//} 0] \; + \; [(0,0) \mathbin{//} 0] \; +$$

	Column 1	Column 2	Column 3	Row 2 Out

$$[0 \mathbin{//} (250,300)] + [0 \mathbin{//} (300,250)] + [0 \mathbin{//} (500,300)] + [0 \mathbin{//} (0,0)].$$

The ledger would usually be written with the plus signs in the equational zero-term left implicit and with the flow accounts last:

Row 1   Row 2

$$[(450,600) \mathbin{//} 0] \qquad [(600,250) \mathbin{//} 0]$$

Column 1   Column 2   Column 3

$$[0 \mathbin{//} (250,300)] \qquad [0 \mathbin{//} (300,250)] \qquad [0 \mathbin{//} (500,300)]$$

Row 2 In   Row 2 Out

$$[(0,0) \mathbin{//} 0] \qquad [(0 \mathbin{//}(0,0)].$$

The transactions occur as fruit is put into or removed from the boxes. Suppose the following three transactions take place:

1. Fifty apples and twenty oranges are taken from Row 1 Column 2,
2. Thirty-five apples and forty oranges are put into Row 2 Column 3, and
3. Twenty apples and thirty oranges are moved from Row 2 to Row 1 in Column 2.

Each transaction is represented by a transaction zero-term. For instance, the first transaction is represented by $[(50,20)\mathbin{//}0] + [0\mathbin{//}(50,20)]$. The list of the transaction zero-terms and the T-accounts to which they are added is the journal:

Journal

Transaction	Description	Accounts	[Debit	//	Credit]
1.	(50,20) out of box at Row 1 Column 2	Column 2 Row 1	[(50,20) [(0,0)	// //	(0,0)] (50,20)]

Journal continued

Transaction	Description	Accounts	[Debit	//	Credit]
2.	(35,40) into box at Row 2 Column 3	Row 2 In Column 3	[(35,40) [(0,0)	// //	(0,0)] (35,40)]
3.	(20,30) moved from Row 2 to Row 1 in Column 2	Row 1 Row 2 Out	[(20,30) [(0,0)	// //	(0,0)] (20,30)]

By adding the T-terms to the appropriate T-accounts in the equation zero-term (that is, by posting the transactions to the ledger), we obtain:

Row 1

[(470,630) // (50,20)]

Row 2

[(600,250) // 0]

Column 1

[0 // (250,300)]

Column 2

[(50,20) // (300,250)]

Column 3

[0 // (535,340)]

Row 2 In

[(35,40) // 0]

Row 2 Out

[(0 //(20,30)].

At any point a trial balance can be performed by adding together all the debit entries and all the credit entries to check that the ledger still is a zero-term:

$$(470,630) + (600,250) + (50,20) + (35,40) = (1155,940),$$

and

$$(50,20) + (250,300) + (300,250) + (535,340) + (20,30) = (1155,940).$$

The following transactions will close the temporary flow accounts into the appropriate permanent account.

Transaction	Description	Accounts	[Debit	//	Credit]
C.	Close *Row* 2 In account into *Row* 2	*Row* 2 *Row* 2 In	[(35,40) [(0,0)	// //	(0,0)] (35,40)]
C.	Close *Row* 2 Out account into *Row* 2	*Row* 2 Out *Row* 2	[(20,30) [(0,0)	// //	(0,0)] (20,30)]

The closing transactions can be added to the ledger, all the T-accounts can be put into reduced form, and the closed temporary accounts can be deleted to obtain:

Row 1   *Row* 2

[(420,610) // (0,0]   [(615,260) // (0,0)]

Column 1   *Column* 2   *Column* 3

[(0,0) // (250,300)]   [(0,0) // (250,230)]   [(0,0) // (535,340)].

An equational zero-term can be decoded into an equation by arbitrarily dividing the T-terms into two groups L and R. A T-term $[d // c]$ in the L group is treated as a LHS T-account by decoding it as $d - c$ on the LHS of the final equation. A T-term $[d // c]$ in the R group is treated as a RHS T-account by decoding it as $c - d$ on the RHS of the final equation. In the equational zero-term above, there is no need to pick the L and R groups arbitrarily since the intent is to treat the *Row* accounts as LHS accounts and the *Column* accounts as RHS accounts. Hence the ledger or equational zero-term decodes as the *final vector equation:*

Row 1   *Row* 2   *Column* 1   *Column* 2   *Column* 3

(420,610) + (615,260) = (250,300) + (250,230) + (535,340).

The double-entry method can still be used if the original equation involved vectors with both positive and negative components (instead of just nonnegative vectors). All that changes is the encoding and decoding process. Given any vector equation, any LHS vector Y is encoded as the T-term $[pos(Y) // neg(Y)]$ and any RHS vector Y is encoded as the T-term

$[neg(Y) // pos(Y)]$. For decoding, a LHS T-account $[d // c]$ is decoded as $d - c$ on the LHS of the resultant equation, and a RHS T-account $[d // c]$ is decoded as $c - d$ on the RHS of the resultant equation.

Multiplicative Double-Entry Bookkeeping

Once the mathematical structure of double-entry bookkeeping is understood, it can be generalized or carried over into totally new domains. We shall sketch in this section and the next section the system of multiplicative double-entry bookkeeping. The idea is to show the double-entry principles in a completely different context. These two sections will not be used elsewhere in the book, so the sections may be skipped without loss of continuity.

In multiplicative double-entry bookkeeping, multiplication replaces addition and the accounts are fractions d/c instead of T-terms $[d // c]$. We will consider the numerator as the debit entry and the denominator as the credit entry, even though the opposite convention could also be adopted. Numerator (or top) and denominator (or bottom) of fractions d/c replaces the left-hand side and the right-hand side of the T-terms $[d // c]$ in additive double-entry bookkeeping. In additive bookkeeping, the debit and credit entries in $[d // c]$ are restricted to nonnegative numbers. In multiplicative bookkeeping, the debit and credit entries in the fractions d/c are restricted to nonzero whole numbers, which in mathematics are called the *nonzero integers*. In general, the integers may be negative in multiplicative bookkeeping, but most specific models will use only positive integers.

Multiplication of integers will usually be indicated by juxtaposition without any times sign (X) so that yz stands for y *times* z. Fractions multiply by multiplying numerator by numerator and denominator by denominator; that is $(w/x)(y/z) = (wy/xz)$. Given two fractions, the cross multiples are the two numbers obtained by multiplying the numerator of one times the denominator of the other. For example, the cross multiples of w/x and y/z are xy and wz. Two fractions are equal if their cross multiples are equal; that is, $w/x = yz$ if $xy = wz$. The multiplicative analogy to the zero T-term $[0 // 0]$ is the unit fraction $1/1$. The inverse of a fraction d/c is its reciprocal c/d: $(d/c)(c/d) = 1/1$.

In mathematics, the algebra of fractions is called the *multiplicative group of fractions* (Bourbaki 1974, p. 20) in contrast to the additive group of differences used in additive double-entry bookkeeping. It could also be called the *multiplicative Pacioli group*.

The notion of an account being in reduced form also carries over, with the appropriate changes, to multiplicative bookkeeping. An additive account or T-term $[d // c]$ is put into reduced form by subtracting the same positive numbers from each side as long as the results are still nonnegative. A multiplicative account or fraction d/c is put into reduced form by dividing the same nonzero integer into numerator and denominator as long as the results are still nonzero integers. As long as some integer (not equal to one) divides both numerator and denominator, the fraction is not in reduced form. Thus a fraction d/c is in reduced form if d and c have no common divisor (other than 1); that is, if the fraction is *in lowest terms*. The quick way to reduce an additive account $[d // c]$ is to subtract the minimum of d and c, in symbols, $min(d,c)$ from both d and c. The quick way to reduce a multiplicative account d/c is to divide the greatest common divisor of d and c, in symbols, $gcd(d,c)$, into both d and c. A T-term $[d // c]$ is already in reduced form if $min(d,c) = 0$. A fraction is in reduced form if $gcd(d,c) = 1$.

There are some subtleties, however, in the analogy between T-terms and fractions that introduce interesting new complications into multiplicative double-entry bookkeeping. If a T-term $[d // c]$ is in reduced form, then either $d = 0$ or $c = 0$. But it is *not* true that if a fraction d/c is in reduced form (that is, is in lowest terms) then either $d = 1$ or $c = 1$. For example, 2/3 is in reduced form but neither numerator nor denominator is equal to unity. The new complications will emerge in the treatment of transactions.

Just as any T-term equal to the zero-term $[0 // 0]$ was called a zero-term, so any fraction equal to the unit fraction 1/1 will be called a *unit*. Then d/c is a unit if and only if $d = c$, so units encode equations in multiplicative bookkeeping just as zero-terms encode equations in additive bookkeeping. Given an equation $w \ldots x = y \ldots z$ between products of nonzero integers, a left-hand-side integer is encoded as a *debit fraction,* such as $w/1$ and $x/1$, and a right-hand-side integer is encoded as a *credit fraction,* such as $1/y$ and $1/z$. The product of all fractions obtained in this manner is equal to 1/1 and is called an *equational unit* in analogy with the equational zero-terms of additive bookkeeping:

$$w \ldots x = y \ldots z \text{ if and only if } (w/1) \ldots (x/1)(1/y) \ldots (1/z)$$
$$= (w \ldots x)/(y \ldots z) = 1/1.$$

If the original equation is an equation between fractions, it can always be first converted into an equation between products of integer by *clearing the fractions,* that is, by converting to the equation of the cross multiples. Alternatively, an equation between fractions can be directly encoded as follows: left-hand-side fractions encode as is and right-hand-side fractions are inverted.

A valid algebraic operation transforms equations into equations. Since equations encode as units, units must be transformed into units. There is only one such operation: multiply by a unit. One times one equals one. A unit times a unit equals a unit. Transactions would therefore be recorded by multiplying the equational unit by another unit, the *transactional unit:*

Original Equational Unit $\times$ Transactional Unit = Final Equational Unit.

In additive bookkeeping, a transactional zero-term, $[d // 0] + [0 // c]$ (where $d = c$), is the sum of two T-terms, one the inverse of the other. Each of the T-terms $[d // 0]$ and $[0 // c]$ has a zero as one entry so it is either a pure debit or pure credit. When the transactional zero-term is added to the equational zero-term in additive bookkeeping, one T-account is debited (that is, has $[d // 0]$ added to it) and another T-account is credited. One could have a seemingly more general form for a transactional zero-term, namely $[x // y] + [y // x]$ where each T-term is again the inverse of the other but where x and y are both nonzero. Then the addition of $[x // y]$ or $[y // x]$ could not be characterized as a pure debit or credit; each would be a mixed debit and credit. But this generality is specious because each T-term can be put into its reduced form so that the transactional zero-term would then have the old form $[d // 0] + [0 // c]$ for some $d = c$.

Here is where the complications about fractions in lowest terms have their effect. The strict analogy to the special form of a transaction zero-term $[d // 0] + [0 // c]$ would be a transactional unit with the form $(d/1)(1/c)$, where $d = c$. The analogy to the general form $[x // y] + [y // x]$ would be $(x/y)(y/x)$. But here the generality is genuine because a fraction x/y could be in reduced form even though neither x nor y are equal to 1. Hence, in this context, the general form of a transactional unit $(x/y)(y/x)$ cannot be reduced to the special case $(d/1)(1/c)$ where $d = c$. This complication should not be "blamed" on the multiplicative nature of fraction accounting because it also occurs in additive bookkeeping using vectors; that is, where the x and y entries in $[x // y]$ are vectors rather than just single numbers (see chapter 8).

In general, we must define a *transactional unit* as a unit that is the product $(x/y)(y/x)$ of two fractions, one fraction the reciprocal or inverse of the other. When a transactional unit is multiplied times an equational unit, one fraction (x/y) is *applied to* (multiplied times) one account (fraction) and the reciprocal fraction (y/x) is applied to some other account. If neither x nor y are 1, then neither application can be characterized as a pure debit or credit; they are mixed debits and credits.

The final equational unit is obtained by multiplying all the transactional units times the original equational unit. We may assume, without loss of generality, that each account is in reduced form; that is, each fraction is in lowest terms. According to any criteria, the fractions in the equational unit can be divided into two groups, L and R. If d/c *is in L,* then the account decodes as the fraction d/c on the LHS of the final equation. If d/c is in R, then the account decodes as the fraction c/d on the RHS of the final equation. The final equation is the equation between the product of the resulting LHS fractions and the resulting RHS fractions. This equation of fractions can be turned into an equation between products of integers by clearing the fractions.

Before turning to an example, we will summarize the relationship between additive and multiplicative double-entry bookkeeping by giving a table of analogies:

Additive	*Multiplicative*
plus	times
T-terms $[d // c]$	fractions d/c
d,c nonnegative numbers	d,c nonzero integers
$[w // x] + [y // z]$	$(w/x)(y/z) = (wy/xz)$
$= [w + y // x + z]$	
cross sums	cross multiples
$[0 // 0]$	$(1/1)$
$[d // c] + [c // d] = [0 // 0]$	$(d/c)(c/d) = 1/1$
group of differences	group of fractions
zero-terms	units
equational zero-term	equational unit
$[d // c]$ reduced if	(d/c) reduced if
$min(d,c) = 0$	$gcd(d,c) = 1$
transactional zero-terms	transactional units

A Multiplicative-Bookkeeping Example

To develop an example of multiplicative accounting, we must review a basic law of counting. Suppose one has to make m different choices. For $i = 1, \ldots, m$ suppose that there are $n(i)$ possibilities to choose from. There are $n(1)$ possibilities for the first choice, $n(2)$ possibilities for the second choice, and so forth for the m choices. In how many different ways can one make the m choices?

For example, suppose there were three choices with 5 possibilities on the first choice, 2 possibilities on the second choice, and 7 possibilities on the third choice; that is, $n(1) = 5$, $n(2) = 2$, and $n(3) = 7$. On the first choice there are 5 possibilities, and for each of those there are 2 possibilities on the second choice, so there are $2 \times 5 = 10$ ways the first two choices could be made. And for each of those 10, there are 7 ways the third choice could be made, so there are in total $2 \times 5 \times 7 = 70$ ways that the three choices could be made. The total is thus the product of the number of possibilities on each choice.

In general, the *law of counting* is that given m choices with $n(i)$ possibilities on the *i-th* choice for $i = 1, \ldots, m,$ the total number of ways the m choices can be made is the *product* of the number of possibilities on each choice; that is $n(1) \times n(2) \times \ldots \times n(m)$ (see Chung 1975, p. 44).

Let us suppose that the choices are arranged in a rectangular array, say, a two-row-by-three-column array. Each cell in the array has a number associated with it, the number of possibilities in that choice. For example, consider the following array of choices.

	Column 1	Column 2	Column 3
Row 1	6	9	4
Row 2	2	7	10

There are six choices in all and the total number of ways of making the six choices is: $6 \times 9 \times 4 \times 2 \times 7 \times 10 = 30,240$. But there are two different ways of arriving at this total. There are $(6)(9)(4) = 216$ ways of making a choice from *Row* 1 and $(2)(7)(10) = 140$ ways of making a choice from *Row* 2. Then there are $(216)(140) = 30,240$ ways of making a choice from the *Row* 1 choices and the *Row* 2 choices. That is the row count.

For a column count, there are $(6)(2) = 12$ ways of choosing from *Column* 1, $(9)(7) = 63$ ways of choosing from *Column* 2, and $(4)(10) = 40$ ways of choosing from *Column* 3. Hence there are $(12)(63)(40) = 30,240$ ways of choosing from the *Column* 1, *Column* 2, and *Column* 3 choices. Equating the row and column counts yields the *initial choices' equation:*

Row 1		*Row* 2		*Column* 1		*Column* 2		*Column* 3
216	$\times$	140	$=$	12	$\times$	63	$\times$	40.

Transactions will change the number of possibilities associated with the cells. If we allow the integral values in the cells to change to any other integer value in a transaction, then the complications will arise where transactions must be represented by mixed debits and credits. To avoid these complications in this introductory treatment, we restrict ourselves to special transactions where the number of possibilities associated with a cell can only change by being multiplied or divided by an integer. Any change in integral values can then be obtained by a succession of these special transactions.

There is a convenient model for these special transactions. Think of each cell as a box containing balls. The balls have numbers on them like billiard balls. The number of possibilities associated with a box is not the number of balls in the box; it is the product of the numbers on the balls in the box. Then adding or removing a ball will have precisely the desired effect of multiplying or dividing the number of possibilities associated with the box by an integer, the integer on the ball.

A *prime number* is an integer with no divisors other than 1 and itself. For example, the first few primes are 2, 3, 5, 7, 11, 13, and 17. Every integer can be uniquely factored into a product of primes. Hence we can, without loss of generality, restrict the balls in the boxes to balls with prime numbers on them. The number of possibilities associated with each box must be a positive integer so there cannot be an empty box. Each otherwise empty box is supplied with a special ball with 1 on it, a 1-ball.

The rectangular array of choices considered above can now be modeled as an array of boxes containing certain balls with prime numbers on them. For example, the *Row* 1 *Column* 1 choice has 6 possibilities and as a product of primes, 6 = (2)(3). Hence that box contains a 2-ball and a 3-ball. In a similar fashion, the other cells can be given balls-in-boxes interpretations.

	Column 1	Column 2	Column 3
Row 1	one 2-ball one 3-ball	two 3-balls	two 2-balls
Row 2	one 2-ball	one 7-ball	one 2-ball one 5-ball

It must be emphasized that the balls themselves are not the choices associated with the boxes; the balls just serve to keep track of the number of possibilities associated with each box.

Transactions occur as balls are added to, removed from, or shuffled around the boxes. Temporary accounts can be used to accumulate the changes in permanent accounts. In multiplicative bookkeeping, the temporary account is a *multiplier* that is multiplied times the old permanent account to get the new permanent account. The temporary account is the *ratio* of the new and the old permanent account, just as in additive accounting it was the difference between the new and old permanent account. Since that difference could be negative, additive temporary accounts were expressed as the difference between two nonnegative accounts; that is:

$$\text{Net Income} = \text{Revenue} - \text{Expenses.}$$

Similarly in multiplicative bookkeeping, the ratio between the new and old integral-valued permanent accounts might not itself be an integer. Hence to keep all accounts as integral valued (prior to being encoded as fractions), a temporary account could be expressed as the ratio of integral accounts:

Ratio Multiplier = (Integral Multiplier)/(Integral Divisor),

or in brief, $RM = IM/ID$.

To illustrate the use of multiplicative temporary accounts, we arbitrarily pick a permanent account such as *Row* 1 and multiply it by its ratio multiplier, *Row* 1 *RM,* set at the initial value of 1/1:

Row 1   *Row* 1 *RM*   *Row* 2

(216)   ×   (1/1)   ×   (140)   =

Column 1   *Column* 2   *Column* 3

(12)   ×   (63)   ×   (40).

The fractional account, *Row* 1 *RM,* can be expressed as a ratio of integral accounts: *Row* 1 *RM* = (*Row* 1 *IM*)/(*Row* 1 *ID*). The above equation can then be expressed in *integral form* as an equation between products of integers by multiplying both sides by the *Row* 1 *ID:*

Row 1   *Row* 1 *IM*   *Row* 2

(216)   ×   (1)   ×   (140)   =

Column 1   *Column* 2   *Column* 3   *Row* 1 *ID*

(12)   ×   (63)   ×   (40)   ×   (1).

This form is analogous to putting the equation in positive form in the additive case.

The equation can now be encoded as an equational unit. The left-hand-side accounts are encoded as *debit fractions,* such as (216/1) and (140/1), while the right-hand-side accounts are encoded as *credit fractions,* such as (1/12), (1/63), and (1/40) with the resultant *initial equational unit:*

Row 1   *Row* 1 *IM*   *Row* 2

(216/1)   ×   (1/1)   ×   (140/1)   ×

Column 1   *Column* 2   *Column* 3   *Row* 1 *ID*

(1/12)   ×   (1/63)   ×   (1/40)   ×   (1/1).

Since there are only times signs between the double-entry fractional accounts, the signs can be left implicit and the accounts can be shuffled around putting the temporary accounts last. This yields the multiplicative ledger:

$$\begin{array}{ccc} Row\ 1 & Row\ 2 & Column\ 1 \\ (216/1) & (140/1) & (1/12) \end{array}$$

$$\begin{array}{cccc} Column\ 2 & Column\ 3 & Row\ 1\ IM & Row\ 1\ ID \\ (1/63) & (1/40) & (1/1) & (1/1). \end{array}$$

We now consider some sample transactions:

1. a 3-ball is put in the *Row 2 Column* 2 box,
2. a 2-ball is taken out of *Row 1 Column* 1 box, and
3. a 5-ball is moved from *Row 2* to *Row 1* in *Column 3*.

   Due to the special nature of the transactions in his model, each transaction takes the classical form of applying an equal (multiplicative) debit and credit to the account. A debit of d to an account means to multiply the account by $(d/1)$ and a credit of c means to multiply by $(1/c)$. Each transactional unit has the form $(d/1)(1/c)$ for some $d = c$. The journal is the list of the transactional units with the accounts being debited and credited.

Journal

Transaction	Description	Accounts	(Debit	/	Credit)
1.	3-ball into *Row 2* Column 2	*Row 2* Column 2	(3 (1	/ /	1) 3)
2.	2-ball out of *Row 1* Column 1	Column 1 *Row 1 ID*	(2 (1	/ /	1) 2)
3.	5-ball from *Row 2* to *Row 1* Column 3	*Row 1 IM* *Row 2*	(5 (1	/ /	1) 5)

   By multiplying these transactional units times the equational unit (*posting to the Ledger*), we obtain the updated ledger:

$$\begin{array}{ccc} Row\ 1 & Row\ 2 & Column\ 1 \\ (216/1) & (420/5) & (2/12) \end{array}$$

$$\begin{array}{cccc} Column\ 2 & Column\ 3 & Row\ 1\ IM & Row\ 1\ ID \\ (1/189) & (1/40) & (5/1) & (1/2). \end{array}$$

For example, the *Row* 2 account was debited with 3 and credited with 5 so it is $(140/1)(3/1)(1/5) = (420/5)$.

The temporary accounts are then closed using the closing transactions.

Transaction	Description	Accounts	(Debit	/	Credit)
C.	Close *Row* 1 *IM* into *Row* 1	*Row* 1 *Row* 1 *IM*	(5 (1	/ /	1) 5)
C.	Close *Row* 1 *ID* into *Row* 1	*Row* 1 *ID* *Row* 1	(2 (1	/ /	1) 2)

Posting to the ledger yields:

Row 1	*Row* 2	*Column* 1
(1080/2)	(420/5)	(2/12)

Column 2	*Column* 3	*Row* 1 *IM*	*Row* 2 *ID*
(1/189)	(1/40)	(5/5)	(2/2).

Putting all the accounts in reduced form; that is, putting the fractions in lowest terms, yields:

Row 1	*Row* 2	*Column* 1
(540/1)	(84/1)	(1/6)

Column 2	*Column* 3	*Row* 1 *IM*	*Row* 1 *ID*
(1/189)	(1/40)	(1/1)	(1/1).

It remains to decode the equational unit (ledger with times signs) to obtain the final-choices equation. Each account is decoded according to the side of the equation it originally came from. Dropping the closed temporary accounts, this leaves the row accounts in *L* and the column accounts in *R*. Hence we have the final-choices' equation:

Row 1		*Row* 2		*Column* 1		*Column* 2		*Column* 3
540	×	84	=	6	×	189	×	40.

7 Introductory Property Theory

Introduction

The subject matter of *property theory* is the abstract theoretical treatment of the appropriation and transfer of property rights and obligations.[1] Descriptive or positive property theory (as in Ellerman, 1980a) must be carefully distinguished from prescriptive or normative property theory (for example, the labor theory of property as in Ellerman 1980b). Our concern here is only with descriptive or positive property theory. In particular, our topic is *property accounting,* which is the use of the formal machinery of vector accounting to describe the subject matter of property theory—such as the appropriation and transfer of the property rights and obligations underlying value accounting. In short:

Property Accounting = Property Theory + Vector Accounting.

Any T-account in the value-accounting model; that is, any value account, has an underlying T-account in the property-accounting model; that is, an underlying property account. Value is the value of property. The values appearing in the value account are the market values of the property rights and obligations in the underlying property account. Symbolically:

Prices × Property T-account = Value T-account.

There are two basic ways in which property rights and obligations change: (1) by *transactions;* that is, bilateral (or multilateral) and unilateral transfers between legal parties and (2) by the *appropriations* of a legal party. These two ways correspond roughly to what are called *external transactions* and *internal transactions* in conventional accounting.

Transactions

Transactions (that is, external transactions) will be analyzed into two types: (a) bilateral *market transactions,* where the *quid* is equal in market value to the *quo* and (b) *unilateral transfers* (also called *nonreciprocal transfers*) such as dividend distributions, subscriptions for newly issued corporate shares, taxes, gifts, and grants. Market transactions include the purchase of the inputs and the sale of outputs. The only unilateral transfers in the model being developed are the dividends and new share subscriptions.[2] A party neither gains nor loses any market value as a result of a market transaction (by definition). A unilateral transfer will generally affect a party's net worth.

In the property-accounting model, there are two new temporary T-accounts: Market Transactions and Unilateral Transfers. The T-account of Transactions is the sum of Market Transactions and Unilateral Transfers. It accounts for all changes in property rights and obligations due to bilateral or unilateral legal transfers between parties—as opposed to changes due to the appropriations of a party. The account unilateral Transfers is the sum of the T-accounts of Dividends and Subscriptions. More detailed models would include other subaccounts such as Taxes, Gifts, and Grants. Market Transactions could be expressed as the sum of T-accounts for Sales and Purchases, and those accounts could be further subdivided if desired. In all the subaccounts of Transactions, property transferred to the firm or party is a credit and property transferred from the party is a debit.

Legal transfers of property between parties are *public* events with legally recognized criteria of transference or conveyance, such as legal contracts. Descriptive property theory takes the criteria for legally valid transfers of property as given. A valid contract for a market exchange will be recorded by respectively crediting and debiting the incoming and outgoing property to Market Transactions or the appropriate subaccounts. A valid unilateral transfer of property will be recorded by respectively crediting or debiting the incoming or outgoing property to Unilateral Transfers or its subaccounts. These accounting transactions, which record legal transfers or exchanges of property, will be called *discharging transactions*.

Appropriation and Expropriation

Before a property right can be transferred, it must first be created or initiated, and it will eventually be terminated. The creation or initial establishment of the property right to an asset, which was previously unowned or is newly produced, is the *appropriation* of the property right. In appropriation, a legal party acquires a property right or legal title to an asset—but not by a transfer from a prior owner. Appropriation establishes the initial right and title. The opposite of appropriation occurs when a party loses, abandons, or otherwise terminates a property right—but not by transferring it to another party. This meaning is the original sense of the word *expropriation*. According to *Black's Law Dictionary;*

This word [expropriation] primarily denotes a voluntary surrender of rights or claims; the act of divesting oneself of that which was previously claimed as one's own, or renouncing it. In this sense, it is the opposite of "appropriation." . . . A meaning has been attached to the term, imported from foreign jurisprudence, which makes it synonymous with the exercise of the power of eminent domain. (1968, p. 692, entry under "Expropriation")

Thus appropriation initiates a property right to an asset and expropriation (in its original sense) terminates it; in between, the property right is transferred. However, since the word *expropriation* is understood commonly today in the other derived sense meaning the compulsory transfer of assets to the government, we may use an alternative expression. Instead of saying the *expropriation of assets,* we may say the *appropriation of liabilities.* Thus instead of the appropriation and expropriation of assets, there is the appropriation of assets and liabilities. When we do use the word *expropriation,* it will be in its original sense as the opposite of appropriation—as the termination of title.

In double-entry property accounting, assets appear as property credits and liabilities appear as property debits in the equity or total ownership property account called *Total Assets and Liabilities.* It is the property account underlying the value account of Net Worth, so:

$$\text{Prices} \times \text{Total Assets and Liabilities} = \text{Net Worth}.$$

Hence the appropriation and expropriation of assets is formulated in property accounting as the appropriation of property credits and property debits. The temporary property T-account, which contains all the appropriated property credits and debits, is called the *Whole-Product T-account* since it represents all the assets and liabilities resulting from production (see Ellerman 1980a, 1980b). Indeed, the Whole-Product T-account is the property account underlying the value T-account of Production in the market-value-accounting model; that is:

$$\text{Prices} \times \text{Whole Product} = \text{Production}.$$

The balance in Production, namely the economic profit, is the net market value of the property credits and debits in the Whole Product.

One of the perennial questions in accounting and economics is the question of what is *Income* (in the sense of net income) or *Profit.* Property accounting allows an answer to that question in terms of the underlying property rights and liabilities. Profit is the net value of the property assets and liabilities that are *appropriated;* that is, Profit is the value of the Whole Product. All changes in the underlying assets and liabilities can be classified as market transactions, unilateral transfers, or appropriations. Market transactions are value swaps, so they cannot contribute to net income. Unilateral transfers are clearly to be treated as special cases and not grouped into any measure of Income resulting from the operations of the firm. That leaves Income or Profit as the net value of what is appropriated, as the value of the Whole Product.

An appropriation, since it only involves one legal party such as a corporation, is not as public as a legal transfer between parties. Indeed, it is only the contested appropriations that involve two or more parties and come to the attention of the legal authorities. For example, a property damage suit arises out of a situation where one party, the plaintiff, has de facto appropriated certain liabilities that the plaintiff believes should be appropriated by another party. If the court agrees, then that decision is an example of a legally enforced appropriation of liabilities by the defendant. But such examples are rare whereas the matter of appropriating liabilities arises whenever property is consumed, used up, or otherwise destroyed in all production or consumption activities. The matter of appropriating assets arises whenever new property is created, such as in any production activities. If contract is the normal legal mechanism for transferring property, what is the normal legal mechanism for the appropriation of the assets and liabilities created in production and consumption?

It is interesting that this question does not seem to be sharply posed in the economic, legal, or philosophical literature. When the question of appropriation is discussed, it concerns not day-to-day production and consumption but some original or primal distributions of property. Moreover, the usual treatment of appropriation considers only assets and neglects the symmetrical treatment of liabilities. Economists sometimes discuss the initial or original distribution of factor ownership or income in their models. Jurists and philosophers contemplate the original appropriation of unowned or commonly owned objects in a manner following Locke's example—which sets the context as a mythical original state of society. Yet new property is created and old property is consumed in everyday production and consumption activities not just in some mythical "original position."

In the economic literature, production is sometimes described as *trading with Nature*. That phrase is a metaphor not a description of a legal mechanism of appropriation. Economists are well aware of the legal mechanism of contract used to acquire and disacquire property rights in market exchanges. But conventional economics has ignored the legal mechanism used to acquire and disacquire property rights in trades with Nature.

The normal legal mechanism of appropriation is indeed invisible in the sense that it is an invisible-hand mechanism; it involves no explicit or overt intervention by the legal authorities. When the law does not intervene to reassign liabilities (for example, a damage suit), then the laissez faire solution prevails; the liabilities lie where they have fallen. Thus the normal legal mechanism for the appropriation of liabilities is quite simple; each party voluntarily accepts the liabilities that fall on that party. If a liability should be involuntarily imposed on a party, then the party may try to overturn the laissez faire solution by seeking legal redress.

The normal legal mechanism for the appropriation of assets follows naturally from the mechanism for the appropriation of liabilities. Nothing comes from nothing. New assets are born out of old liabilities. Producing outputs requires using up inputs. Revenues require expenses. The new asset-appropriation mechanism is based on the appropriation of the associated or *matched* liabilities. When new assets are produced, the party who appropriated the matching liabilities for the used-up inputs has the legally defensible claim on the new assets. Hence we have the *laissez faire mechanism of appropriation:* Let the liabilities generated by an activity lie where they have fallen, and then let that party that assumed the liabilities claim any appropriate new assets resulting from the activity. This is the legal mechanism of appropriation that governs normal day-to-day production and consumption activities.

In the market-value-accounting model, revenues and expenses were determined on a production basis. The purchase of inventoried inputs is not equivalent to the appropriation of the liability for using up the inputs (that is, the expropriation of the inputs). As long as a unit of the input remains in inventory, the unit could be resold so that some other party would end up appropriating the liability for using up that asset. It is only as the inputs are consumed in production that the firm laissez faire appropriates those liabilities (that is, expropriates those assets). Thus the expropriation of an asset is reflected in the value-accounting model as the expiration of the cost of the asset; that is, the recognition of the asset's value as an expense. That event is recorded as a debit of the asset's value to the Production account in value accounting and as a debit of the asset itself to the underlying Whole-Product account in property accounting. The laissez faire appropriation of the produced-output assets is reflected in the value-accounting model as the recognition of the asset's value as revenue. That event is recorded as a credit of the asset's value to the Production account in market-value accounting and as a credit of the asset itself to the Whole-Product account in property accounting.

Since property rights and obligations can change only by (1) transactions and (2) appropriations, the difference between the *equity* property account of Total Assets and Liabilities at the beginning and end of the time period is the Transactions account plus the Whole-Product account:

Change in Assets and Liabilities = Transactions + Whole Product.

The value of the Whole Product is the economic profit, $\pi(T)$. The Transactions account is the sum of Market Transactions and Unilateral Transfers. The net value of Market Transactions is zero by definition. The credit balance in Unilateral Transfers is $SUBS(T) - DIV(T)$. Hence the change in the value of Total Assets and Liabilities; that is, the increase in the value account of Net Worth, between the beginning and end of the period is:

$$\text{Change in Net Worth} = SUBS(T) - DIV(T) + \pi(T)$$

as shown on the Income Statement of the value-accounting model.

Introductory Property Accounting

Before proceeding with a detailed property-accounting model in the next chapter, we will present an ultra-simple property-accounting model in this section. A number of theoretical shortcuts will be employed, and detailed explanations will be postponed until the full development. In particular, time will be ignored—as if all the activities took place at the same time.

There are only three types of assets: (1) cash, (2) outputs, and (3) inputs. There are no fixed assets. The initial balance sheet has cash, output inventory, and input inventory as assets. The property vectors will have three components: cash, outputs, inputs. The initial asset vector is Assets = (5000,20,15), so there is $5,000 cash on hand, the output inventory contains 20 physical units of the outputs, and the input inventory contains 15 physical units of the inputs. The debt will be represented by its current balance, the amount of cash that would just pay it off. The debt vector is Debts = (2000,0,0). This yields the initial balance-sheet equation (or *identity*):

$$\begin{array}{ccccc}
\text{Assets} & = & \text{Debts} & + & (\text{Assets} - \text{Debts}) \\
(5000,20,15) & = & (2000,0,0) & + & (3000,20,15).
\end{array}$$

This equation encodes as the following equational zero-term (with the temporary property accounts added in):

Assets   Liabilities   Total Assets and Liabilities

$[(5000,20,15) // 0]$ + $[0 // (200,0,0)]$ + $[0 // (3000,20,15)]$

         Change in Assets   Whole Product   Sales   Purchases
         and Liabilities

   + $[0 // 0]$ + $[0 // 0]$ + $[0 // 0]$ + $[0 // 0]$

There are only two market transactions: 120 units of the input are purchased for $10 each, and 100 units of the output are sold for $15 each. In the internal transactions of production, 110 units of the inputs are used up in production, and 90 units of the outputs are produced. The journal lists the transactional zero-terms added to the initial equational zero-term. Usually several property accounting transactions will underlie a single-value-accounting transaction. For instance, the first three property-accounting transactions record the purchase of the inputs.

Journal

See next page ⟶ ➤

Ledger

	Assets					Liabilities		
	[(5000,20,15)	//	(0,0,0)]		[(0,0,0)	//	(2000,0,0)]
(1)	[(0,0,120)	//	(0,0,0)]				
(2)	[(0,0,0)	//	(1200,0,0)]		Suppliers		
(4)	[(0,0,0)	//	(0,0,110)]	(1)	[(0,0,0)	//	(0,0,120)]
(5)	[(0,90,0)	//	(0,0,0)]	(2)	[(1200,0,0)	//	(0,0,0)j
(6)	[(0,0,0)	//	(0,100,0)]	(3)	[(0,0,120)	//	(1200,0,0)]
(7)	[(1500,0,0)	//	(0,0,0)]				

	[(6500,110,135)	//	(1200,100,110)]
	= [(5300,10,25)	//	(0,0,0)]

		Customers		
(6)	[(0,100,0)	//	(0,0,0)]
(7)	[(0,0,0)	//	(1500,0,0)]
(8)	[(1500,0,0)	//	(0,100,0)]

	Purchases		
(3)	[(1200,0,0)	//	(0,0,120)]
(9)	[(0,0,120)	//	(1200,0,0)]

	Sales		
(8)	[(0,100,0)	//	(1500,0,0)]
(11)	[(1500,0,0)	//	(0,100,0)]

	Total Assets and Liabilities		
	[(0,0,0)	//	(3000,20,15)]
(12)	[(1200,100,110)	//	(1500,90,120)]

	[(1200,100,110)	//	(4500,110,135)]
	= [(0,0,0)	//	(3300,10,25)]

	Change in Assets and Liabilities		
(9)	[(1200,0,0)	//	(0,0,120)]
(10)	[(0,0,110)	//	(0,90,0)]
(11)	[(0,100,0)	//	(1500,0,0)]
(12)	[(1500,90,120)	//	(1200,100,110)]

	Whole Product		
(4)	[(0,0,110)	//	(0,0,0)]
(5)	[(0,0,0)	//	(0,90,0)]
(10)	[(0,90,0)	//	(0,0,110)]

Since there are no unilateral transfers, the preclosing balance in Change in Assets and Liabilities:

$$[(1200,100,110) \,// \,(1500,90,120)] = [(0,10,0) \,// \,(300,0,10)],$$

Journal

Transaction	Description	Accounts	[Debit	//	Credit]
1.	In-transfer of the inputs	Assets Suppliers	[(0,0,120) [(0,0,0)	// //	(0,0,0)] (0,0,120)]
2.	Out-transfer of the cash	Supplier Assets	[(1200,0,0) [(0,0,0)	// //	(0,0,0)] (1200,0,0)]
3.	Discharge transaction	Supplier Purchases	[(0,0,120) [(1200,0,0)	// //	(1200,0,0)] (0,0,120)]
4.	Use inputs in production	Whole product Assets	[(0,0,110) [(0,0,0)	// //	(0,0,0)] (0,0,110)]
5.	Production of the outputs	Assets Whole product	[(0,90,0) [(0,0,0)	// //	(0,0,0)] (0,90,0)]
6.	Out-transfer of the outputs	Customers Assets	[(0,100,0) [(0,0,0)	// //	(0,0,0)] (0,100,0)]

7.	In-transfer of the cash	Assets	[(1500,0,0)	//	(0,0,0)]
		Customer	[0,(0,0)	//	(1500,0,0)]
8.	Discharge transaction	Sales	[(0,100,0)	//	(1500,0,0)]
		Customers	[(1500,0,0)	//	(0,100,0)]
9.	Close purchases into summary dA&L	Change in A&L	[(1200,0,0)	//	(0,0,120)]
		Purchases	[(0,0,120)	//	(1200,0,0)]
10.	Close whole product into summary dA&L	Change in A&L	[(0,0,110)	//	(0,90,0)]
		Whole product	[(0,90,0)	//	(0,0,110)]
11.	Close sales into summary dA&L	Change in A&L	[(0,100,0)	//	(1500,0,0)]
		Sales	[(1500,0,0)	//	(0,100,0)]
12.	Close summary dA&L into total A&L	Total A&L	[(1200,100,110)	//	(1500,90,120)]
		Change in A&L	[(1500,90,120)	//	(1200,100,110)]

is the sum of (the preclosing balances in) the Market Transactions, Sales and Purchases, and Whole Product:

Sales   Purchases   Whole Product

$[(0,100,0)//(1500,0,0)] + [(1200,0,0)// (0,0,120)] + [(0,0,110)//(0,90,0)]$

The Whole-Product T-account specifies that 90 units of output were appropriated (priced at \$15 each) and 110 units of the inputs were expropriated (priced at \$10 each), so the economic profit or value of the whole product is (\$15 × 90) − (\$10 × 110) = \$250. By the change in Assets and Liabilities T-account in reduced form, $[(0,10,0)//(300,0,10)]$, we see that the net cash flow was \$300, that the input inventory investment was 10 physical units, and that the output inventory disinvestment was 10 physical units. The \$300 of net cash flow results from the \$250 profit plus the net inventory disinvestment of \$50 = (\$15 × 10) − (\$10 × 10).

After totaling each property T-account in the ledger and taking its balance (putting it in reduced form), we can drop the closed temporary accounts and reinsert the plus signs between the permanent accounts to yield the *final equational zero-term:*

Assets   Liabilities   Total Assets and Liabilities

$[(5300,10,25)//(0,0,0)] + [(0,0,0)//(2000,0,0)] +   [(0,0,0)//(3300,10,25)]$

This decodes to the *final balance-sheet equation:*

$$\text{Assets} = \text{Debts} + \text{Assets} - \text{Debts}$$
$$(5300,10,25) = (2000,0,0) + (3300,10,25).$$

Notes

1. Property theory should be distinguished from what is called *the economics of property rights* (Furubotn and Pejovich, 1974). The latter is a part of price theory in economics; it takes a broader approach to price-theoretic models by taking the structure of property rights as variable rather than always fixed. The tools of price-theoretic analysis are applied to a wide range of institutional frameworks of property rights to analyze the effects on the economic behavior of producers and consumers. In contrast, property theory is not a part of price theory; the subject matter is the property-rights structure itself not its effects on economic behavior. That is, the subject matter is the theory of property rights itself, not the economics of property rights. Property theory could be considered as a part of theoretical

jurisprudence if it were not so intimately related to accounting and economics. Perhaps it is best to resist the temptation to stuff property theory into an academic pidgeonhole; the world is not always split into departments like a university. There is an older conception of *political economy,* as in J.S. Mill's *Principles of Political Economy* (1848, esp. book II, chapters I and II, "Of Property" and "The Same Subject Continued") that encompassed parts of jurisprudence, accounting, and political theory in addition to the modern narrow definition of economics. Property theory is a part of that broader conception of political economy (Ellerman, 1980a).

2. It might be questioned whether dividend distributions and new share subscriptions are unilateral transfers between the corporation and individual shareholders as separate legal parties. If an individual buys a new share for one-hundred dollars, then doesn't the person just engage in a market transaction receiving one-hundred dollars of property (the share) in return for the one-hundred dollars cash? That would only be the case if the person purchased a debt instrument from the corporation. In that instance, the corporation's assets and liabilities increase by one-hundred dollars so there is no change in the corporate net worth and no change in the individual's net worth. But when a corporation issues a new equity instrument for one-hundred dollars, that paid in capital increases the company's assets with no corresponding increase in liabilities. Hence the net worth of the corporation increases by one-hundred dollars. If the individual received *another* hundred dollars in the form of the share, then that would be two increases of one-hundred dollars offset only by the individual's one-hundred-dollars payment. Thus total social wealth would have increased by $100 (= $200 − $100) as a result of the share sale—which is absurd.

It is double-counting to count the share's value as distinct from the increase in the corporate net worth. The one-hundred-dollars increase in the corporate net worth is reflected just in the one-hundred dollars of value in the hands of the new shareholder. The individual participates in two separate legal parties—the corporation as a legal person and the individual himself or herself as a legal person. The one-hundred-dollars increase in net worth is enjoyed by the corporation (and thus by its individual owners or members) while the one-hundred-dollars decrease is suffered by the individual as a separate legal person. Thus the purchase of a new share is a unilateral transfer from an individual as a separate legal person to a corporation having the individual as a member or part owner. A dividend distribution is similarly a unilateral transfer in the opposite direction from the corporation as a legal person to the individual owners as separate legal persons.

8

The Property-Accounting Model

The Property Balance Sheet

Different components in a property vector represent different types of property. The same commodity at different points in time is treated as distinct types of property requiring different vector components. Our accounting model has been kept relatively simple so the vectors are manageable for expository purposes. There are ten components required in the property vectors. The components in order represent:

component 1   = Cash at time T,

component 2   = Final goods at time T,

component 3   = Raw materials at time T,

component 4   = Vintage $m-1$ machines at time T,

component 5   = Cash at time $T + 1$,

component 6   = Final goods at time $T + 1$,

component 7   = Raw materials at time $T + 1$,

component 8   = Vintage m machines at time $T + 1$,

component 9   = Labor during the time period from T to $T + 1$, and

component 10 = Cash at time $T + 2$.

Let $ASSETS(t)$ be the vector of balance-sheet assets at any time t and let $DEBTS(t)$ be the vector of balance-sheet liabilities (legal obligations for future-dated out transfers of assets) at time t. At T, the assets are:

$$ASSETS(T) = (CASH(T), FG(T), RM(T), 1, 0, 0, 0, 0, 0, 0),$$

and the liabilities are:

$$DEBTS(T) = (0, 0, 0, 0, D, 0, 0, 0, 0, D).$$

Hence we have the: property balance sheet equation at time T:

$$ASSETS(T) = DEBTS(T) + (ASSETS(T) - \text{DEBTS}(T)).$$

A price vector has in its i-th component the price per unit of the i-th commodity (the i-th commodity being represented by the i-th component in the property vectors). Since time differences are already reflected in distinct components in the property vectors, any change in the price of a commodity over time would be reflected in the distinct components of a price vector. In our model, we have assumed constant prices to focus attention on property changes rather than pure value phenomena such as unrealized capital gains or losses. There is essentially one price vector except for changes in the unit of value such as time T dollars or time $T + 1$ dollars. The price vector with all prices expressed in time T dollars is:

$$PRICES(T) = (1, P, P', C(m - 1), 1/(1 + r), P/(1 + r), P'/(1 + r),$$
$$C(m)/(1 + r), W/(1 + r), 1/(1 + r)^2).$$

For example, the price at time T of a unit of raw materials at time $T + 1$ is $P'/(1 + r)$. Since the unit of value, time T dollars, is transformed into time $T + 1$ dollars by multiplying by $(1 + r)$, we have:

$$PRICES(T + 1) = (1 + r)PRICES(T).$$

The value of a property vector when evaluated at a certain price vector is the scalar product of the price vector and the property vector. This scalar product is computed by multiplying each price times the corresponding component of the property vector and summing the results. Hence the value in time T dollars of the assets at time T is:

$$\text{PRICES}(T) \times ASSETS(T) = CASH(T) + PFG(T) + P'RM(T)$$
$$+ C(m - 1) = GBV(T),$$

and the value of the debts is:

$$PRICES(T) \times DEBTS(T) = D/(1 + r) + D/(1 + r)^2 = D(T).$$

The value of $ASSETS(T) - DEBTS(T)$ is the difference:

$$PRICES(T) \times (ASSETS(T) - DEBTS(T)) = GBV(T) - D(T)$$
$$= NBV(T).$$

Hence if each property vector in the property balance sheet is multiplied by the price vector, we obtain the value balance-sheet equation:

$$GBV(T) = D(T) + NBV(T).$$

If the unit of value is changed to time $T + 1$ dollars, then the same property vectors are multiplied by $PRICES(T + 1)$ to obtain the time T balance sheet expressed in time $T + 1$ dollars:

$$(1 + r)GBV(T) = (1 + r)D(T) + (1 + r)NBV(T).$$

Double-entry property accounting requires that the vectors in the original property equation be encoded as T-terms to obtain the original equation zero-term. The T-terms used here have the form $[d // c]$ where d and c are nonnegative vectors with ten components each. The symbol 0 will be used, according to the context, to represent both the zero vector and the scalar zero; that is, $(0, \ldots, 0) = 0$. Any vector v, possibly with some negative components, can always be represented as the difference between two nonnegative vectors, $v = pos(v) - neg(v)$. The nonnegative vector $pos(v)$ has as its components any positive components of v and otherwise its components are zero. The nonnegative vector $neg(v)$ selects the absolute value of any negative components of v, and otherwise its components are zero. For example, for:

$$v = (1, -2,3, -4,5, -6,7, -8,9, -10),$$

$$pos(v) = (1,0,3,0,5,0,7,0,9,0),$$

$$neg(v) = (0,2,0,4,0,6,0,8,0,10), \text{ and}$$

$$v = pos(v) - neg(v).$$

If a vector v is on the LHS of the original vector equation, then it is encoded as the T-term $[pos(v) // neg(v)]$, and if v is on the RHS of the equation, it is encoded as $[neg(v) // pos(v)]$. Thus a vector equation $x = y + z$ is encoded to obtain the equation zero-term:

$$[pos(x) // neg(x)] + [neg(y) // pos(y)] + [neg(z) // pos(z)].$$

Decoding reverses the process. A LHS T-account $[d // c]$ is decoded as $d - c$ and a RHS T-account $[d // c]$ is decoded as $c - d$ on the respective sides of the resultant vector equation.

We can now encode the original property-balance-sheet equation:

$$ASSETS(T) = DEBTS(T) + (ASSETS(T) - DEBTS(T)).$$

The LHS vector $ASSETS(T)$ is encoded as the property T-account of Assets: $[ASSETS(T) // 0]$. The RHS vector $DEBTS(T)$ is encoded as the property T-account of Liabilities: $[0 // DEBTS(T)]$. The RHS vector $ASSETS(T) - DEBTS(T)$ is encoded at the property T-account of Total Assets and Liabilities (Total A&L) or (A&L): $[DEBTS(T) // ASSETS(T)]$. This yields the equation zero-term:

Assets	Liabilities	Total Assets and Liabilities

$$[ASSETS(T) // 0]   +   [0 // DEBTS(T)]   +   [DEBTS(T) // ASSETS(T)].$$

The original equation zero-term, which is the starting point in the accounting process for the time period, is like the above equation zero term except that the temporary T-accounts (introduced below) must be added in with their initial zero balances.

The product of a price vector times a T-term with vector entries is defined as the T-term with scalar entries, each scalar being the scalar product of the price vector times the vector entry. For example:

$$PRICES(T) \times [DEBTS(T) // ASSETS(T)] =$$

$$= [PRICES(T) \times DEBTS(T) // PRICES(T) \times ASSETS(T)]$$

$$= [D(T) // GBV(T)]$$

$$= [0 // NBV(T)]$$

(assuming that $NBV(T)$ is nonnegative). In general, the relation is:

Prices × Property T-account = Value T-account.

In this relationship, the property account is said to *underlie* the value account, and the value account *corresponds* to the property account. Hence the property T-account of Total Assets and Liabilities:

$$[DEBTS(T) // ASSETS(T)]$$

underlies the value T-account of Net Worth:

$$PRICES(T) \times [DEBTS(T) // ASSETS(T)] = [0 // NBV(T)].$$

(where we assume that $NBV(T)$ is nonnegative).

The property account of Total Assets and Liabilities helps one to understand the metaphorical nature of a common view of assets and liabilities.

> Corresponding to the dollar value of every asset—tangible or intangible—there must necessarily be an exact equal total amount of *claims or ownership*. The value of a $40,000 house is exactly matched by somebody's claim on its ownership consisting, say, of $25,000 owed a creditor and $15,000 owned by its owner. (Samuelson 1976, p. 120)

The idea is to reinterpret liabilities or debts metaphorically as joint claims on assets. Thus the creditor is pictured as claiming part of the asset and the owner as owning the remainder of the asset. If this metaphor of *liabilities cancellation* were consistently applied, it would yield a picture of property relations where there were no liabilities, only jointly claimed assets. The metaphor is clearly inspired by the value cancellation between the value of the assets and the value of the liabilities to yield the net worth. However, this cancellation is only at the value level, not at the underlying property level. A liability is a future-dated asset transfer so it would be represented in a different component of any property vector from a present asset and thus the liability could not cancel with the asset. The cancellation or *netting* only applies to value, not to property. There is the net value of assets, but there is no such thing as *net assets*. In Samuelson's example, the house owner owns 100 percent of the $40,000 house and holds the legal obligation for a series of future-dated asset transfers (the loan payments) with the present value of $25,000. These distinct and noncancellable property rights and obligations are precisely what would be represented in the party's Total Assets and Liabilities property T-account.

A similar metaphor is at work in the view of both the creditors and the shareholders of a corporation as *claimants* on the assets of the corporation. For the reasons stated above, that metaphor is not a correct picture of the structure of property rights in a corporation. The creditors are not joint owners of the corporate assets. The corporation is itself a legal party that owns 100 percent of the corporate assets and holds certain liabilities for future-dated out-transfers of assets to the creditors. The creditors have claims against the corporation whereas the shareholders are the members of the corporation. The liability-cancellation metaphor also does not correctly account for the structure of control rights in a corporation. If the creditors and shareholders were really joint claimants of the corporate assets, then they would share the control rights, jointly elect the board of directors, and so forth. But the direct discretionary decision-making rights over corporate affairs are held by the agents of the shareholders. If one desires to make the point that the shareholders' control over their nominal agents is more fictitious than real in large corporations, then that point should be made explicitly—but it is not an excuse to misrepresent metaphorically the legal structure of a corporation.

The Temporary T-accounts

Let the Total-Assets-and-Liabilities T-account at any time t be symbolized as:

$$A\&L(t) = [DEBTS(t) \; // \; ASSETS(t)].$$

Then the temporary T-account *Change in Assets and Liabilities* for the T-*th* time period could be defined as:

$$dA\&L(T) = A\&L(T + 1) - A\&L(T).$$

This Change-in-Assets-and-Liabilities-property account represents all the party's changes in property rights and obligations during the time period that are channeled through the temporary accounts. It is the property account underlying the Change-in-Net-Worth value account. Property changes either by (external) transactions or appropriations, and these changes are presented by the temporary property accounts of Transactions and the Whole Product. If we symbolize the T-terms in these accounts for the T-*th* period as $Tr(T)$ and $WP(T)$ respectively, then:

$$dA\&L(T) = Tr(T) + WP(T).$$

The account of Transactions is subdivided into Market Transactions, symbolized $MTr(T)$, and Unilateral Transactions, symbolized $UTr(T)$, so:

$$Tr(T) = MTr(T) + UTr(T).$$

The Market Transactions are separated into Purchases, symbolized *Purchases*(T), and Sales, symbolized *Sales*(T), so:

$$MTr(T) = Sales(T) + Purchases(T).$$

An account, such as Purchases, could be further subdivided into purchases of cash (loans), labor, raw materials, and equipment but that would serve no present theoretical purpose. In all the subaccounts of Change in Assets and Liabilities, incoming or appropriated property is a credit and the outgoing or expropriated property is a debit. The tree of subaccounts of the temporary account of Change in Assets and Liabilities is:

Change in Assets and Liabilities	{	Whole Product				
		Transactions	{	Market Transactions	{	Sales
						Purchases
				Unilateral Transfers		

The Personal and Impersonal T-accounts

The property transactions recorded in Transactions and its subaccounts should not be confused with the broader notion of *accounting transactions,* namely the journal entries involving an equal debit and credit. The accounting transactions in value accounting, involving equal debit and credit value, may have one or more underlying accounting transactions in property accounting involving equal debit and credit property vectors. Due to the cancellations at the value level, there may be two or more property-accounting transactions underlying a single value-accounting transaction.

For example, the cash purchase of the raw materials X' from the suppliers was recorded as a single value-accounting transaction crediting Cash and debiting Raw-Materials Inventory with the value $P'X'$. Several property-accounting transactions underlie that value transaction. In property accounting, the suppliers would have a personal balance-sheet T-account, Suppliers, to record transactions with them. Raw-Materials Inventory is debited and the account Suppliers is credited with the property vector having X' in the raw materials at time $T + 1$ component with zeros elsewhere. And Cash is credited and Suppliers is debited with the property vector having $P'X'$ in the cash at time $T + 1$ component with zeros elsewhere.

All external legal parties involved with bilateral or unilateral transfers with the firm have personal balance-sheet T-accounts. For our purposes, it is sufficient to have the personal accounts, Customers, Suppliers, Workers, Creditor 1, and Shareholders. All dealings with each of these parties are channeled through their account. The debit and credit entries in the personal accounts have their naive meanings: property transferred to the party is debited or charged to the party's account and the external party is credited with property transferred to the firm. Ordinarily, Customers is a LHS subaccount of Assets, and Suppliers, Workers, Creditor 1, and Shareholders are RHS subaccounts of Liabilities.

In the example above, the property credit of X' (actually the vector with X' as the seventh component) and the property debit of $P'X'$ (the vector with $P'X'$ as its fifth component) cannot cancel out at the property level (since different vector components are involved). However, those property rights do have the same value so there is a cancellation at the value level. The two entries in the Suppliers account cancel in value so the Suppliers account is not needed in value accounting to record cash transactions. The cash purchase was recorded as a single transaction between Cash and Raw-Materials Inventory (leaving out the intermediate account Suppliers). In property accounting, the two entries in Suppliers do not cancel so it was necessary to explicitly use the personal account of Suppliers to record the cash purchase.

When market transactions involve future-dated assets (that is, credit transactions), the personal account of the outside party is needed even in value accounting. Many personal accounts, such as Accounts Payable, appear in conventional value accounting without the explicit name of the outside party or parties. Indeed, all balance-sheet accounts listed as liabilities as well as Accounts Receivable (for example, Customers) are personal accounts.

After the property accounting transactions recording the cash purchase of raw materials, the Suppliers T-account is $[(0,0,0,0,P'X',0, \ldots 0)$ $//$ $(0,0,0,0,0,0,X',0,0,0)]$. Since the $P'X'$ and X' can never cancel out in property accounting (as their values did in value accounting), some new machinery is needed to *clear* or *discharge* the suppliers' account. This new machinery will be motivated with some intuitive reasoning. If the suppliers had just transferred X' to the firm and got nothing in return for the credit, then they might well expect the commodities X' to be returned. If the firm had just transferred $P'X'$ to the suppliers and got nothing in return for the debit, the firm might well expect the cash returned. If both the raw materials and cash were returned, that would clear the credit and debit in the suppliers' account. We need similarly to clear or discharge the suppliers' account—not because the goods and cash were returned but because they were a swap, a market exchange, a contract. The fact that the in-transfer of X' and the out-transfer of $P'X'$ were a market transaction is recorded by a new accounting transaction that discharges Suppliers into Market Transactions—or in this case into the subaccount of Purchases. In this discharging transaction, the T-term $[(0, \ldots ,0,X',0,0,0)$ $//$ $(0,0,0,0,P'X',0, \ldots)]$ is added to Suppliers thus clearing or discharging it, and the reverse T-term $[(0,0,0,0,P'X',0, \ldots)$ $//$ $(0, \ldots ,0,X',0,0,0)]$ is added to Purchases.

In general, any bilateral or unilateral transfer of property that represents a valid legal transference of property between the firm and an outside party is recorded in property accounting by a discharge of the transferred property from the party's personal account into the appropriate subaccount of Transactions.

The discharging transactions illustrate another new feature in vector accounting in general and in property accounting in particular. The effect of an accounting transaction on a T-account cannot always be reduced to a credit or debit. For example, the T-term:

$$[(0, \ldots ,0,X',0,0,0) \ // \ (0,0,0,0,P'X',0, \ldots ,0)]$$

was added to Suppliers, but that T-term has nonzero entries on both the debit and credit sides. In value accounting, a T-term $[d \ // \ c]$, with nonnegative scalars d and c, can always be reduced to a form $[0 \ // \ c - d]$ or $[d - c \ // \ 0]$ so that its addition to a T-account is either a straight credit or a straight debit. However, when d and c are nonnegative vectors, the T-term cannot in general be reduced to a form where either the debit or credit side is the zero vector. The general reduced form is:

$$[neg(c - d) \text{ // } pos(c - d)]$$

where for each i, the i-th component on either the debit or credit side is zero. Thus both $neg(c - d)$ and $pos(c - d)$ can have positive components, but no component is positive in both vectors. The T-term:

$$[(0, \ldots ,0,X',0,0,0) \text{ // } (0,0,0,0,P'X',0, \ldots ,0)]$$

is in reduced form. Its addition to the T-account Suppliers cannot be characterized as simply a debit or a credit since both are involved. The convention of listing the debit part of a transaction first in the journal is irrelevant for these transactions where each part is a mixture of debits and credits.

The economic activity being modeled does not involve any credit transactions. However, for completeness, we will indicate the property-accounting treatment of a credit transaction. Suppose that in addition to the cash purchase of X' units of raw materials, an additional X'' units were purchased to be paid for with $(1 + r)P'X''$ dollars at time $T + 2$. Then after the in-transfer of the raw materials and the out-transfer of cash at time $T + 1$ (but before the discharge), the suppliers' account is:

$$[(0,0,0,0,P'X',0, \ldots ,0) \text{ // } (0, \ldots ,0,X' + X'',0,0,0)].$$

The discharge records the market transaction, and the market transaction is the exchange of $X' + X''$ units of raw materials for $P'X'$ dollars at time $T + 1$ and $(1 + r)P'X''$ dollars at time $T + 2$. Hence in the discharging transaction, the T-term added to Suppliers, with its reverse added to Purchases, is:

$$[(0, \ldots ,0,X' + X'',0,0,0) \text{ // } (0,0,0,0,P'X',0,0,0,0,(1 + r)P'X'')].$$

With no more activity, the balance-sheet T-account Suppliers has at time $T + 1$ the reduced form:

$$[(0, \ldots ,0) \text{ // } (0, \ldots ,0,(1 + r)P'X'')].$$

The corresponding value account is found by multiplying by *PRICES* $(T + 1)$ to obtain $[0 \text{ // } P'X'']$, which is the Account Payable to the suppliers.

To record the property-accounting transactions, we need to specify the remaining property T-accounts. Aside from the temporary accounts and the personal permanent accounts, there are the impersonal permanent accounts. We will use the same names for these property accounts as the corresponding value accounts. The impersonal permanent balance-sheet accounts are Cash, Final-Goods Inventory, Raw-Materials Inventory, Fixed Equipment, and Labor. These accounts are all subaccounts (see the next section) of Assets.

Subaccounts

We have heretofore used the notion of *subaccount* intuitively, but a more exact definition can now be given. The basic idea is that an account is the sum of its subaccounts, but this idea has a different meaning depending on whether the subaccounts are permanent or temporary. The account of Assets is just the sum of the permanent accounts of Cash, Final-Goods Inventory, Raw-Materials Inventory, Fixed Equipment, Labor, and Customers. Hence at any time *t*, we could take the balance in all the subaccounts of Assets and write the equation:

$$Assets(t) \ = \ Cash(t) \ + \ Final\text{-}Goods \ Inventory(t)$$
$$+ \ Raw\text{-}Materials \ Inventory(t) \ + \ Fixed \ Equipment(t)$$
$$+ \ Labor(t) \ + \ Customers(t).$$

This account, Assets, will appear in formulas where it would be unwieldy to write out all the subaccounts, but only the subaccounts will appear in the ledger.

A slightly different notion of subaccount is appropriate for temporary accounts. The temporary account of Change in Assets and Liabilities (dA&L) is the summary account for the other temporary accounts of Whole Product, Sales, Purchases, and Unilateral Transfers. This means that the other temporary accounts are closed into dA&L at the end of the accounting period. Let the closing balances in the other temporary accounts be $WP(T)$, $Sales(T)$, $Purchases(T)$, and $UTr(T)$. The initial balance in dA&L (and in any temporary account) is [0 // 0] so if the other temporary accounts are closed into dA&L, then its closing balance is:

$$\begin{array}{ccc} Closing \ Balance \ = & Initial \ Balance & + \ Closing \ Balance \\ dA\&L & dA\&L & Whole \ Product \end{array}$$

$$\begin{array}{ccc} + \ Closing \ Balance & + \ Closing \ Balance & + \ Closing \ Balance \\ Sales & Purchases & Unilateral \\ & & Transfer. \end{array}$$

This equation would usually just be written as:

$$dA\&L(T) = WP(T) + Sales(T) + Purchases(T) + UTr(T).$$

The account, dA&L is closed in Total Assets and Liabilities (A&L) so dA&L and its subaccounts could all be referred to as subaccounts of A&L:

$$A\&L(T + 1) = A\&L(T) + dA\&L(T)$$
$$= A\&L(T) + WP(T) + Sales(T) + Purchases(T)$$
$$+ UTr(T).$$

The Property Journal

The journal records the property-accounting transactions. Each transaction is recorded using a transaction zero-term of the form $[d // c] + [c // d]$; that is, a T-term plus its reverse. Each part, such as $[d // c]$ and $[c // d]$, is added to some property T-account that is named in the journal. For example, in the first transaction below, the transaction zero-term is:

$$[(\ldots ,0,X',0, \ldots) // (0, \ldots)] + [(0, \ldots) // (\ldots ,0,X',0, \ldots)].$$

The first T-term is added to the Raw-Materials Inventory T-account and the reverse of the T-term is added to the Suppliers T-account. These T-accounts are in the ledger, which is the collection of T-accounts (labeled T-terms) in the equation zero-term. By adding the transaction zero-term to the equation zero-term (posting to the ledger), a new equation zero-term is obtained. After all the transaction zero-terms have been added, the original equation zero-term is transformed into the resultant equation zero-term.

Before recording any transactions, the original equation zero-term has the form:

	Assets		Liabilities		A&L
	$[ASSETS(T) // 0]$	+	$[0 // DEBTS(T)]$	+	$[DEBTS(T) //$
					$ASSETS(T)]$

	dA&L		WP		Sales		Purchases		UTr
+	$[0 // 0]$	+	$[0 // 0]$	+	$[0 // 0]$	+	$[0 // 0]$	+	$[0 // 0]$,

where the temporary accounts start off with zero balances. The T-account Assets is just shorthand for the sum of Cash, Final-Goods Inventory, Raw-Materials Inventory, Labor, Fixed Equipment, and Customers. The T-account Liabilities is just the sum of the accounts Creditor 1, Suppliers, Workers, and Shareholders.

Since many property-accounting transactions may underlie a single value-accounting transaction, a special numbering system will be used in the property journal so that the relationship will be evident. For example, the property-accounting-transactions 1 *a* and 1 *b* underlie the value-accounting-transaction 1.

Journal

See journal on next page ⟶

Journal

Transaction	Description	Accounts	[Debit	//	Credit]
1a.	In-transfer of raw materials	Raw-materials inventory Suppliers	$[(\ldots,0,X',0,\ldots)$ $[(0,\ldots)$	// //	$(0,\ldots)]$ $(\ldots,0,X',0,\ldots)]$
1b.	Out-transfer of cash	Suppliers Cash	$[(\ldots,0,P'X',0,\ldots)$ $[(0,\ldots)$	// //	$(0,\ldots)]$ $(\ldots,0,P'X',0,\ldots)]$
1c.	Discharge suppliers	Suppliers Purchases	$[(\ldots,X',\ldots)$ $[(\ldots,P'X',\ldots)$	// //	$(\ldots,P'X',\ldots)]$ $(\ldots,X',\ldots)]$
2a.	In-transfer of labor	Labor Workers	$[(\ldots,0,L,0)$ $[(0,\ldots)$	// //	$(0,\ldots)]$ $(\ldots,0,L,0]$
2b	Out-transfer of wages	Workers Cash	$[(\ldots,0,WL,0,\ldots)$ $[(0,\ldots)$	// //	$(0,\ldots)]$ $(\ldots,0,WL,0,\ldots)]$
2c.	Discharge workers account	Workers Purchases	$[(\ldots,0,L,0)$ $[(\ldots,0,WL,\ldots)$	// //	$(\ldots,0,WL,\ldots)]$ $(\ldots,0,L,0]$
3.	Begin aging final-goods inventory	Whole product Final-goods inventory	$[(0,FG(T),0,\ldots)$ $[(0,\ldots)$	// //	$(0,\ldots)]$ $(0,FG(T),0,\ldots)]$
4.	End aging final-goods inventory	Final-goods inventory Whole product	$[(\ldots,0,FG(T),0,\ldots)$ $[(0,\ldots)$	// //	$(0,\ldots)]$ $(\ldots,0,FG(T),0,\ldots)]$
5.	Begin aging cash inventory	Whole product Cash	$[(CASH(T),0,\ldots)$ $[(0,\ldots)$	// //	$(0,\ldots)]$ $(CASH(T),0,\ldots)]$
6.	End aging cash inventory	Cash Whole product	$[(\ldots,0,CASH(T),0,\ldots)$ $[(\ldots)$	// //	$(\ldots)]$ $(\ldots,0,CASH(T),0,\ldots)]$
7.	Begin aging raw-materials inventory	Whole product Raw-materials inventory	$[(0,0,RM(T),0,\ldots)$ $[(0,\ldots)$	// //	$(0,\ldots)]$ $(0,0,RM(T),0,\ldots)]$
8.	End aging raw-materials inventory	Raw-materials inventory Whole product	$[(\ldots,0,RM(T),0,\ldots)$ $[(0,\ldots)$	// //	$(0,\ldots)]$ $(\ldots,0,RM(T),0,\ldots)]$

Journal continued

Transaction	Description	Accounts	[Debit	//	Credit]
9.	Use of raw-materials in production	Whole product	$[(\ldots, 0, X, 0, \ldots)$	//	$(0, \ldots)]$
		Raw-materials inventory	$[(0, \ldots)$	//	$(\ldots, 0, X, 0, \ldots)]$
10.	Use of labor in production	Whole product	$[(\ldots, 0, L, 0)$	//	$(0, \ldots)]$
		Labor	$[(0, \ldots)$	//	$(\ldots, 0, L, 0]$
11.	Begin use of the machine	Whole product	$[(0,0,0,1,0, \ldots)$	//	$(0, \ldots)]$
		Fixed equipment	$[(0, \ldots)$	//	$(0,0,0,1,0, \ldots)]$
12.	End use of the machine	Fixed equipment	$[(\ldots, 0,1,0,0)$	//	$(0, \ldots)]$
		Whole product	$[(0, \ldots)$	//	$(\ldots, 0,1,0,0]$
13.	Production of the final goods	Final-goods inventory	$[(\ldots, 0, Q, 0, \ldots)$	//	$(0, \ldots)]$
		Whole product	$[(0, \ldots)$	//	$(\ldots, 0, Q, 0, \ldots)]$
14.	Out-transfer of sold goods	Customers	$[(\ldots, 0, Q', 0, \ldots)$	//	$(0, \ldots)]$
		Final-goods inventory	$[(0, \ldots)$	//	$(\ldots, 0, Q', 0, \ldots)]$

No.	Transaction	Accounts	Entry
14b.	In-transfer of cash	Cash	$[(\ldots,0,PQ',0,\ldots) \;//\; (0,\ldots)]$
		Customers	$[(0,\ldots) \;//\; (\ldots,0,PQ',0,\ldots)]$
14c.	Discharge customers	Customers	$[(\ldots,PQ',\ldots) \;//\; (\ldots,Q',\ldots)]$
		Sales	$[(\ldots,Q',\ldots) \;//\; (\ldots,PQ',\ldots)]$
15.	Debt payment	Creditor 1	$[(\ldots,0,D,0,\ldots) \;//\; (0,\ldots)]$
		Cash	$[(0,\ldots) \;//\; (\ldots,0,D,0,\ldots)]$
16a.	Payment of dividends	Shareholders	$[(\ldots,0,DIV(T),0,\ldots) \;//\; (0,\ldots)]$
		Cash	$[(0,\ldots) \;//\; (\ldots,0,DIV(T),0,\ldots)]$
16b.	Discharge shareholders	Unilateral transfer	$[(\ldots,DIV(T),\ldots) \;//\; (0,\ldots,0)]$
		Shareholders	$[(0,\ldots,0) \;//\; (\ldots,DIV(T),\ldots)]$
17a.	Receipt of subscriptions	Cash	$[(\ldots,0,SUBS(T),0,\ldots) \;//\; (\ldots)]$
		Shareholders	$[(\ldots) \;//\; (\ldots,0,SUBS(T),0,\ldots)]$
17b.	Discharge shareholders	Shareholders	$[(\ldots,SUBS(T),\ldots) \;//\; (0,\ldots)]$
		Unilateral transfer	$[(0,\ldots) \;//\; (\ldots,SUBS(T),\ldots)]$

The remaining property-accounting transactions close the temporary accounts into the summary temporary account, namely, Change in Assets and Liabilities. When the Whole-Product account is summed, it is:

$$WP(T) = [NEGPROD(T) \; // \; POSPROD(T)]$$

where the *negative product* is:

$$NEGPROD(T) = (CASH(T), FG(T), RM(T), 1, 0, 0, X, 0, L, 0)$$

and the *positive product* is:

$$POSPROD(T) = (0, 0, 0, 0, CASH(T), FG(T) + Q, RM(T), 1, 0, 0).$$

The positive product and the negative product represent the property that was respectively appropriated and expropriated during the time period.

Journal continued

Transaction	Description	Accounts	[Debit	//	Credit]
C.	Close whole product	Whole product	[(POSPROD(T)	//	NEGPROD(T)]
		Change in A&L	[NEGPROD(T)	//	POSPROD(T)]
C.	Close sales	Sales	[($\ldots, 0, PQ', 0, \ldots$)	//	($\ldots, 0, Q', \ldots$)]
		Change in A&L	[($\ldots, Q', \ldots$)	//	($\ldots, 0, PQ', 0, \ldots$)]
C.	Close purchases	Purchases	[($\ldots, X', 0, L, 0$)	//	($\ldots, P'X' + WL, \ldots$)]
		Change in A&L	[($\ldots, P'X' + WL, \ldots$)	//	($\ldots, X', 0, L, 0$)]
C.	Close unilateral transfer	Unilateral transfer	[($\ldots, SUBS(T), \ldots$)	//	($\ldots, DIV(T), \ldots$)]
		Change in A&L	[($\ldots, DIV(T), \ldots$)	//	($\ldots, SUBS(T), \ldots$)]

Summing the account Change in Assets and Liabilities yields:

$$dA\&L = [(CASH(T),FG(T),RM(T),1,P'X'$$
$$+ \ WL \ + \ DIV(T),Q',X,0,L,0) \ // \ (0,0,0,0,CASH(T)$$
$$+ \ PQ' \ + \ SUBS(T),FG(T) \ + \ Q,RM(T)$$
$$+ \ X',1,L,0)]$$

which in reduced form is:

$$dA\&L(T) = [(CASH(T),FG(T),RM(T),1,0, \ . \ . \ . \ ) \ //$$
$$(\ . \ . \ . \ ,0,CASH(T \ + \ 1) \ + \ D,FG(T \ + \ 1),RM(T \ + \ 1),$$
$$1,0,0)].$$

The final closing transaction closes Change in Assets and Liabilities into Total Assets and Liabilities.

Transaction	Description	Accounts	[Debit	//	Credit]
C.	Close dA&L	dA&L	$-dA\&L(T)$		
		A&L			$dA\&L(T)$

The Property Ledger

The ledger is the set of T-accounts or labeled T-terms in the equation zero-term. The sum of the T-accounts is the equation zero-term. In each T-account, there are listed the T-terms added to it by the transactions. The numbers in parentheses are the numbers of the transactions in the property journal, ($<$) marks the entries that total the T-account and (C) marks the entries that close the temporary accounts.

Ledger

See Ledger next page ⟶ ▶▶

Ledger

Cash

(1b) $[(CASH(T),0,\ldots)$ // $(0,\ldots,0)]$
(2b) $[(0,\ldots)$ // $(\ldots,0,P'X',0,\ldots)]$
(5) $[(0,\ldots)$ // $(\ldots,0,WL,0,\ldots)]$
(6) $[(\ldots,0,CASH(T),0,\ldots)$ // $(CASH(T),0,\ldots)]$
(14b) $[(\ldots,0,PQ',0,\ldots)$ // $(0,\ldots)]$
(15) $[(0,\ldots)$ // $(\ldots,0,D,\ldots)]$
(16a) $[(0,\ldots)$ // $(\ldots,0,DIV(T),0,\ldots)]$
(17a) $[(\ldots,0,SUBS(T),0,\ldots)$ // $(\ldots,0,CASH(T+1),\ldots)]$
(<) $[(0,\ldots)$ //

(<) $[(\ldots,CASH(T+1),\ldots)$ // $(0,\ldots)]$

Raw-Materials Inventory

(1a) $[0,0,RM(T),0,\ldots$ // $(0,\ldots)]$
(7) $[(\ldots,0,X',0,\ldots)$ // $(0,\ldots)]$
(8) $[(0,\ldots)$ // $(0,0,RM(T),0,\ldots)]$
(9) $[(\ldots,0,RM(T),0,\ldots)$ // $(\ldots,0,X,0,\ldots)]$
(<) $[(0,\ldots)$ // $(\ldots,0,RM(T+1),\ldots)]$

(<) $[(\ldots,0,RM(T+1),\ldots)$ // $(0,\ldots)]$

Fixed Equipment

(11) $[(0,0,0,1,0,\ldots)$ // $(0,\ldots,0)]$
(12) $[(0,\ldots)$ // $(0,0,0,1,0,\ldots)]$
(<) $[(\ldots,0,1,0,0)$ // $(0,\ldots)]$

(<) $[(0,\ldots,0,1,0,0)$ // $(0,\ldots,0)]$

Final-Goods Inventory

(3) $[(0,FG(T),0,\ldots)$ // $(0,\ldots,0)]$
(4) $[(0,\ldots)$ // $(0,FG(T),0,\ldots)]$
(13) $[(\ldots,0,FG(T),0,\ldots)$ // $(0,\ldots)]$
(14a) $[(\ldots,0,Q,0,\ldots)$ // $(\ldots,0,Q',0,\ldots)]$
(<) $[(0,\ldots)$ // $(\ldots,0,FG(T+1),\ldots)]$

(<) $[(\ldots,0,FG(T+1),\ldots)$ // $(0,\ldots)]$

Labor

(2a) $[(\ldots,0,L,0)$ // $(0,\ldots)]$
(1l) $[(0,\ldots)$ // $(\ldots,0,L,0,)]$

Creditor 1

(15) $[(0,\ldots)$ // $(\ldots,0,D,0,\ldots,0,D)]$
(<) $[(\ldots,0,D,0,\ldots)$ // $(0,\ldots,0,D)]$
(<) $[(0,\ldots,0,D)$ // $(0,\ldots,0)]$

(<) $[(0,\ldots,0)$ // $(0,\ldots,D)]$

Ledger continued

Suppliers

(1a) $[(0, \ldots) \quad // \quad (\ldots ,0,X',0, \ldots)]]$
(1b) $[(\ldots ,0,P'X',0, \ldots) \quad // \quad (0, \ldots)]]$
(1c) $[(\ldots ,X', \ldots) \quad // \quad (\ldots ,P'X', \ldots)]]$

Customers

(14a) $[(\ldots ,0,Q',0, \ldots) \quad // \quad (0, \ldots)]]$
(14b) $[(0, \ldots) \quad // \quad (\ldots ,0,PQ',0, \ldots)]]$
(14c) $[(\ldots ,PQ', \ldots) \quad // \quad (\ldots ,Q', \ldots)]]$

Total Assets and Liabilities

(C) $[DEBTS(T) \quad // \quad ASSETS(T)]$
(<) $[ASSETS(T+1) \quad dA\&L(T) \quad // \quad DEBTS(T+1) \quad]$
(<) $[DEBTS(T+1) \quad // \quad ASSETS(T+1)]$

Workers

(2a) $[(0, \ldots ,0) \quad // \quad (0, \ldots ,0,L,0)]$
(2b) $[(\ldots ,0,WL,0, \ldots) \quad // \quad (0, \ldots)]]$
(2c) $[(\ldots ,0,L,0) \quad // \quad (\ldots ,0,WL, \ldots)]]$

Shareholders

(16a) $[(\ldots ,0,DIV(T),0, \ldots) \quad // \quad (\ldots)]]$
(16a) $[(\ldots) \quad // \quad (\ldots ,0,DIV(T),0, \ldots)]]$
(17a) $[(\ldots) \quad //(\ldots ,0,SUBS(T),0, \ldots)]]$
(17b) $[(\ldots ,0,SUBS(T),0, \ldots) \quad // \quad (\ldots)]]$

Whole Product

(3) $[(0,FG(T),0, \ldots) \quad // \quad (0, \ldots)]]$
(4) $[(0, \ldots) \quad // \quad (\ldots ,0,FG(T),0, \ldots)]]$
(5) $[(CASH(T),0, \ldots) \quad // \quad (\ldots ,0,CASH(T),0, \ldots)]$
(6) $[(\ldots) \quad // \quad (\ldots ,0,CASH(T),0, \ldots)]]$
(7) $[(0,0,RM(T),0, \ldots) \quad // \quad (0, \ldots)]]$
(8) $[(0, \ldots) \quad // \quad (\ldots ,0,RM(T),0, \ldots)]]$
(9) $[(\ldots ,0,X,0, \ldots) \quad // \quad (0, \ldots)]]$
(10) $[(0, \ldots ,0,L,0) \quad // \quad (0, \ldots ,0)]$
(11) $[(0,0,0,1,0, \ldots) \quad // \quad (0, \ldots ,0)]$
(12) $[(0, \ldots ,0) \quad // \quad (0, \ldots ,0)]$
(13) $[(0, \ldots ,0) \quad // \quad (\ldots ,0,Q,0, \ldots)]$
(C) $[POSPROD(T) \quad // \quad NEGPROD(T)]$

Sales

(14c) $[(\ldots, Q', \ldots) \quad // \quad (\ldots, PQ', \ldots)]$

(C) $[(\ldots, PQ', \ldots) \quad // \quad (\ldots, Q', \ldots)]$

Unilateral Transfer

(16b) $[(\ldots, 0, DIV(T), 0, \ldots) \quad // \quad (0, \ldots, 0]$

(17b) $[(0, \ldots, 0) \quad // \quad (\ldots, 0, SUBS(T), \ldots)]$

(C) $[(\ldots, SUBS(T), \ldots) \quad // \quad (\ldots, DIV(T), \ldots)]$

Change in Assets and Liabilities

(C) $[NEGPROD(T) \quad // \quad POSPROD(T)]$

(C) $[(\ldots, DIV(T), \ldots) \quad // \quad (\ldots, SUBS(T), \ldots)]$

(C) $[(\ldots, P'X' + WL, \ldots) \quad // \quad (\ldots, X', 0, L, 0)]$

(C) $[(\ldots, 0, Q', 0, \ldots) \quad // \quad (\ldots, 0, PQ', 0, \ldots)]$

(C) $[\quad -dA\&L(T) \quad]$

Purchases

(1c) $[(\ldots, P'X', 0, \ldots) \quad // \quad , \quad (\ldots, X', \ldots)]$

(2c) $[(\ldots, 0, WL, 0, \ldots) \quad // \quad (\ldots, 0, L, 0)]$

(C) $[(\ldots, X', 0, L, 0) \quad // \quad (\ldots, P'X' + WL, \ldots)]$

The Property-Flow Statement and Balance Sheet

The income statement in value accounting provides the connection between the Net-Worth accounts on the beginning and ending balance sheets. The income statement presents a breakdown of the account Change in Net Worth by giving the balances in its subaccounts (that is, the other temporary value accounts closed into it). The property account underlying Change in Net Worth is Change in Assets and Liabilities. The property-accounting statement that underlies the income statement is the statement that gives the closing balances in the subaccounts of Change in Assets and Liabilities (that is, the other temporary property accounts closed into it). It will be called the *property-flow statement* since it provides the connection between the stocks of property specified in the beginning and ending Total-Assets-and-Liabilities accounts.

The closing balance in the summary temporary account, Change in Assets and Liabilities, can be expressed as the sum of the closing balances in the other temporary accounts:

$$dA\&L(T) = WP(T) + Sales(T) + Purchases(T) + UTr(T).$$

The property-flow statement presents $dA\&L$ as the sum of its subaccounts:

$WP(T)$ $= [(CASH(T),FG(T),RM(T),1,0,0,X,0,L,0) \;//$

                 $(\ldots ,0,CASH(T),FG(T) + Q,RM(T),1,0,0)]$

$Sales(T)$ $= [(0, \ldots ,0,Q',0, \ldots ,0) \;// \; (0, \ldots ,0,PQ',0, \ldots ,0)]$

$Purchases(T)$ $= [(\ldots ,0,P'X' + WL,0, \ldots) \;// \; (0, \ldots ,0,X',0,L,0)]$

$UTr(T)$ $= [(0, \ldots 0,DIV(T),0, \ldots ,0) \;// \; (0, \ldots ,0,SUBS(T),$

                 $0, \ldots ,0)]$

$dA\&L(T)$ $= [(CASH(T),FG(T),RM(T),1,P'X' + WL + DIV(T),$

                $Q',X,0,L,0) \;// \; (0,0,0,0,CASH(T) + SUBS(T)$

                $+ PQ',FG(T) + Q,RM(T) + X',1,L,0)]$

             $= [(CASH(T),FG(T),RM(T),1,0, \ldots) \;//$

                 $(\ldots ,0,CASH(T + 1) + D,FG(T + 1),RM(T + 1),1,0,0)].$

A streamlined form of the value-accounting income statement can be obtained by multiplying the property-flow statement by the price vector.

The net values of the Sales and Purchases accounts are zero since they represent market transactions. The value of the Whole Product is the economic profit $\pi(T)$ and the value of the Unilateral Transfers is $SUBS(T)$ – $DIV(T)$. The sum of those values is $NBV(T + 1) - (1 + r)NBV(T)$, the balance in the Change in Net Worth account, which in turn is the value of the underlying Change-in-Assets-and-Liabilities property account.

The end-of-the-period Total-Assets-and-Liabilities account is:

$$A\&L(T + 1) \quad = A\&L(T) + dA\&L(T)$$

$$= [DEBT(T) \text{ // } ASSETS(T)] + dA\&L(T)$$

$$= [(\ldots ,0,D,) \text{ // } (\ldots ,0, CASH(T + 1), FG(T + 1),$$
$$RM(T + 1),1,0,0)]$$

Summing the subaccounts of Assets in the ledger yields:

$$Assets(T + 1) = [(\ldots ,0, CASH(T + 1), FG(T + 1), RM(T + 1),1,0,0)$$
$$\text{ // } (0, \ldots ,0)]$$

$$= [ASSETS(T + 1) \text{ // } (0, \ldots ,0)],$$

where one might note the difference between the T-account $Assets(T + 1)$ and the vector $ASSETS(T + 1)$. The liabilities are:

$$Liabilities(T + 1) \quad = [(0, \ldots ,0) \text{ // } (0, \ldots ,0,D)]$$

$$= [(0, \ldots ,0) \text{ // } DEBTS(T + 1)].$$

Hence the end-of-the-period resultant equation zero-term is:

Assets

$$[(\ldots ,0, CASH(T + 1), FG(T + 1), RM(T + 1),1,0,0) \text{ // } (0, \ldots)]$$

Liabilities

$$+ [(0, \ldots ,0) \text{ // } (0, \ldots ,0,D)]$$

Total Assets and Liabilities

$$+ [(0, \ldots ,0,D) \text{ // } (\ldots ,0, CASH(T + 1), FG(T + 1),$$
$$RM(T + 1),1,0,0)],$$

where the zeroed temporary accounts are not listed. This decodes as the *property balance sheet equation at time T + 1*:

$$ASSETS(T + 1) = DEBTS(T + 1) + (ASSETS(T + 1) - DEBTS(T + 1)).$$

A valuation of property is realized whenever the property is exchanged for other property as in a purchase or sale. Since a realized valuation is expressed objectively in the property paid or received in the purchase or sale, it would show up in property accounting. Realized valuations are non-controversial since they are realized as property. Value accounting diverges from property accounting by using unrealized valuations such as the valuation of unsold outputs (at market value or cost) or the valuation of inputs when the current price differs from the historical purchase price. In other words, valuation in itself, as distinct from the simple recording of property paid or received, is only necessary for unrealized valuations. It is in that sense that property accounting avoids valuation; it avoids any valuation not realized as property.

Prices show up in property accounting only in the context of realized valuations, such as in the determination of the cash payments involved in purchases and sales. Thus prices appear only in the transactions involving the Cash account, the personal accounts, and the Purchases and Sales accounts (and thus in the larger accounts having these accounts as subaccounts).

9

A Simplified Property-Accounting Model

The Simplified Property Accounts

Property accounting can be simplified to obtain a version of property accounting that is more in the spirit of conventional accounting. Conventional value accounting does not, in general, treat commodities at different times as distinct commodities. The main, practical difficulty in simply ignoring time distinctions is in the treatment of debt—where time is of the essence. If cash at two different times simply was treated as being the same, then a debt could be repaid by paying back only the principal after (say) ten years. Interest would appear to be only an exploitative surcharge. Indeed, a failure to appreciate the difference that time makes seems to be the basis for some theories about the "exploitative" nature of the rate of interest (for example, Morishima 1973).

A debt is established when current cash is obtained in exchange for some series of future cash payments. In full-blown property accounting, the debt is represented by the series of future cash payments. However, if we are going to simplify by not having a different type of cash for each time period, then a different means of representing the debt is necessary.

A debt will be represented in the simplified model by the current balance, the amount of current cash that just would pay off the loan. Time will be incorporated by interpreting carrying the debt for a time period as purchasing that amount of capital services for the period. The interest rate r is the price of a dollar-year of capital services. A new component for capital services (dollar-years) is required in the property vectors. The capital services are consumed in production. Logic requires showing the year's services of all capital being consumed in production—regardless of whether the capital had its source in debt or equity. The capital services having their source in debt will be purchased in a market transaction. The remaining capital services having their source in equity will be treated as being unilaterally transferred to the firm from the shareholders.

In the simplified model, only seven components will be needed for the property vectors. In order, the components are:

component 1 = Cash,

component 2 = Final goods,

component 3 = Raw materials

component 4 = Vintage $m - 1$ machines,

component 5 = Vintage m machines,

component 6 = Capital services, and

component 7 = Labor services.

An asterisk (*) is used to indicate that a property vector or a property T-account is in the simplified model. At time T, the balance-sheet assets are:

$$ASSETS^*(T) = (CASH(T), FG(T), RM(T), 1, 0, 0, 0),$$

and the liabilities are:

$$DEBTS^*(T) = (D(T), 0, 0, 0, 0, 0, 0).$$

The balance-sheet equation at time T is:

$$ASSETS^*(T) = DEBTS^*(T) + (ASSETS^*(T) - DEBTS^*(T)).$$

At time T, the price vector is:

$$PRICES^*(T) = (1, P, P', C(m - 1), C(m), r, W).$$

Since we are assuming constant prices and are not distinguishing between time T dollars and time $T + 1$ dollars in the simplified model:

$$PRICES^*(T + 1) = PRICES^*(T).$$

The market value of the assets at time T is the scalar product:

$$PRICES^*(T) \times ASSETS^*(T) = CASH(T) + PFG(T) + P'RM(T)$$
$$+ C(m - 1)$$
$$= GBV(T),$$

and the value of the liabilities is:

$$PRICES^*(T) \times DEBTS^*(T) = D(T).$$

The value of $ASSETS^*(T) - DEBTS^*(T)$ is the difference:

$$PRICES^*(T) \times (ASSETS^*(T) - DEBTS^*(T)) = GBV(T) - D(T)$$
$$= NBV(T).$$

The property balance sheet equation may be encoded as before. The LHS vector $ASSETS^*(T)$ is encoded as the property T-account of Assets: $[ASSETS^*(T) \,/\!/\, 0]$. The RHS vector $DEBTS^*(T)$ is encoded as the property T-account of Liabilities: $[0 \,/\!/\, DEBTS^*(T)]$. And the RHS vector $ASSETS^*(T) - DEBTS^*(T)$ is encoded as the property T-account of Total Assets and Liabilities: $[DEBTS^*(T) \,/\!/\, ASSETS^*(T)]$. The original zero-term is:

Assets	Liabilities	Total Assets and Liabilities

$$[ASSETS^*(T)/\!/0] \;+\; [0/\!/DEBTS^*(T)] \;+\; [DEBTS^*(T)/\!/ASSETS^*(T)]$$

Except for the new permanent LHS account for Capital Services, the set of property T-accounts, such as the personal, impersonal, and temporary accounts, are all the same in the simplified model. The main differences in the transactions are the deletions of the transactions to age the assets and the addition of transactions to record the purchase, receipt, and use of capital services. The vectors involved in all the entries are shortened from ten to seven components to reflect the simplifications. The transactions are numbered to correspond as closely as possible to the numbering in the journal for the conventional value-accounting model.

The Simplified Property Journal

See journal next page————————————————➤ ➤

The Simplified Property Journal

Transaction	Description	Accounts	[Debit	//	Credit]
1a.	In-transfer of raw materials	Raw-materials Inventory	[(0,0,X',0, . . .)	//	(0, . . . ,0)]
		Suppliers	[(0, . . . ,0)	//	(0,0,X',0, . . .)]
1b.	Out-transfer of cash	Suppliers	[(P'X',0, . . . ,0)	//	(0, . . . ,0)]
		Cash	[(0, . . . ,0)	//	(P'X',0, . . .)]
1c.	Discharge suppliers	Suppliers	[(0,0,X',0, . . .)	//	(P'X',0, . . .)]
		Purchases	[(P'X',0, . . .)	//	(0,0,X',0, . . .)]
2a.	In-transfer of labor	Labor	[(0, . . . ,0,L)	//	(0, . . . ,0)]
		Workers	[(0, . . . ,0)	//	(0, . . . ,0,L)]
2b.	Out-transfer of wages	Workers	[(WL,0, . . . ,0)	//	(0, . . . ,0)]
		Cash	[(0, . . . ,0)	//	(WL,0, . . . ,0)]
2c.	Discharge workers account	Workers	[(0, . . . ,0,L)	//	(WL,0, . . . ,0)]
		Purchases	[(WL,0, . . . ,0)	//	(0, . . . ,0,L)]
2d.	Use of labor in production	Whole product	[(0, . . . ,0,L)	//	(0, . . . ,0)]
		Labor	[(0, . . . ,0)	//	(0, . . . ,0,L)]
3.	Use of raw materials in production	Whole product	[(0,0,X,0, . . . ,0)	//	(0, . . . ,0)]
		Raw-materials inventory	[(0, . . . ,0)	//	(0,0,X,0, . . . ,0)]
4a.	Production of the final goods	Final-goods inventory	[(0,Q,0, . . . ,0)	//	(0, . . . ,0)]
		Whole product	[(0, . . . ,0)	//	(0,Q,0, . . . ,0)]
4b.	Out-transfer of sold goods	Customers	[(0,Q',0, . . . ,0)	//	(0, . . . ,0)]
		Final-goods inventory	[(0, . . . ,0)	//	(0,Q',0, . . . ,0)]
4c.	In-transfer of cash	Cash	[(PQ',0, . . . ,0)	//	(0, . . . ,0)]
		Customers	[(0, . . . ,0)	//	(PQ',0, . . . ,0)]
4d.	Discharge customers	Customers	[(PQ',0, . . . ,0)	//	(0,Q',0, . . .)]
		Sales	[(0,Q',0, . . .)	//	(PQ',0, . . . ,0)]

No.	Transaction	Account	Vector
6.	Debt payment	Creditor 1	$[(D - rD(T),0,\ldots,0)$ // $(0,\ldots,0]$
		Cash	$[0,\ldots,0)$ // $(D - rD(T),0,\ldots,0]$
7a.	In-transfer of capital services	Capital services	$[(0,\ldots,0,D(T),0)$ // $(0,\ldots,0]$
		Creditor 1	$[(0,\ldots,0)$ // $(0,\ldots,0,D(T),0]$
7b.	Out-transfer of interest	Creditor 1	$[(rD(T),0,\ldots,0)$ // $(0,\ldots,0]$
		Cash	$[0,\ldots,0)$ // $(rD(T),0,\ldots,0]$
7c.	Discharge creditor 1	Creditor 1	$[(0,\ldots,0,D(T),0)$ // $(rD(T),0,\ldots)]$
		Purchases	$[(rD(T),0,\ldots,)$ // $(0,\ldots,0,D(T),0]$
7d.	In-transfer of capital services	Capital services	$[(0,\ldots,NBV(T),0)$ // $(0,\ldots,0]$
		Shareholders	$[0,\ldots,0)$ // $(0,\ldots,NBV(T),0]$
7e.	Discharge shareholders	Shareholders	$[(0,\ldots,0,NBV(T),0)$ // $(0,\ldots,0]$
		Unilateral transfer	$[0,\ldots,0)$ // $(0,\ldots,NBV(T),0]$
7f.	Use of capital services in production	Whole product	$[(0,\ldots,0,GBV(T),0)$ // $(0,\ldots,0]$
		Capital services	$[0,\ldots,0)$ // $(0,\ldots,0,GBV(T),0]$
8a.	Begin use of the machine	Whole product	$[(0,\ldots,0,1,0,0,0)$ // $(0,\ldots,0]$
		Fixed equipment	$[0,\ldots,0)$ // $(0,\ldots,0,1,0,0,0]$
8b.	End use of the machine	Fixed equipment	$[(0,\ldots,0,1,0,0)$ // $(0,\ldots,0]$
		Whole product	$[0,\ldots,0)$ // $(0,\ldots,0,1,0,0]$
9a.	Payment of dividends	Shareholders	$[(DIV(T),0,\ldots,0)$ // $(0,\ldots,0]$
		Cash	$[0,\ldots,0)$ // $(DIV(T),0,\ldots,0]$
9b.	Discharge shareholders	Unilateral transfer	$[(DIV(T),0,\ldots,0)$ // $(0,\ldots,0]$
		Shareholders	$[0,\ldots,0)$ // $(DIV(T),0,\ldots,0]$
10.	Receipt of subscriptions	Cash	$[(SUBS(T),0,\ldots,0)$ // $(0,\ldots,0]$
		Shareholders	$[0,\ldots,0)$ // $(SUBS(T),0,\ldots,0]$
10b.	Discharge shareholders	Shareholders	$[(SUBS(T),0,\ldots,0)$ // $(0,\ldots,0]$
		Unilateral transfer	$[0,\ldots,0)$ // $(SUBS(T),0,\ldots,0]$

The remaining property transactions close the temporary accounts into the summary temporary account, Change in Assets and Liabilities (dA&L). When the Whole-Product account is summed, it is:

$$WP^*(T) = [NEGPROD^*(T) // POSPROD^*(T)]$$

where the negative product is:

$$NEGPROD^*(T) = (0,0,X,1,0,GBV(T),L),$$

and the positive product is:

$$POSPROD^*(T) = (0,Q,0,0,1,0,0).$$

Summing the other temporary accounts yields:

$$Sales^*(T) = [(0,Q',0, \ldots) // (PQ',0, \ldots ,0)],$$

$$Purchases^*(T) = [(P'X' + WL + rD(T),0, \ldots ,0) // (0,0,X',0,0,D(T),L)],$$

and

$$UTr^*(T(= [(DIV(T),0, \ldots ,0) // (SUBS(T),0, \ldots ,NBV(T),0)].$$

Journal continued

Transaction	Description	Accounts	[Debit	//	Credit]
C.	Close Whole product	Whole product	$[POSPROD^*(T)]$	//	$NEGPROD^*(T)]$
		Change in A&L	$[NEGPROD^*(T)]$	//	$POSPROD^*(T)]$
C.	Close Sales	Sales		$-Sales^*(T)$	
		Change in A&L		$Sales^*(T)$	
C.	Close Purchases	Purchases		$-Purchases^*(T)$	
		Change in A&L		$Purchases^*(T)$	
C.	Close Unilateral transfer	Unilateral transfer		$-UTr^*(T)$	
		Change in A&L		$UTr^*(T)$	

Summing the Change-in-Assets-and-Liabilities account yields:

$$dA\&L^*(T) = [(P'X' + WL + rD(T) + DIV(T),Q',X,1,0,GBV(T),L)$$
$$// (SUBS(T) + PQ',Q,X,0,1,GBV(T),L)].$$

The balance in the cash component is not equal to the net cash flow $NCF(T)$ since the cash-principal payment $D - rD(T)$ was directly charged to the Creditor's account instead of being channeled through the temporary accounts. Adding back that principal payment yields $NCF(T) + D - rD(T)$, which we assume is positive. To put $dA\&L^*(T)$ in reduced form we assume that there was net disinvestment in the raw-material inventory and net investment in the final-goods inventory. Then $dA\&L^*(T)$ in reduced form is:

$$dA\&L^*(T) = [(0,0,RM(T) - RM(T + 1),1,0,0,0) // (NCF(T)$$
$$+ D - rD(T),FG(T+ 1) - FG(T),0,0,1,0,0)]$$

The final closing transaction closes Changes in Assets and Liabilities into Assets and Liabilities.

Transaction	Description	Accounts	[Debit // Credit]
C.	Close dA&L	dA&L	$-dA\&L^*(T)$
		A&L	$dA\&L^*(T)$

The whole-product T-account $[NEGPROD^*(T) // POSPROD^*(T)]$ is a RHS account so it decodes as the whole-product vector for this model:

$$POSPROD^*(T) - NEGPROD^*(T) = (0,Q, -X, -1,1, -GBV(T), - L).$$

The market value of the whole product is the scalar product of the price vector times the whole-product vector:

$$(1,P,P',C(m - 1),C(m),r,W) \times (0,Q, -X, -1,1, -GBV(T), -L)$$
$$= PQ - P'X - WL - [C(m - 1)$$
$$- C(m)] - rGBV(T)$$
$$= \pi(T),$$

which is the economic profit in the market-value accounting model. The whole product gives the property that was recorded as appropriated (positive product) and expropriated (negative product) in the model. The accounting profit in the conventional model depends not only on what is appropriated and expropriated but also on what is sold. Hence the conventional accounting profit would not be determined as the value of the whole product.

Market-value accounting can be arrived at as the image of full-blown property accounting under evaluation at market prices:

Market Prices × Full Property Accounting = Market-Value Accounting

The image of simplified property accounting under evaluation at market prices is not conventional value accounting because conventional accounting does not evaluate produced outputs at market value (only sold outputs). The version of value accounting obtained by the market-price evaluation of simplified property accounting will be called *simplified market-value accounting.*

Market Prices × Simplified Property Accounting

= Simplified Market-Value Accounting.

The Simplified Property Ledger

The pair of T-terms in each transaction add together to make the transaction zero-term. These transaction zero-terms are added to the equation zero-term. The T-accounts are the labeled T-terms whose sum is the equation zero-term. The set of these T-accounts is the ledger.

See ledger next page——————————————————————▶▶

The Simplified Property Ledger

Cash

(1b)	[(CASH(T),0, ...) // (0, ...)]
(2b)	[(0, . . . ,0) // ($P'X'$,0, ...)]
(4c)	[(0, . . . ,0) // (WL,0, . . . ,0)]
	[(PQ',0, . . .) // (0, . . . ,0)]
(6)	[(0, ...) // ($D - rD(T)$,0, ...)]
(7b)	[(0, . . . ,0) // ($rD(T)$,0, ...)]
(9a)	[(0, . . . ,0) // ($DIV(T)$,0, ...)]
(10a)	[($SUBS(T)$,0, ...) // (0, ...)]
(<)	[(0, ...) // ($CASH(T + 1)$,0, ...)]
(<)	[($CASH(T + 1)$,0, ...) // (0, ...)]

Raw-Materials Inventory

(1a)	[(0,0,$RM(T)$,0, ...) // (0, ...)]
(3)	[(0,0,X',0, ...) // (0, . . . ,0)]
(<)	[(. . . .) // (0,0,X,0, ...)]
	// (0,0,$RM(T + 1)$,0, ...)]
(<)	[(0,0,$RM(T + 1)$,0, ...) // (. . . .)]

Capital Services

(7a)	[(. . . . ,0,$D(T)$,0) // (0, . . . ,0)]
(7d)	[(. . . . ,0,$NBV(T)$,0) // (. . . ,0)]
(7f)	[(. . . . ,0) // (. . . . ,$GBV(T)$,0)]

Final-Goods Inventory

(4a)	[(0,$FG(T)$,0, ...) // (0, ...)]
(4b)	[(0,Q,0, ...) // (0, . . . ,0)]
	[(0, . . . ,0) // (0,Q',0, . . .)]
(<)	[(0, . . .) // (0,$FG(T + 1)$,0, ...)]
(<)	[(0,$FG(T + 1)$,0, ...) // (0, ...)]

Labor

(2a)	[(. . . . ,0,L) // (0, . . . ,0)]
(2d)	[(0, . . . ,0) // (. . . ,0,L,)]

Fixed Equipment

(8a)	[(0,0,0,1,0,0,0) // (0, . . . ,0)]
(8b)	[(0, . . . ,0) // (0,0,0,1,0,0,0)]
	[(0,0,0,0,1,0,0) // (0, . . . ,0)]
(<)	[(0, . . . 0) // (0,0,0,0,1,0,0)]
(<)	[(0,0,0,0,1,0,0) // (0, . . . ,0)]

Creditor 1

(6)	$[0, \ldots ,0]$	$//$	$(D(T),0, \ldots ,0)]$
(7a)	$[(D - rD(T),0, \ldots)$	$//$	$(0, \ldots ,0)]$
	$[0, \ldots ,0]$	$//$	$(\ldots ,0,D(T),0)]$
(7b)	$[(rD(T),0, \ldots)$	$//$	$(0, \ldots ,0)]$
(7c)	$[(\ldots ,D(T),0)$	$//$	$(rD(T),0, \ldots)]$
(<)	$[(D(T + 1),0, \ldots)$	$//$	$(0, \ldots ,0)]$
(<)	$[0, \ldots ,0]$	$//$	$(D(T + 1),0, \ldots)]$

Workers

(2a)	$[0, \ldots ,0]$	$//$	$(0, \ldots ,0,L)]$
(2b)	$[(WL,0, \ldots ,0)$	$//$	$(0, \ldots ,0)]$
(2c)	$[0, \ldots ,0,L)$	$//$	$(WL,0, \ldots ,0)]$

Shareholders

(7d)	$[0, \ldots ,0]$	$//$	$(\ldots ,0,NBV(T),0)]$
(7e)	$[(\ldots ,0,NBV(T),0)$	$//$	$(0, \ldots ,0)]$
(9a)	$[(DIV(T),0, \ldots)$	$//$	$(0, \ldots ,0)]$
(9b)	$[0, \ldots ,0]$	$//$	$(DIV(T),0, \ldots)]$
(10a)	$[0, \ldots ,0]$	$//$	$(SUBS(T),0, \ldots)]$
(10b)	$[(SUBS(T),0, \ldots)$	$//$	$(0, \ldots ,0)]$

Whole Product

(2d)	$[0, \ldots ,0,L)$	$//$	$(0, \ldots ,0)]$
(3)	$[(0,0,X,0, \ldots)$	$//$	$(0, \ldots ,0)]$
(4a)	$[0, \ldots ,0]$	$//$	$(0,Q,0, \ldots)]$
(7f)	$[(\ldots ,0,GBV(T),0)$	$//$	$(0, \ldots ,0)]$
(8f)	$[(0,0,1,0,0,0)$	$//$	$(0, \ldots ,0)]$
(8b)	$[0, \ldots ,0]$	$//$	$(0,0,0,1,0,0)]$
(C)	$[POSPROD^*(T)$	$//$	$NEGPROD^*(T)]$

Suppliers

(1a)	$[0, \ldots ,0]$	$//$	$(0,0,X',0, \ldots)]$
(1b)	$[(P'X,0, \ldots)$	$//$	$(0, \ldots ,0)]$
(1c)	$[(0,0,X',0, \ldots)$	$//$	$(P'X,0, \ldots)]$

Customers

(4b)	$[(0,Q',0, \ldots ,0)$	$//$	$(0, \ldots ,0)]$
(4c)	$[(0, \ldots ,0)$	$//$	$(PQ',0, \ldots ,0)]$
(4d)	$[(PQ',0, \ldots ,0)$	$//$	$(0,Q',0, \ldots)]$

Total Assets and Liabilities

(C)	$[DEBTS^*(T)$	$//$	$dA\&L^*(T) \qquad ASSETS^*(T)]$
(<)	$[\; ASSETS^*(T +)$	$//$	$DEBTS^*(T + 1)]$
(<)	$[DEBTS^*(T + 1)$	$//$	$ASSETS^*(T + 1)]$

Sales

(4d)	$[(0,Q',0, \ldots)$	$//$	$(PQ',0, \ldots ,0)]$
(C)	$[(PQ',0, \ldots)$	$//$	$(0,Q',0, \ldots)]$

The Simplified Property Ledger continued

Purchases

(1c)	$[(P'X',0,\ldots)$	$//$	$(0,0,X',0,\ldots)]$
(2c)	$[(WL,0,\ldots,0)$	$//$	$(0,\ldots,0,L)]$
(7c)	$[(rD(T),0,\ldots)$	$//$	$(\ldots,D(T),0)]$
(C)	$[(0,0,X',0,0,D(T),L)$	$//$	$(P'X' + WL + rD(T),0,\ldots)]$

Unilateral Transfers

(7e)	$[(0,\ldots,0)$	$//$	$(0,\ldots,0,NBV(T),0)]$
(9b)	$[(DIV(T),0,\ldots,)$	$//$	$(0,\ldots,0)]$
(10b)	$[(0,\ldots,0)$	$//$	$(SUBS(T),0,\ldots,0)]$
(C)	$[(SUBS(T),\ldots,NBV(T),0)$	$//$	$(DIV(T),0,\ldots,0)]$

Change in Assets and Liabilities

(C)	$[NEGPROD^*(T)$	$//$ $POSPROD^*(T)]$
(C)	$Sales^*(T)$	
(C)	$Purchases^*(T)$	
(C)	$UTr^*(T)$	
(C)	$-dA\&L^*(T)$	

The Simplified Property-Flow Statement

The property-flow statement is the property-accounting version of the income statement. The summary temporary account, Change in Assets and Liabilities, gives (as its names indicates) the changes in the assets and liabilities—which are channeled through the temporary accounts. The sum of the closing balances in the temporary accounts Whole Product, Sales, Purchases, and Unilateral Transfers gives the closing balance in Change in Assets and Liabilities:

$$dA\&L^*(T) = WP^*(T) + Sales^*(T) + Purchases^*(T) + UTr^*(T).$$

The property-flow statement presents $dA\&L^*(T)$ as this sum:

$$
\begin{aligned}
WP^*(T) &= [(0,0,X,1,0,GBV(T),L) \, // \, (0,Q,0,0,1,0,0)] \\
Sales^*(T) &= [(0,Q',0, \ldots ,0) \, // \, (PQ',0, \ldots ,0)] \\
Purchases^*(T) &= [(P'X' + WL + rD(T),0, \ldots ,0) \, // \, (0,0,X',0,0,D(T),L)] \\
UTr^*(T) &= [(DIV(T),0, \ldots ,0) \, // \, (SUBS(T), \ldots ,NBV(T),0)]
\end{aligned}
$$

$$
\begin{aligned}
dA\&L^*(T) &= [(P'X' + WL + rD(T) + DIV(T),Q',X,1,0,GBV(T),L) \\
&\quad // \, (PQ' + SUBS(T),Q,X',0,1,GBV(T),L)] \\
&= [(0,0,RM(T) - RM(T+1),\, 1,\, 0,0,0) \, // \, (NCF(T) + D \\
&\quad - rD(T),FG(T+1) - FG(T),0,0,1,0,0)]
\end{aligned}
$$

A streamlined income statement for simplified market-value accounting can be obtained by multiplying the property-flow statement through by the price vector. As noted above, the market value of the whole product $WP^*(T)$ is the economic profit $\pi(T)$. The market values of $Sales^*(T)$ and $Purchases^*(T)$ are each zero, and the market value of $UTr^*(T)$ is $SUBS(T) + rNBV(T) - DIV(T)$. Hence the market value of the Change in Assets and Liabilities is:

$$
\begin{aligned}
PRICES^*(T) \times dA\&L^*(T) &= \pi(T) + SUBS(T) + rNBV(T) - DIV(T) \\
&= NBV(T+1) - NBV(T),
\end{aligned}
$$

the change in the net worth over the time period.

The time $T + 1$ Total Assets and Liabilities are obtained by adding the (closing balance in) Change in Assets and Liabilities to the time T Total Assets and Liabilities:

$$A\&L^*(T + 1) = A\&L^*(T) + dA\&L^*(T)$$

$$= [DEBTS^*(T) \text{ // } ASSETS^*(T)] + dA\&L^*(T)$$

$$= [(D(T),0,RM(T) - RM(T + 1),1,0,0,0) \text{ // } (CASH(T)$$
$$+ NCF(T) + D - rD(T),FG(T + 1),RM(T), 1,1,0,0)]$$

$$= [(D(T) - D + rD(T),0, \ldots) \text{ // } (CASH(T) + NCF(T),$$
$$FG(T + 1),RM(T + 1),0,1,0,0)]$$

$$= [(D(T + 1),0, \ldots) \text{ // } (CASH(T + 1),FG(T + 1),$$
$$RM(T + 1),0,1,0,0)]$$

$$= [DEBTS^*(T + 1) \text{ // } ASSETS^*(T + 1)].$$

Summing the asset T-accounts in the ledger yields the T-account:

$$Assets^*(T + 1) = [(CASH(T + 1),FG(T + 1),RM(T + 1),0,1,0,0)$$
$$\text{ // } (0, \ldots ,0)]$$

$$= [ASSETS^*(T + 1) \text{ // } (0, \ldots ,0)],$$

where it might be noted that the T-account $Assets^*(T + 1)$ is distinct from but related to the vector $ASSETS^*(T + 1)$. Summing the liability T-accounts in the ledger (Creditor 1, Suppliers, Workers, and Shareholders) yields the T-account:

$$Liabilities^*(T + 1) = [(0, \ldots ,0) \text{ // } (D(T + 1),0, \ldots ,0)]$$
$$= [(0, \ldots ,0) \text{ // } DEBTS^*(T + 1)].$$

Hence the end-of-the-year resultant-equation zero-term is:

Assets

$$[ASSETS^*(T + 1) \text{ // } (0, \ldots ,0)]$$

Liabilities

$$+ [(0, \ldots ,0) \text{ // } DEBTS^*(T + 1)]$$

Total Assets and Liabilities

$$+ [DEBTS^*(T + 1) \text{ // } ASSETS^*(T + 1)].$$

This decodes as the property balance-sheet equation at time $T + 1$:

$$ASSETS^*(T + 1) = DEBTS^*(T + 1) + (ASSETS^*(T + 1) - DEBTS^*(T + 1)).$$

10 Simplified Market-Value Accounting

Derivation of Value Accounting

Using the schema:

$$\text{Prices} \times \text{Property Accounting} = \text{Value accounting,}$$

we will derive simplified market-value accounting by multiplying market prices times simplified property accounting. This will allow us to systematically see how a value-accounting model can be derived from a property-accounting model by evaluating at some given prices or other valuation coefficients. It will also allow us to develop a value-accounting model using the formal machinery of the algebra of T-accounts.

The price vector is:

$$PRICES^*(T) = (1, P, P', C(m - 1), C(m), r, W).$$

The product of a price vector times a vector T-term or T-account is the scalar T-term or T-account with the two entries being the scalar product of the price vector times the two vector entries; for example:

$$PRICES^*(T) \times [DEBTS^*(T) \; // \; \text{ASSETS}^*(T)]$$

$$= [PRICES^*(T) \times DEBTS^*(T) \; // \; PRICES^*(T) \times ASSETS^*(T)]$$

$$= [D(T) \; // \; GBV(T)] = [0 \; // \; NBV(T)].$$

In this manner, the product of the market price vector times all the vector T-terms and T-accounts of simplified property accounting will yield the scalar T-terms and T-accounts of simplified market-value accounting.

A price vector times a property T-account yields a value T-account called the *corresponding* value T-account. A property account is said to *underlie* its corresponding value account. Most property accounts and the corresponding value accounts have the same name. The exceptions are:

Property T-accounts   *Corresponding Value T-accounts*

Total Assets and Liabilities   Net Worth
Change in Assets and Liabilities   Change in Net Worth
Whole Product   Production

Some property T-accounts, such as Sales and Purchases, will disappear when evaluated at market prices since the net value of a market transaction is by definition zero, so those accounts will be deleted in the value-accounting model. The personal accounts of parties not involved in credit transactions will also not be needed in the value-accounting model.

The market price vector times the property-balance-sheet equation at time T:

$$ASSETS^*(T) = DEBTS^*(T) + (ASSETS^*(T) - DEBTS^*(T))$$

yields the value-balance-sheet equation at time T:

$$GBV(T) = D(T) + NBV(T).$$

The market price vector times the original equation zero-term of the simplified property-accounting model:

| | | Total Assets |
Assets	Liabilities	and Liabilities
$[ASSETS^*(T) // 0]$ +	$[0 // DEBTS^*(T)]$ +	$[DEBTS^*(T) //$
		$ASSETS^*(T)]$

Change in A&L	WP	Sales	Purchases	UTr
+ $[0 // 0]$	+ $[0 // 0]$ +	$[0 // 0]$ +	$[0 // 0]$ +	$[0 // 0]$

yields the original equation zero-term of the value-accounting model:

Assets	Liabilities	Net Worth
$[GBV(T) // 0]$ +	$[0 // D(T)]$ +	$[0 // NBV(T)]$

Change in NW	Production	UTr
+ $[0 // 0]$ +	$[0 // 0]$ +	$[0 // 0]$,

where Sales and Purchases have been deleted in the value-accounting model.

It would be possible to multiply each property-accounting transaction by the price vector to obtain a value-accounting transaction. However, this would be needlessly complex in some cases since several property-accounting transactions can often be collapsed into one value-accounting transaction. For example, by multiplying transactions 1 a and 1 b in the simplified property-accounting journal by the market prices, we would arrive at two value transactions, one that debited $P'X'$ to Raw-Materials Inventory and credited it to Suppliers and the other that debited $P'X'$ to Suppliers and credited it to Cash. Clearly these two value transactions can be combined by canceling out Suppliers so that the transaction debits $P'X'$ to Raw-Materials Inventory and credits the same amount to Cash. This combined value transaction will be referred to as 1 a–1 b in the journal. Some property accounting transactions will just disappear when evaluated at market prices. For example, any transaction that discharges a market transaction, such as 1 c, will be applying a debit and credit of zero at the value-accounting level.

The Journal

See journal next page ⟶

The closing balance in the Whole-Product T-account for the simplified property model is:

$$WP^*(T) = [NEGPROD^*(T) \; // \; POSPROD^*(T)]$$

where the negative product is:

$$NEGPROD^*(T) = (0,0,X,1,0,GBV(T),L),$$

and the positive product is:

$$POSPROD^*(T) = (0,Q,0,0,1,0,0).$$

Evaluating at market prices yields:

$$
\begin{aligned}
PRICES^*(T) \times WP^*(T) &= [P'X + C(m-1) + rGBV(T) + WL \; // \\
&\quad PQ + C(m)] \\
&= [0 \; // \; PQ - P'X - WL - (C(m-1) \\
&\quad - C(m)) - rGBV(T)] \\
&= [0 \; // \; \pi(T)],
\end{aligned}
$$

Transaction	Description	Accounts	[Debit	//	Credit]
1a-1b.	Purchase raw materials	Raw-materials inventory / Cash	$[P'X$ / 0	// / //	$0]$ / $P'X']$
2a-2b.	Purchase labor	Labor / Cash	$[WL$ / 0	// / //	$0]$ / $WL]$
2d.	Use of labor in production	Production / Labor	$[WL$ / 0	// / //	$0]$ / $WL]$
3.	Use of Raw-materials in production	Production / Raw-materials inventory	$[P'X$ / 0	// / //	$0]$ / $P'X]$
4a.	Production of final goods	Final-goods inventory / Production	$[PQ$ / 0	// / //	$0]$ / $PQ]$
4b-4c.	Sale of the final goods	Cash / Final-goods inventory	$[PQ'$ / 0	// / //	$0]$ / $PQ']$
6.	Debt payment	Creditor 1 / Cash	$[D - rD(T)$ / 0	// / //	$0]$ / $D - rD(T)]$
7a-7b.	Purchase of capital services	Capital services / Cash	$[rD(T)$ / 0	// / //	$0]$ / $rD(T)]$
7d-7e.	Receipt of capital services	Capital services / Unilateral transfer	$[rNBV(T)$ / 0	// / //	$0]$ / $rNBV(T)]$
7f.	Use of capital services in production	Production / Capital services	$[rGBV(T)$ / 0	// / //	$0]$ / $rGBV(T)]$
8a.	Begin use of the machine	Production / Fixed equipment	$[C(m - 1)$ / 0	// / //	$0]$ / $C(m - 1)]$
8b.	End use of the machine	Fixed equipment / Production	$[C(m)$ / 0	// / //	$0]$ / $C(m)]$
9a-9b.	Payment of dividends	Unilateral transfer / Cash	$[DIV(T)$ / 0	// / //	$0]$ / $DIV(T)]$
10a-10b.	Receipt of subscriptions	Cash / Unilateral transfer	$[SUBS(T)$ / 0	// / //	$0]$ / $SUBS(T)]$

assuming that the economic profit $\pi(T)$ is nonnegative. The value of the closing balance of the Unilateral-Transfers property account is the closing balance in the Unilateral-Transfers value account:

$$PRICES^*(T) \times UTr^*(T) = PRICES^*(T) \times [DIV(T),0, \ldots) // (SUBS(T),$$

$$0, \ldots, NBV(T),0)]$$

$$= [DIV(T) // SUBS(T) + rNBV(T)]$$

$$= [0 // rNBV(T) + SUBS(T) - DIV(T)]$$

assuming that $rNBV(T) + SUBS(T)$ is larger than or equal to $DIV(T)$. It remains to close Production and Unilateral Transfers into Change in Net Worth.

Transaction	Description	Accounts	[Debit	//	Credit].
C.	Close Production	Production	[$\pi(T)$	//	0]
		Change in net worth	[0	//	$\pi(T)$]
C.	Close unilateral transfer	Change in net worth	[0//$rNBV(T)$ + $SUBS(T)$		$- DIV(T)$]
		Unilateral transfer	[$rNBV(T)$ + $SUBS(T)$		$- DIV(T)$ // 0]

Assuming that the change in net worth:

$$\pi(T) - DIV(T) + rNBV(T) + SUBS(T) = NBV(T + 1) - NBV(T),$$

is nonnegative, the final transaction closes Change in Net Worth into Net Worth (or an appropriate subaccount such as Retained Earnings).

Transaction	Description	Accounts	[Debit	//	Credit]
C.	Close Change in net worth	Change in net worth	[$\pi(T) - DIV(T) +$ $rNBV(T) + SUBS(T)//0$]		
		Net worth	[0 // $\pi(T) - DIV(T) +$ $rNBV(T) + SUBS(T)$]		

The Ledger

See ledger next page ⟶➤

The Ledger

Each journal entry involved a pair of T-terms, one the reverse of the other. Their sum is the transaction zero-term. Each transaction zero-term is added to the equation zero-term. The equation zero-term is the sum of a set of labeled T-terms or T-accounts. The set of T-accounts in the equation zero-term is the ledger. The addition of the two T-terms in a transaction zero-term to the equation zero-term, each being added to the appropriate T-account, is the operation of posting to the ledger.

Ledger

Cash

	$[CASH(T)$	//	$0]$
(1a–1b)	$[0$	//	$P'X']$
(2a–2b)	$[0$	//	$WL]$
(4b–4c)	$[PQ'$	//	$0]$
(6)	$[0$	//	$D - rD(T)]$
(7a–7b)	$[0$	//	$rD(T)]$
(9a–9c)	$[0$	//	$DIV(T)]$
(10a–10b)	$[SUBS(T)$	//	$0]$
(<)	$[0$	//	$CASH(T+1)]$
(<)	$[CASH(T+1)$	//	$0]$

Final-Goods Inventory

	$[PFG(T)$	//	$0]$
(4a)	$[PQ$	//	$0]$
(4b–4c)	$[0$	//	$PQ']$
(<)	$[0$	//	$PFG(T+1)]$
(<)	$[PFG(T+1)$	//	$0]$

Raw-Materials Inventory

	$[P'RM(T)$	//	$0]$
(1a–1b)	$[P'X'$	//	$0]$
(3)	$[0$	//	$P'X']$
(<)	$[0$	//	$P'RM(T+1)]$
(<)	$[P'RM(T+1)$	//	$0]$

Labor

(2a–2b)	$[WL$	//	$0]$
(2d)	$[0$	//	$WL]$

Capital Services

(7a–7b)	$[rD(T)$	//	$0]$
(7d–7e)	$[rNBV(T)$	//	$0]$
(7f)	$[0$	//	$rGBV(T)]$

Fixed Equipment

	$[C(m-1)$	//	$0]$
(8a)	$[0$	//	$C(m-1)]$
(8b)	$[C(m)$	//	$0]$
(<)	$[0$	//	$C(m)]$
	$[C(m)$	//	$0]$

Creditor 1

	$[0$	//	$D(T)]$
(6)	$[D - rD(T)$	//	$0]$
(<)	$[D(T+1)$	//	$0]$
(<)	$[0$	//	$D(T+1)]$

Net Worth

	$[0$	//	$NBV(T)]$
(C)	$[0// \pi(T) - DIV(T) + rNBV(T) + SUBS(T)]$		
(<)	$[NBV(T+1)$	//	$0]$
(<)	$[0$	//	$NBV(T+1)]$

Ledger continued

	Production				Unilateral Transfers		
(2d)	[WL	//	0]	(7d–7e)	[0	//	$rNBV(T)$]
(3)	[$P'X$	//	0]	(9a–9b)	[$DIV(T)$	//	0]
(4a)	[0	//	PQ]	(10a–10b)	[0	//	$SUBS(T)$]
(7d)	[$rGBV(T)$	//	0]	(C)	[$rNBV(T + SUBS(T)$		
(8a)	[$C(m - 1)$	//	0]			$- DIV(T) // 0$]	
(8b)	[0	//	$C(m)$]				
(C)	[$\pi(T)$	//	0]				

The Income Statement

A streamlined form of the income statement could be obtained by multiplying market prices times the Property-Flow Statement of Simplified property accounting. A more ordinary form for the income statement would be as follows:

Income Statement

$$\text{Sales} = PQ'$$
$$\text{Ending final-goods inventory} = PFG(T+1)$$
$$-\ \text{Beginning final-goods inventory} = -PFG(T)$$

$$\text{Revenue} = PQ$$

$$\text{Labor expense} = WL$$

$$\text{Raw-materials purchases} = P'X'$$
$$\text{Beginning raw-materials inventory} = P'RM(T)$$
$$-\ \text{Ending raw-materials inventory} = P'RM(T+1)$$

$$\text{Raw-materials expense} = P'X$$

$$\text{Fixed equipment purchases} = 0$$
$$\text{Beginning fixed equipment inventory} = C(m-1)$$
$$-\ \text{Ending fixed equipment inventory} = -C(m)$$

$$\text{Depreciation} = C(m-1) - C(m)$$

$$\text{Capital-services Expense} = rGBV(T)$$

$$\text{Economic profit} = \pi(T)$$

$$-\ \text{Dividends} = -DIV(T)$$
$$\text{Subscriptions} = SUBS(T)$$
$$\text{Capital-services contributions} = rNBV(T)$$

$$\text{Change in net worth} = \pi(T) - DIV(T) + rNBV(T) + SUBS(T)$$
$$= NBV(T+1) - NBV(T).$$

Inserting plus signs between the closing balances of the T-accounts of the ledger will yield the end-of-the-year resultant equation zero-term:

Cash		Final-Goods Inventory		Raw-Materials Inventory
$[CASH(T + 1) // 0]$	$+$	$[PFG(T + 1) // 0]$	$+$	$[P'RM(T + 1) // 0]$

	Fixed Equipment		Creditor 1		Net Worth
$+$	$[C(m) // 0]$	$+$	$[0 // D(T + 1)]$	$+$	$[0 // NBV(T + 1)].$

This could also be obtained by multiplying market prices times the resultant equation zero-term in the simplified property-accounting model.

A LHS T-account $[d // c]$ in the equation zero-term decodes as $d - c$ on the LHS of the resultant equation, and a RHS T-account $[d // c]$ decodes as $c - d$ on the RHS of the resultant equation. Hence decoding the above resultant equation zero-term yields the resultant balance-sheet equation at time $T + 1$:

$$CASH(T + 1) + PFG(T + 1) + P'RM(T + 1) + C(m) = D(T + 1) + NBV(T + 1)$$

In more conventional form, this is the:

Balance Sheet at Time $T + 1$

Assets		Liabilities	
Cash	$CASH(T + 1)$	Creditor 1	$D(T + 1)$
Final-goods inventory	$PFG(T + 1)$		
Raw-materials inventory	$P'RM(T + 1)$		
Fixed equipment	$C(m)$	Net Worth	$NBV(T + 1)$
Total assets	$GBV(T + 1)$	Total Liabilities and net worth	$D(T + 1) +$ $NBV(T + 1)$

11 Comments on the Accounting Literature

The Meaning of Double Entry

The mathematical formulation of double-entry bookkeeping allows clarity on some basic questions such as: (1) what is *double* about double-entry bookkeeping, and (2) what is single-entry bookkeeping. There is surprising confusion on these questions in the literature.

In chapter 6, a simple balance-sheet example was developed using the Pacioli group. It can be simplified further by deleting the temporary accounts (which can however be used in both single- and double-entry bookkeeping) and by recording the relevant debits and credits directly to Net Worth. The double-entry and single-entry treatments will be presented so that they can be compared and contrasted. Both treatments begin with the balance-sheet equation:

$$\begin{array}{ccccc}
\text{Assets} & & \text{Liabilities} & & \text{Net Worth} \\
6000 & = & 3500 & + & 2500.
\end{array}$$

The three transactions were:

1. $1400 is expended on productive inputs,
2. $1600 of outputs is produced and sold, and
3. $900 of principal is paid on a loan.

The double-entry and the single-entry systems of accounting are both methods of recording the effects of the transactions so that the initial balance-sheet equation is transformed into the ending balance-sheet equation. Both methods must yield the same ending balance sheet (using the same accounting principles), otherwise at least one method would be incomplete or incorrect. The difference lies in how the transactions are recorded and applied to the balance-sheet equation.

In the *double-entry* system, the initial balance sheet is encoded as the *initial equational zero-term:*

Assets	Liabilities	Net Worth
[6000 // 0] +	[0 // 3500] +	[0 // 2500].

Each transaction is encoded as a transactional zero-term in the form $[d // 0] + [0 // c]$ where $d = c$, and then the debit and credit T-terms are added to the appropriate T-accounts.

	Assets	Liabilities	Net Worth
	[6000 // 0] +	[0 // 3500] +	[0 // 2500]
(1)	[0 // 1400]	+	[1400 // 0]
(2)	[1600 // 0]	+	[0 // 1600]
(3)	[0 // 900] +	[900 // 0]	
	[7600 // 2300] +	[900 // 3500] +	[1400 // 4100].

Putting each resulting T-term in reduced form yields the *final equational zero-term:*

Assets	Liabilities	Net Worth
[5300 // 0] +	[0 // 2600] +	[0 // 2700],

which decodes to the *ending balance-sheet equation:*

Assets	Liabilities	Net Worth
5300 =	2600 +	2700.

In the *single-entry* bookkeeping system, the transactions are applied directly to the relevant accounts. The accounts are not encoded as T-accounts, and both addition and subtraction (equals addition of the negative of a number) are used; that is, both positive and negative numbers are used:

	Assets	Liabilities	Net Worth
	6000 =	3500 +	2500
(1)	− 1400		− 1400
(2)	+ 1600		+ 1600
(3)	− 900	− 900	
	5300 =	2600 +	2700.

The ending balance-sheet equation is obtained by summing the positive and negative numbers in each account to get the account's total. A more complicated example of a complete single-entry system of bookkeeping is developed in chapter 1 of Gordon and Shillinglaw (1969), although it is not called single-entry bookkeeping. The single-entry system often is used in computerized systems of accounting where a single memory location is assigned to an account and it is updated with additions and subtractions.

The characteristic features of each system can now be seen. The characteristic feature of the double-entry system is the T-account or T-term. The *doubleness* is the two-sidedness of the T-account. There are no negative numbers in the T-terms, although negative numbers can arise on the financial statements obtained by decoding the T-terms. The characteristic feature of single-entry bookkeeping is the single-sidedness of the accounts. Positive and negative entries are made in one column, instead of using only positive entries in two-sided T-accounts.

There is a remarkably wide range of opinion in the literature about the meaning of double entry and single entry. The most common confusion is that double entry derives from the fact that each transaction changes two (or more) accounts. This is the "every-stick-has-two-ends" theory of double-entry bookkeeping. Representative expressions of this view are as follows:

> Every event that is recorded in the accounts affects at least two items; there is no conceivable way of making only a single change in the accounts. Accounting is therefore properly called a "double-entry" system. (Anthony 1970, p. 32)

> A business transaction does not affect just one item alone. There are at least two items to be considered in each transaction. . . . The dual aspect of each transaction forms the basis underlying what is called *double-entry accounting*. (Moore and Jaedicke 1967, pp. 648–649)

The double- and single-entry systems are methods of *recording* transactions to transform the beginning equation into the ending equation. The doubleness of a transaction, the fact that it affects two accounts, is a property of the transaction itself, not a property of the recording method. The transaction affects exactly the same accounts in the single-entry system as in the double-entry system (as inspection of the above example shows). Otherwise it could hardly produce the same balance sheet in the end. Every stick has two ends in both single- and double-entry bookkeeping since it is the same stick, or transaction, being recorded by two different methods. The fact that two or more terms must be changed is a general mathematical fact about equations and has nothing in particular to do with the balance sheet or accounting. Given any equation between sums such as:

$$a + b + \cdots + c = x + y + \cdots + z,$$

there is no way that only one term, such as *b*, could be changed and the equation still be true. Two or more terms must be changed.

The confusion over double entry has been compounded by the unfortunate use of the expression *single entry* to describe bookkeeping with an incomplete set of accounts where only one end of a transaction is recorded. For example, it is said that a household checkbook is single entry because only one entry is made. The household checkbook is indeed single entry but not because of the one entry. It would still be single entry if a complete set of household accounts were maintained, so that there were always two entries for each transaction. A household checkbook is single entry because it is a single-column account updated by additions and subtractions. Often minus signs are suppressed by having subtraction understood by the context or by other notational conventions, so one should not infer double entry from the mere absence of minus signs. There is no bookkeeping system using a complete set of accounts where a transaction is only recorded in one account. Throwing away half the T-accounts in a double-entry system does not create a single-entry system. Without a complete set of accounts, one just has a fragment of a single-entry or double-entry system.

Another view of the doubleness of double-entry bookkeeping derives from the two sides of the balance-sheet equation.

> The heart of the double-entry bookkeeping system, . . . is the idea that the total value of assets which a firm holds may be categorized or partitioned from two different viewpoints: (i) by the type of the assets, such as cash, inventories, machinery, etc., and (ii) by the claimants on the total value of the assets, such as trade creditors, banks, stockholders, etc. (Ijiri 1965, pp. 82–83)

But the exact same balance-sheet equation is the starting point of the single-entry bookkeeping system. There is no reason to call the balance-sheet equation, "the fundamental equation of the double-entry bookkeeping system" (Ijiri 1965, p. 84), since it plays the same role in the single-entry system. In spite of calling it double-entry, Ijiri goes on to develop a matrix treatment of an accounting system that involves no T-accounts and freely uses positive and negative numbers (1965, p. 91). It is in fact an interesting matrix treatment of a single-entry system. The transaction matrix from double-entry bookkeeping (see below) is introduced, but then it is transformed into an appropriate matrix for a single-entry system (with positive and negative entries) and is used in the latter form.

The doubleness of double-entry bookkeeping is not the two-sidedness of transactions and is not the two-sidedness of equations. Transactions have the same number of ends, and equations have the same number of sides in single-entry bookkeeping. The doubleness of double-entry bookkeeping is the two-sidedness of the T-account, and the singleness of single-entry book-keeping is the one-sidedness of the one-column plus-and-minus account.

Transactions Matrices

There is a well-known connection between rectangular arrays of (positive or negative) numbers and equations; for example, the cross-classification tables of statistics. Each number in the array is cross-classified as a row entry and as a column entry. The additive equation associated with the array states that the sum of the row sums equals the sum of the column sums. A multiplicative equation can be associated with an array of numbers by substituting *product* for *sum*. These cross-classification or double-classification tables were used in chapter 6 to generate the beginning equations in the vector-accounting and the multiplicative-accounting examples. There is no intrinsic connection between these rectangular double-classification tables and double-entry bookkeeping. We could have just as well developed single-entry treatments starting with the same tables and equations.

Not all equations can be meaningfully derived from a double-classification table. In particular, the balance-sheet equation cannot be meaningfully derived from a double-classification table. When a corporation draws one-hundred dollars cash from its checking account, there is no meaningful sense in which it could be characterized as, say, sixty dollars debt capital and forty dollars equity capital. In the Pacioli-group treatment of balance-sheet accounting, the equation associated with the equational zero-term thus does not derive from a double-classification table.

The equation associated with the sum of the transactional zero-terms, however, does derive from a not only rectangular but also square array called a *transaction matrix*. Instead of the usual two-vertical-column T-account format, transpose the right-hand or credit column into a row. By overlaying the horizontal rows and vertical columns, one has a square array where each account has a column for debits and a row for credits. Given a transaction zero-term in the simple classical form, $[X // 0] + [0 // X]$, suppose the credit part is added to the i-th account and the debit part is applied to the j-th account. This transaction could then be recorded in the transaction matrix by entering X once in the intersection of the i-th row and the j-th column. In the simple example developed above, the *transactions array* would be as shown in figure 11-1.

The use of transactions arrays in accounting was popularized by Kemeny, Schleifer, Snell, and Thompson (1962). Transactions matrices are usually traced in economics to Leontief's input-output theory (1951) and, in accounting, to Gomberg (1927) and Kohler (1952) (see Mattessich 1964, pp. 88–94). But the transaction array goes back at least to the midnineteenth-

Debits

	A	L	NW
A		900	1400
L			
NW	1600		

Credits (label spanning the L row on the left)

Figure 11–1. A Transactions Array

century mathematician, Augustus DeMorgan, who introduced it in a short essay, "On the Main Principle of Bookkeeping" (1869). Being long before the current fad of calling all rectangular arrays or tables, *matrices,* and even before the full development of matrix algebra, DeMorgan simply called it a "table of *double-entry*" (1869, p. 183), and compared it to a multiplication table.

The confusion over double-entry bookkeeping was deepened by Kemeny et al.'s attempt to relabel double-entry bookkeeping as *double-classification bookkeeping.*

> A little reflection shows that the important point about double-entry book-keeping is not that each transaction is *recorded* twice but rather that each transaction is *classified* twice—once as a debit and once as a credit. (1962, p. 347)

However, the premise that double entry derives from each transaction being recorded twice is incorrect. Each transaction is also recorded twice in single-entry bookkeeping. Hence the clever *one-write system* of overlaying rows and columns so that only one entry need be made does not give grounds to rename the system *double-classification bookkeeping*—since that wasn't what made it double entry in the first place. It is the two-column T-account that is unique to double entry, and that is still present in the transactions table where the credit columns have been transposed as rows.

The treatment of double-entry bookkeeping using transactions tables, for example, Kemeny et al. (1962), has been vastly overplayed. It obscures the algebraic structure of double-entry bookkeeping and it does not generalize well to vector or multiplicative bookkeeping. The *matrix formulation* does not promote the crucial step of seeing the T-accounts as algebraic objects in the Pacioli group. Moreover, it is not a complete mathematical formulation of double-entry bookkeeping, in spite of the relatively superficial and nongeneralizable use of matrix algebra. For example, the row sum and the column sum for an account must still be informally compared to find the balance in the account.

For each balance-sheet account, the total debits are *balanced* against the
total credits. That is, we subtract a given total credits entry from the corresponding total debit entry and record the absolute value of the result next
to whichever entry is larger. (Kemeny et al. 1962, pp. 355–356)

That operation is not a *matrix treatment* to be compared to the group-theo-
retical treatment. It is a concrete example and special case of what is
abstractly characterized as reducing a T-term to its reduced form in the
Pacioli group.

The matrix formulation also does not generalize well. It exploits the
fact that a transaction zero-term in scalar accounting can always be put in
the classical form $[X // 0] + [0 // X]$ so that only X can be entered in the
table. In general vectorial bookkeeping, transactional zero-terms have the
form $[X // Y] + [Y // X]$ *where neither X nor Y are zero vectors.* The
discharging transactions were examples. In the example of multiplicative
bookkeeping, we were careful to keep the multiplicative transactional units
in the classical form, $(X/1)(1/X)$. But, in general, they can have the form
$(X/Y)(Y/X)$ where X/Y is in lowest terms and neither X nor Y are unity.
In these cases, the simple transaction-table treatment breaks down.

There are two equivalent ways to treat the general transaction zero-
term, $[X // Y] + [Y // X]$. The simplest method is to factor it into two
classical transactional zero-terms:

$$\{[X // 0] + [0 // X] + [Y // 0] + [0 // Y]\},$$

and then to apply each one separately. This is an economically artificial
treatment of the general transaction to make it fit a transaction table with
nonnegative vector entries.

The other treatment is to appropriately modify the table. Draw a northwest to southeast diagonal in each square of the transaction table. Then
entries can be made both below and above the diagonal in a square so that a
square has the form $X\backslash Y$. This is to be interpreted in opposite ways from
the row or column viewpoint. The entry $X\backslash Y$ in the intersection of the *i–th*
row and *j–th* column means to add $[X // Y]$ to the column account and to
add the reverse $[Y // X]$ to the row account. The rows and columns can no
longer be labeled *credit* and *debit,* respectively, since the addition of a general T-term $[X // Y]$ to an account is a mixed debit and credit. Each row
and each column has become a T-account. For an entry $X\backslash Y$ in a square, the
X below the diagonal line is a debit to the column and a credit to the row,
while the Y above the diagonal has the opposite significance. Then the general transaction zero-term $[X // Y] + [Y // X]$ can be recorded by a *single
entry* in the form $X\backslash Y,$ which is double classified by the rows and columns.

The equivalence between the two treatments can be seen as follows.
When the divided squares are used, only the triangle of squares above (or

below) the main diagonal in the transaction matrix is needed. It is a transaction *triangle* instead of a square array. Indeed, the transaction triangle can be derived from the transaction matrix by folding the matrix along its main diagonal. If the general transaction zero-term had been factored into two classical transactions, then the transaction would be recorded by entering the vector X in the *i–th* row and *j–th* column, and the vector Y in the *j–th* row and the *i–th* column. When the transaction matrix is folded along its main diagonal, the X and the Y are mapped to the same square but with the opposite significance. That can be seen as the origin of the diagonal-divided squares with the entries on either side of the diagonal having the opposite significance.

Similar considerations apply in multiplicative accounting. There is no need to consider more details here. The point is that when the matrix entries are vectors in vectorial accounting or integers to be multiplied along rows and columns in multiplicative accounting, the superficial connection with ordinary matrix algebra is severed. Vectors do not appear as matrix entries, and no matrix operation takes the product of the elements in a row or column. The so-called matrix treatment, while of limited use, has on the whole hindered the mathematical treatment of double-entry bookkeeping by obscuring the algebraic structure of the Pacioli group.

Arthur Cayley (1821–1895) was one of the few mathematicians who wrote about double-entry bookkeeping. In the year before his death, he published a small pamphlet entitled *The Principles of Book-keeping by Double Entry,* in which he wrote:

> The Principles of Book-keeping by Double Entry constitute a theory which is mathematically by no means uninteresting: it is in fact like Euclid's theory of ratios an absolutely perfect one, and it is only its extreme simplicity which prevents it from being as interesting as it would otherwise be. (1894 Preface)

In the pamphlet, Cayley only described double-entry bookkeeping in practical informal terms and did not present a mathematical formulation.

Cayley was also one of the founders of matrix algebra. Charnes, Cooper, and Ijiri cite this connection as evidence that "the concepts of matrices and double-entry principles" (1963, p. 39) are closely related to one another. However, the evidence does not support this conclusion. Cayley never mentioned matrices in the pamphlet on double-entry bookkeeping even though he was surely familiar with DeMorgan's use of a square array as a table of double entry (DeMorgan 1869, p. 183) a quarter of a century earlier. Moreover, it would seem that Cayley's interest in, and knowledge of, double-entry bookkeeping was due not to matrix algebra but to the fact that Cayley was also a lawyer. He made his living for fourteen years as a solicitor before accepting an appropriate professorship in mathematics (without the religious prerequisites that prevented his earlier appointment).

The mathematical basis for double-entry bookkeeping lies not in matrix algebra but in the group-of-differences (herein called the Pacioli group) construction. That construction uses the double-entry format; that is, the T-account format, to extend an additive algebraic system to include additive inverses and thus to include the effect of negative quantities. As Cayley pointed out in his presidential address to the British Association for Advancement of Science, the "notion of a negative magnitude" is "used in a very refined manner in bookkeeping by double entry" (1896, p. 434).

Precursors of Property Accounting

The full development of property accounting was built on two foundations: (1) descriptive property theory and (2) the mathematical formulation of double-entry bookkeeping using the Pacioli group.

The nontrivial part of descriptive property theory is the *discovery* and analysis of the laissez faire mechanism of appropriation involved in normal production. The conventional treatment of production tends to ignore appropriation in several ways: (1) by describing production only in value terms (not in terms of property), (2) by viewing the right to the product as being included in some previous ownership right (see chapters 12 and 13), or (3) by viewing appropriation metaphorically as a trade with Nature. In property accounting, the abstract concepts of property theory are applied to describe, using the customary double-entry-accounting framework, the stocks and flows of property rights in a productive enterprise. In the later chapters 12 and 13, we will consider the literature in capital theory, finance theory, and general-equilibrium theory from the viewpoint of descriptive property theory.

The necessary formal machinery for property accounting arose out of the mathematical formulation of double-entry bookkeeping. One of the purposes of formalizing a discipline is to see how it can be generalized in new directions. Since double-entry bookkeeping had not been previously put in complete mathematical terms, the easy extensions of the double-entry method to vectors and fractions were unknown. The overemphasis on the matrix treatment may be partly responsible for this lack of development.

The mathematics for single-entry vectorial accounting is just the ordinary algebra of vectors where the vectors have positive and negative components. The use of vector-space methods in economics (as opposed to just multivariable calculus) has become widespread due to the development of linear and nonlinear programming, activity analysis, and game theory. Whole product vectors, under a variety of names such as *production vec-*

tors, activity vectors, and *input-output vectors,* have become standard in modern mathematical economics. Hence the mathematical description of production using production sets of whole-product vectors or input-output vectors could be viewed as a highly abstract single-entry-property-accounting treatment (without a theory of appropriation) of a firm with no balance sheet (that is, a pure rental firm). The treatment can be easily expanded to include vectors representing stocks of assets and liabilities and to give a more complete single-entry-property-accounting treatment of a productive enterprise (for example, Ellerman 1981).

The challenge, however, was to develop a theory of double-entry property accounting. Value accounting is usually double entry, so a double-entry-property-accounting system was needed as the objective underlying property structure, the physical skeleton, behind value accounting. By applying prices or other valuation coefficients, one wanted to be able to derive a double-entry-value-accounting system as the image of the property-accounting system (see chapters 9 and 10).

The only significant work towards property accounting has been the pioneering developments of Professor Yuji Ijiri (1965, 1966, 1967, 1979). Ijiri clearly states the idea of a property-accounting system that he calls *multi-dimensional physical accounting* (1966, p. 155). He shows that vectors can be used to deal with incommensurate physical units in different components of the vectors—which is a basic idea of vectorial accounting.

Other writers have used vectors in scalar accounting to keep track of not only the scalar amount of the transaction but also the numbers of the accounts debited and credited, the date, and other auxiliary numerical information, for example, Kemeny et al. (1962, p. 358) and Mattessich (1964, p. 94). This is clearly a part of scalar accounting, and (unlike Ijiri's work) it is not a part of vectorial accounting. It is also a loose use of the technical term *vector.* Any self-respecting vector, unlike a garden variety ordered *n*-tuple or one-dimensional array, should at least have a meaningful addition operation defined on its components so that the vectors could be meaningfully added together. The addition of two account numbers or two dates is without significance.

While Professor Ijiri clearly had the right idea, his actual development of multidimensional physical accounting was bound to be fragmentary as long as it was without the proper mathematical framework of the Pacioli group and the property-theoretic content. In Ijiri (1965), he presents an example of the starting point of any single-entry or double-entry-property-accounting system, the property balance-sheet equation using vectors of physical quantities (1965, p. 86). That is a real advance. As noted in the previous section on the meaning of double entry, there is nothing particularly double entry (as opposed to single entry) about the balance-sheet equation in either its scalar or vector form, even though Ijiri calls it double entry.

Without the Pacioli-group machinery, Ijiri does not move to the next step of introducing genuine double-entry concepts by encoding the property balance-sheet equation in T-accounts.

In two later works (1966 and 1967), Ijiri makes his most determined attempt to develop a multidimensional physical-accounting model in the double-entry format. He does introduce T-accounts here, but he mysteriously does not use the vector balance-sheet equation of Ijiri (1965). Moreover, Ijiri never took the step of using vectors in the T-accounts. The balance sheet is presented simply as a set of physically incommensurate quantities (debts are called *negative assets*) reminiscent of Boulding's *physical balance sheet* (1962, p. 45). Without an initial balance-sheet equation, one cannot get very far in a double-entry system. Ijiri introduces T-accounts as stock accounts called *asset accounts* and as flow or temporary accounts called *activity accounts*. None of the T-accounts use vectors, which is another reason why the development will be fragmentary. With the Pacioli-group formulation, the extension of the algebra of T-accounts to vector T-accounts is straightforward.

Ijiri (1966, 1967) describes several sample physical transactions and is careful to record each as an equal debit and credit. The debit and credit entries for different transactions are made in terms of incommensurate scalars rather than vectors. This system creates no problem in the asset or stock accounts since each asset account deals with only one type of physical quantity (for example, the Cash account in dollars, the Materials account in pounds, the Finished-Goods account in cases, and so forth). But the incommensurate physical quantities get jumbled together in the activity or flow accounts.

> It will be noted that entries in each asset account are homogeneous (additive), but entries in each activity account are not. (Ijiri 1967, p. 113)

This feature means that no meaningful additions can be performed in the activity or flow accounts (all for want of vector T-accounts). In particular, the activity accounts cannot be summed, put in reduced form, or closed. Since Ijiri cannot do anything with the activity accounts, he simply *rules* them as if they had been closed and abandons them.

It might be asked, if Ijiri just abandons the temporary accounts without any closing transactions, how can he arrive at the appropriate figures for the Proprietorship account on the closing balance sheet? The answer is that there is no Proprietorship account because, unlike Ijiri (1965), Ijiri (1966, 1967) does not start off with a property balance-sheet equation. The initial balance sheet just gives physical totals for the assets and debts. There is no Proprietorship account to balance an equation. That fact also explains why the promising vector balance-sheet equation of Ijiri (1965, p. 86) with its

Proprietorship account disappears in the later development (1966, 1967). A balance-sheet equation and a Proprietorship account would require making sense out of the jumble of incommensurate quantities in the activity accounts and would require an orderly closing of those accounts into the Proprietorship account. Without any Proprietorship (or Total A&L) account to worry about, Ijiri can just rule and abandon the activity accounts such as Sales (1966, p. 157; 1967, p. 113) which has two debit entries of 3,500 cases of finished goods and 600 man-hours of labor and one credit entry of $63,000 of cash.

Attention can then be turned to the asset or stock accounts, each of which deals with commensurate quantities. Hence those accounts can be summed and balanced to find the appropriate balances for the closing balance-sheet asset and debt amounts. In a separate table called an "Asset-Activity Statement" (1966, p. 159; 1967, p. 114), Ijiri repeats the same calculations of the asset and debt totals using a single-entry format; that is, single-column accounts with positive and negative entries.

Since the side of each transaction that affected the activity or flow accounts was never utilized, one might wonder why Ijiri bothered to rigorously record each transaction with an equal debit and credit entry. The double-entry method is used to perform algebraic operations on an equation, and Ijiri did not begin with an equation. Apparently he wished to illustrate the trial balance in the context of multidimensional physical accounting.

> Since every number is entered twice, once on the debit side and once on the credit side, the flash total of entries on the debit side of all accounts is equal to the flash total of entries on the credit side of all accounts. (Ijiri 1966, p. 158; with a similar statement in 1967, p. 113)

Firstly, this *trial balance* (unlike the trial balance in vectorial accounting) adds incommensurates together. For instance, on the debit side of the Sales account, the trial balance would be adding 3,500 cases of finished goods and 600 man-hours together to get 4,100 "whatevers". Secondly, the trial balance does not work. A genuine trial balance in a ledger assumes that one starts off with an equation. Then the transactions will be adding equals to equals so the trial balance will, errors aside, give equal debit and credit totals. Since Ijiri does not begin with an equation as explained above, his flash totals are doomed to be unequal. He adds equals to unequals and, of course, gets unequals as a result. When one adds up the debits and the credits in his ledger (1966, pp. 156–157; 1967, pp. 112–113), one finds that there are 12,500 more whatevers on the credit side of the ledger than on the debit side.

This analysis of Professor Ijiri's model of multidimensional physical accounting serves two functions: (1) to give Ijiri credit for formulating and starting to develop the system of physical or property accounting and (2) to point out some of the reasons for the fragmentary nature of his development. Although the model of property accounting presented here grew out of our recent work in mathematics, economics, and property theory, Ijiri clearly envisioned the same goal over fifteen years ago. It is our unfortunate task to point out the problems in Ijiri's model because, to our knowledge, there has been no public criticism of the model. In the fifteen years since the model was published (twice in Ijiri 1966 and 1967), no one seems to have pointed out such matters as: (1) the lack of a balance-sheet equation, (2) the lack of a Proprietorship or similar account, (3) the nonclosure and unworkability of the activity accounts, and (4) the nonbalancing trial balance. All these matters are corrected in property accounting. Without seeing some of the inherent problems in the earlier attempts, it might be difficult to understand why we have gone to the trouble to rebuild property accounting from the ground up on the basis of the mathematical formulation of double-entry bookkeeping, the Pacioli group.

12 Appropriation in Capital Theory, Finance Theory, and Accounting

The Discovery of Appropriation

Property accounting brings into sharp relief a largely neglected aspect of production, the *appropriation* of the assets and liabilities produced in production. For a variety of reasons (some investigated below), work in the fields of economics and accounting has neglected or ignored the entire phenomenon of appropriation as it occurs in production. With the development of property accounting, the stocks and flows of property rights involved in production are directly accounted for, so the role of appropriation becomes clear and distinct. A recognition of the unique aspects of appropriation has direct and profound implications for a number of doctrines in economics and accounting. Our purpose is to outline some of these implications.

In the previous chapter on property theory, we outlined the laissez faire mechanism of appropriation. In the normal day-to-day activities of production and consumption, commodities are consumed as inputs to production or as consumer goods. The owner of the goods loses the goods but not by transfer to another party. The goods have been used up and consumed with the knowledge and intent of the owner of the goods, so that party has no legally defensible claim against another party for compensation against the loss. That is expropriation, the voluntary legal expropriation of those goods, or, equivalently, the voluntary legal appropriation of the liabilities for those goods. Since no explicit legal imputation or assignment of the liabilities for those goods was involved, we have termed this a *laissez faire appropriation of the liabilities.* In property accounting, an expropriation of assets is recorded by debiting the assets to the Whole-Product account. If the goods had been consumed, used up, or destroyed in circumstances against the consent of the owner, then the owner would presumedly have a plausible claim against some other party for compensation. Legal proceedings could be commenced that could overturn the laissez faire solution and reassign the liability to the other party.

In production, new goods, commodities, or assets are produced. Under normal circumstances, a party has already voluntarily appropriated the liabilities for the matching inputs that gave rise to the produced outputs.

Hence, in the absence of any reassignment of the input liabilities, that party would have the legally defensible claim on the produced outputs. Since no explicit legal assignment is involved, we have termed this the *laissez faire appropriation of those assets*. In property accounting, an appropriation of assets is recorded by crediting the assets to the Whole-Product account.

In this manner, a party laissez faire appropriates the assets and liabilities produced in production. Having borne the costs of the inputs used up in production, that party is the last legal owner of the inputs. In a market economy, that party, the whole-product appropriator, is not always the prior owner of some specific input. Usually owners of capital hire labor, but workers can borrow or hire capital and an entrepreneur could hire both the labor and capital. The whole-product appropriator is determined by the direction of the hiring contracts, by *who hires what or whom*. Whichever party hires all the inputs (and does not resell them) will bear those costs as the inputs are consumed in production and thus will appropriate the whole product. The whole-product appropriator (or, in value terms, the residual or profit claimant) is that last legal owner of the consumed inputs; that is, the hiring party.

Being the hiring party, and thus the whole-product appropriator, is a contractual role. It is not the ownership of some specific asset or the performance of any specific service. The whole product is thus not a return to some asset or to some service. It is a return to a contractual role, the role of being the hiring party (the last legal owner of the used-up inputs). Moreover, it is a return in terms of property, not simply a value return. In the textbook model of perfectly competitive equilibrium, there are no pure or economic profits so the net value of the whole product is zero. This does not mean that the hiring party gets nothing. The hiring party gets no net value in that instance but still gets the whole product in terms of property. Moreover, the property mechanism of laissez faire appropriation operates regardless of whether the price mechanism is in equilibrium or disequilibrium and regardless of whether the markets are competitive or noncompetitive.

There is a widespread tendency, especially in economics, to "explain" any income as the return to some factor. The whole product is not a return to some factor. It is of no avail to postulate hidden or implicit factors. At best, some hidden factor might be priced so that the profits would be exactly zero when the factor is taken into account. Hidden factors don't change the structure of property rights involved in production. The whole product, even if of zero value, still accrues to the contractual role of being the hiring party.

The explanation that profit is a return to risk bearing is quite tautologous when *risk bearing* means bearing the costs (appropriating the negative product). Of course, the party that appropriates the negative product also appropriates the positive produce and thus nets the profits. But why in the first place did that party, rather than some other, appropriate the negative product and thus the whole product? That party did so only by being the *last* owner of the inputs. The inputs might have changed hands several times. But it is the party whose name is on the input contracts when the inputs are consumed in production (and thus are not resold) who will bear, or swallow, the costs of the inputs rather than pass the costs on. Having one's name on the contracts is a contractual role.

We will consider the import of the *discovery of appropriation* for various aspects of economic and accounting theory. The general form of the argument is as follows. Broadly speaking, economic resources have two types of uses, the so-called active use and the passive use. A resource is used passively when it is sold or rented out in return for some market price or rental. A resource is used actively when, instead of being evaluated directly on the market, it is used up in production, usually along with other resources. Then the liabilities for the used-up resources and the rights to any produced assets are appropriated. Thus appropriation is involved in the active use, not in the passive use of resources.

Difficulties arise in the conventional treatment of the active case, since conventional economics and accounting tend to ignore appropriation. The economic return in the active case is not just the value of the original resource but the extra value of the appropriated property. But the total return in the active case is typically imputed only to the original resource, as if the ownership of the appropriated property were already included in ownership of the original resource. Property that is appropriated cannot be previously owned; otherwise it could not be appropriated. The extra value of the appropriated property (for example, the whole product) is not a return to the original resource. In the context of the laissez faire appropriation mechanism, it is a return to the role of being the last legal owner of the used-up resources.

One general form of the mistaken imputation of the appropriated property to the original resource is often involved in *opportunity-cost* reasoning. The opportunity cost is the return from the best alternative use of the resource. But if the alternative use is the active use of the resource, then the return is not just the return to the resource but the additional value of the appropriated property. Hence the discovery of appropriation vitiates many of the loose applications of the opportunity-cost doctrine. We turn now to specific examples of this *imputation fallacy* in capital theory and finance theory.

Appropriation in Capital Theory

One reason for the customary neglect of appropriation seems to lie in the tendency to interpret *profit* as the implicit factor payment to some hidden factor. If the distribution of value is definitionally explained by the distribution of explicit or implicit factors and if economists are only concerned with value-theoretic questions, then the question of the appropriation of the property rights and obligations in the whole product will not arise (since the whole product then has zero value).

Another way to neglect appropriation is to construe the right to the whole product as if it were part of a preexistent property right. This practice is part of the Marxist view of the capitalist economic system where the preexistent property right is the "ownership of the means of production." This is also a common practice in capital theory, where the preexistent right is the ownership of a capital asset. For example, in Professor Samuelson's treatment of capital theory, he assumes not only that future property (for example, future whole products) has a present value but that it has a present owner.

> All potential income must be capitalized. That is to say, we start with institutional property rights. Each income account "belongs" to some "person." (Samuelson 1937, p. 477; reprinted in Samuelson 1966, p. 169)

Property *appropriated* in the future can have a present capitalized value (which could be zero) but it cannot have a present owner, since otherwise it could not be appropriated.

In the first chapter, a simple example of a capital asset was developed. The asset had a market cost of C, yielded K units of capital services per year for n years, and then had a salvage value of S. Capital services had a market value of R per unit and the interest rate was r. Under competitive conditions, arbitrage between buy and lease markets would enforce equality between the present values of the outlays to obtain the same real services through buying and leasing:

$$C - S/(1 + r)^n = RKa(n,r)$$

where:

$$a(n,r) = 1/(1 + r) + 1/(1 + r)^2 + \cdots + 1/(1 + r)^n$$

is the present value of an ordinary annuity of one. Hence the market value of the capital asset C is the discounted present value of the rentals plus the scrap value:

$$C = RKa(n,r) + S/(1 + r)^n.$$

Consider a simple production possibility where K units of capital services combined with L units of labor yield Q units of output each year. Let W be the wage rate and P the unit price of output, all payments being made at the end of the period. Hence the economic profit each period is:

$$\pi = PQ - RK - WL.$$

One of the basic concepts of capital theory is the notion of the *capitalized value of an asset*. The definition is usually stated in a rather general fashion; owning the asset *yields* a future income stream and the discounted present value of the income stream is the capitalized value of the asset. But there are quite different ways in which *owning an asset* can yield an income stream. In particular, there are the active and the passive uses of capital. The capitalized-value concept is unproblematic if the income stream is simply the stream of net rentals plus the scrap value. The capitalized value of that stream is, under competitive conditions, just the market value C of the asset. Bonds and annuities provide similar examples of income streams generated by renting out or loaning out capital assets; that is, by the passive use of capital.

Capital theory would be somewhat less controversial if it stuck to such examples of hired-out capital. However, the capitalized-value definition is also applied to the quite different active case where, instead of hiring out the capital, labor is hired in, a product is produced and sold, and the net proceeds are all imputed to the capital assets. In the example above, the owner of the capital asset could hire L units of labor and produce Q units of output each year for n years. This action would yield net proceeds of $PQ - WL$ each year plus the scrap value of S the last year. The present discounted value of this income stream is:

$$V = (PQ - WL)a(n,r) + S/(1 + r)^n.$$

This present value is then called *the capitalized value of the capital asset* as if to impute the net proceeds to the capital asset.

The economic profits were π each year so the present value of the profit stream is:

$$V_0 = \pi a(n,r).$$

The net proceeds $PQ - WL = RK + \pi$ can be analyzed as the implicit rental RK plus the profits π. Hence the capitalized value can be analyzed into two parts:

$$V = RKa(n,r) + S/(1 + r)^n + \pi a(n,r) = C + V_0.$$

Thus the capitalized value V is the market value of the asset C plus the present value V_0 of the future profits. The profits are the market value of the whole product so V_0 is the present value of the whole products appropriated each of the n years. Value is the value of property, and the property whose value is V consists of the capital asset *plus* the stream of whole products appropriated each year. Hence, strictly speaking, it is incorrect to label V as the capitalized value *of the capital asset* by itself.

When the profits are imputed to the capital asset by calling V the capitalized value of the capital asset, then the role of appropriation is overlooked. One might then think that by purchasing the asset, or the means of production, one is thereby purchasing the outputs and the net proceeds—so there is no need to appropriate the outputs.

> When a man buys an investment or capital-asset, he purchases the right to the series of prospective returns, which he expects to obtain from selling its output, after deducting the running expenses of obtaining that output, during the life of the asset. (Keynes 1936, p. 135)

But in fact one thereby purchases only the asset. Any further return will depend on one's contracts. If one rents out the asset and sells the scrap, then one receives only the rental-plus-scrap income stream. If, instead, one hires in labor, bears the costs of the used-up labor and capital services, and claims and sells the outputs, *then* one receives the net proceeds mentioned by Keynes. In each case, one owned the asset. The difference was in the subsequent contracts. By making the contracts so that one was the hiring party, one could additionally appropriate the whole product each time period with its positive or negative value. The capitalized value V is the return to the asset C *plus* the return V_0 to the contractual role that allows one to appropriate the stream of whole products.

Another example of assigning the whole product to the capital asset is involved in the notions of *marginal efficiency of capital* or *net productivity of capital*. We have seen how competitive arbitrage will enforce the equation:

$$C = RKa(n,r) + S/(1 + r)^n.$$

In other words, the interest rate r will discount the rental-plus-scrap income stream back to the market cost C of the asset. Since:

$$V = (RK + \pi)a(n,r) + S/(1 + r)^n,$$

the interest rate r discounts the rental-plus-scrap and profit streams back to the value $V = C + V_0$. If the profits are positive, then V is larger than C. Some higher discount rate r' would be necessary to discount the rental-plus-scrap and profit streams back to C, since the interest rate r discounts them back to V. Such a rate r', which satisfies the equation:

$$C = (RK + \pi)a(n,r') + S/(1 + r')^n,$$

is sometimes called an *internal rate of return* or *average rate of return over cost*. However, the rate r' is also presented as the *yield rate* of the capital asset and then it is called the *marginal efficiency of capital* (Keynes 1936, p. 135) or the *net productivity of capital* (Samuelson 1976, p. 600). This usage presents the profit stream as if it were part of the return to owning the capital asset when in fact it is the return to having the contractual role of being the hiring party.

Yet another method of imputing the whole product and its value, the profits, to capital is the *quasi-rent doctrine*. In a genuinely competitive model, all factors including the services of plant and equipment would have a competitively determined price. Capital assets would have a competitive rental such as RK in the example. In conventional microeconomics, it is held that capital assets might "earn" a short-run quasi-rent due to the short-run inelasticities of supply in capital assets. In the example, the *gross quasi rent* would be $PQ - WL = RK + \pi$ and the *net quasi rent* is $PQ - WL - RK = \pi$, the profits. There is no merit in the argument that short-run inelasticities require a special notion of quasi rents in addition to the usual competitive rentals. Short-term competitive rentals reflect such scarcities, and thus the short-run rental RK might be higher than the rental in the longer term. The quasi-rent doctrine is another example of the penchant in conventional economic theory to fallaciously impute the profits to capital. The value of the appropriated whole product, the profit, is added to the machine's competitive rental, and the result, $RK + \pi = PQ - WL$, is dubbed the "quasi-rent earned by the machine" (Stonier and Hague 1973, p. 328)

There is a pattern here. Capital has a passive use and an active use. Thus capital theory will always have a pair of concepts associated with capital, one concept derived for the passive case and one concept for the active case. The value concept associated with the active case includes the concept for the passive case plus the value of the whole product (the profits), that is appropriated by the capital owner in the active case. Thus a capital asset has a market cost (passive) and a *capitalized value* (active). A physical capital good has a marginal productivity (passive) and a *net productivity* (active). Financial capital has a marginal rate of return over cost (passive) and an *average rate of return over cost* or *marginal efficiency* (active). And a capital asset has a market rental (passive) and a quasi rent (active). The difference between the passive and active case is the appropriation of the whole product, which is the return to a contractual role not a return to the capital. But conventional capital theory neglects appropriation and imputes the whole product and its value, the profits, to capital.

One traditional reason for the neglect of the entire question of the appropriation of the whole product is that it doesn't matter, for the purposes of price theory, if attention is restricted to zero-profit perfectly competitive equilibrium.

Remember that in a perfectly competitive market it really doesn't matter who hires whom: so have labor hire "capital". (Samuelson 1957, p. 894; reprinted in Samuelson 1966, p. 351)

[U]nder constant returns to scale and statical conditions of certainty, it is immaterial which factor hires which. . . . Labor as much hires capital goods and land as capital hires labor and land. (Samuelson 1967, p. 114; reprinted in Samuelson 1972, p. 27)

The same zero-profit condition occurs in capital theory where it hides the imputation of the whole product. The capitalized value definition and the net productivity definition assign to an asset, such as a machine, not only the stream of future services it yields but the whole products produced by using up the machine services. The right to the machine's services is indeed a part of the legal ownership of the machine. The value of each year's services is the rental, and the discounted value of the rentals is the market cost of the machine C. However the capital-theoretic definitions also impute (fallaciously) the annual whole products to the machine. The value of each year's whole product is the pure profit and the discounted value of the future whole products is V_0. The capitalized value V is the sum $C + V_0$, and the net productivity of the capital good presents the rental-plus-profit stream as being the yield of the machine.

When that capital-theoretic assignment of the whole products to the capital assets is challenged, the all-too-typical response is that it really doesn't matter because in perfectly competitive equilibrium the pure profits are zero. Since $V_0 = 0$ in that instance, Professor Samuelson can claim to have demonstrated that "equality of capitalized value and reproduction cost" (Samuelson 1961, p. 42; reprinted in Samuelson 1966, p. 309); that is, $V = C$. Similarly, a prominent capital theorist shows that the competitive "equilibrium price of a one-year-old machine in terms of 'costs' " is equal to the "present discounted value of the future *net* output which a one-year-old machine can produce." (Burmeister 1974, p. 443)

Any such justification of the capital-theoretic imputations that must assume perfectly competitive equilibrium is on rather thin ice. And even then, there is no property-theoretic explanation: it is simply a moot point from the price-theoretic viewpoint since the whole products have zero value in that razor-thin special case. Moreover, the capital-theoretic definitions of capitalized value or net productivity are by no means restricted to the competitive model. When professor Samuelson asserts that *"capital goods have a 'net' productivity"* (1976, p. 661) (while the other factors have only a marginal productivity), there is no limitation to competitive equilibrium. The capital-theoretic definitions are used throughout the literature on capital budgeting and finance theory—which is hardly restricted to competitive equilibrium. It is ultimately of no avail always to retreat ostrichlike to the special case of zero-profit perfectly competitive equilibrium whenever the fallacious imputation of the whole products to capital, and thus the neglect of appropriation, is challenged. The real problem (aside from the obvious ideological bias) is that the consideration of appropriation carries economics beyond the neoclassical conceptual orbit of price theory into the domain of property theory.

Professor Samuelson's dictum that the cash value of a doctrine is in its vulgarization applies not only to Marxism but to the fallacious imputations of capital theory. For instance, in a book called *The Capitalist Manifesto,* one reads that:

> The essence of property in productive wealth is the right to receive its product. (Kelso and Adler 1958, p. 210)

The return to property is its rental or selling price. The product; that is, the whole product, must be appropriated. Historians of economic thought can sort out the question of priority. Is capitalist ideology a vulgarization of capital theory or are the imputation fallacies of capital theory an attempt to rationalize capitalist ideology?

The Value of a Corporation in Finance Theory

In our discussion of capital theory, we considered how the economic profits produced using a capital asset are added into the capitalized value of the asset as if the right to the whole product was part and parcel of the ownership right to the capital asset. In the influential work of Merton H. Miller and Franco Modigliani in finance theory, this capitalized-value definition is applied to a corporation itself.

> Consider now the so-called discounted cash flow approach familiar in discussions of capital budgeting. There, in valuing any specific machine we discount at the market rate of interest the stream of cash receipts generated by the machine; plus any scrap or terminal value of the machine; and minus the stream of cash outlays for direct labor, materials, repairs, and capital additions. The same approach, of course, can also be applied to the firm as a whole which may be thought of in this context as simply a large, composite machine. (Merton H. Miller and Franco Modigliani, "Dividend Policy, Growth, and the Valuation of Shares," *The Journal of Business* 34 (October 1961):415. Reprinted with permission.)

Miller and Modigliani (MM) showed that, under perfectly competitive conditions, the capitalized value of a corporation is independent of the corporation's policy on dividends versus retained earnings. They proved the dividend irrelevance thesis by developing formulas for the value of a corporation that are the same regardless of the dividend decision. Our interest is less in the dividend irrelevance thesis than in analyzing the capitalized-value definition to discern the underlying property rights.

Miller and Modigliani (1961) present four distinct but equivalent approaches to the capitalized value of a corporation:

1. the discounted-cash-flow approach,
2. the current-earnings-plus-future-investment-opportunities approach,
3. the stream-of-dividends approach, and
4. the stream-of-earnings approach.

All these approaches yield the same capitalized value, but none of them allows one to readily analyze the underlying property rights so as to separate the property actually owned by the corporation from the property that the corporation is *assumed to appropriate* in the future. This job is performed by a fifth equivalent approach, the *net-book-value-plus-future-economic-profits* approach or, in short, the *book-plus-profits* approach. We saw in the simple capital-theory example how the capitalized value V could be split into the value C of the asset itself plus the value V_0 of the future whole products that could be appropriated. The fifth approach simply extends this analysis to the corporation itself.

Two of the formulas used by Miller and Modigliani as well as the fifth approach will be developed by further articulation of the market-value-accounting model used before. The balance-sheet accounts, such as the gross book value $GBV(T)$, the debt $D(T)$, and the net book value $NBV(T)$, are what economists call *stock variables* since they represent a value at a point in time. Other accounts such as the income-statement accounts are *flow variables,* which represent a change in value over a period of time. The change in any stock variable over a time period is a flow variable denoted by prefixing the stock variable with a d. Hence we have the additional flow variables, $dGBV(T) = GBV(T + 1) - GBV(T)$, $dD(T) = D(T + 1) - D(T)$, and $dNBV(T) = NBV(T + 1) - NBV(T)$. The difference between the balance-sheet equations at time $T + 1$ and time T yields the following flow variable equation: $dGBV(T) = dD(T) + dNBV(T)$. The change $dGBV(T)$ in the gross book value is the *net investment* during that time period, and the *gross investment,* denoted $I(T)$, is the net investment plus depreciation:

$$I(T) = dGBV(T) + \{C(m - 1) - C(m)\}.$$

The corporation starts operation at time 0. Hence the value of any stock variable at time T can be obtained by summing the initial value and all the intervening changes. Thus the net book value at time T is:

$$NBV(T) = NBV(0) + dNBV(0) + dNBV(1) + \cdots + dNBV(T - 1).$$

We will now have need for the following notation concerning the shares of the corporation:

$n(t)$ = number of shares outstanding at time t,

$v(t)$ = price per share at time t,

$V(t) = n(t)v(t)$ = value of all outstanding shares at time t,

$div(t)$ = dividends per share at time $t + 1$ to holders of record at time t, and

$DIV(t) = n(t)div(t)$ = total dividends paid at time $t + 1$.

The Stream-of-Dividends Formula

The value $V(t)$ of the outstanding shares is called the *value of the corporation*. Formulas for $V(t)$ can be developed from the arbitrage principle that, under conditions of perfect competitive markets and certainty, capital must yield the same rate of return whether it is loaned out at interest or invested in corporate shares.

If one share is purchased for $v(T)$ at time T, then the return at the end of the period is the dividends $div(T)$ plus the capital gains $v(T + 1) - v(T)$. If the same capital was loaned out at interest, the end of the period return is $rv(T)$. If the returns were unequal, that would induce the appropriate buying and selling of corporate shares so that the price per share would adjust to equalize the returns. Thus arbitrage activity between the loan and stock markets would enforce the following *arbitrage equation:*

$$rv(T) = div(T) + v(T + 1) - v(T).$$

Solving for $v(T)$ and multiplying through by $n(T)$ yields:

$$V(T) = [n(T)div(T) + n(T)v(T + 1)]/(1 + r).$$

This formula expresses the value $V(T)$ of the corporation at time T in terms of the dividends and the value of the shares held at time $T + 1$ by the shareholders of record at time T. Using the arbitrage-enforced equation in the time period $T + 1$ yields $v(T + 1) = [div(T + 1) + v(T + 2)]/(1 + r)$, so plugging that into the previous equation for $V(T)$ gives:

$$V(T) = n(T)div(T)/(1 + r) + n(T)div(T + 1)/(1 + r)^2$$
$$+ n(T)v(T + 2)/(1 + r)^2$$

Continued use of the arbitrage equation in future time periods and substitutions will finally give the valuation using the *stream-of-dividends formula:*

$$V(T) = \sum_{t=1}^{\infty} \frac{n(T)div(T + t - 1)}{(1 + r)^t}.$$

Hence the total market value of the corporation at time T is the discounted present value of the future dividends that will accrue to the shareholders of record at time T (for example, Fama and Miller 1972, p. 87, formula 2.19b). Dividends accruing to new shares purchased at a later date are not added into the value of the corporation at time T.

The above derivation of the stream-of-dividends formula does not require the assumption that the corporation appropriates the whole products produced using its capital. For example, if the corporate assets were all hired out, then the rate of return would be the interest rate and the gross return would be $rGBV(T$. After servicing the debt, the net return or accounting profits $A(T)$ would be just the interest on equity, $rNBV(T)$. That amount could be paid out as dividends, and then the same pattern could be repeated each year. The discounted present value of the annual payout $rNBV(T)$ is just $NBV(T)$, so, under the assumption that the capital is hired out, the value $V(T)$ of the corporation is its net book value $NBV(T)$. But that is not the usual assumption.

The usual assumption is that the complementary inputs are hired in so that the outputs are produced, appropriated, and sold. We have made that assumption up to now (apart from the last paragraph) and we will continue to do so.

The Discounted-Cash-Flow Formula

We turn now to the discounted-cash-flow formula for the value $V(T)$. Let $dn(T) = n(T + 1) - n(T)$ be the change in the outstanding shares during the time period T. Multiplying each side of $n(T) = n(T + 1) - dn(T)$ by $v(T + 1)$ yields $n(T)v(T + 1) = V(T + 1) - dn(T + 1) - SUBS(T)$, where $SUBS(T) = dn(T)v(T + 1)$ is the net subscriptions for the period T. If the corporation hires in the complementary inputs and appropriates the whole product, then the accounting profit is:

$$A(T) = PQ - P'X - WL - \{C(m - 1) - C(m)\} - rD(T)$$
$$= \pi(T) + rNBV(T).$$

The change in the net book value is:

$$dNBV(T) = NBV(T + 1) - NBV(T) = A(T) - DIV(T) + SUBS(T).$$

These results can be substituted into the equation:

$$V(T) = [n(T)div(T) + n(T)v(T + 1)]/(1 + r),$$

to yield the following equations:

$$V(T) = [DIV(T) + V(T + 1) - SUBS(T)]/(1 + r)$$

$$= [A(T) - dNBV(T) + V(T + 1)]/(1 + r).$$

In our accounting models, only a few future years were considered to keep the notation as simple as possible. By extending the vectors, the formulas developed for time period T could be extended to any future time period. In particular, the above formula for $V(T)$ could be extended to any future period:

$$V(T + t) = [A(T + t) - dNBV(T + t) + V(T + t + 1)]/(1 + r) \text{ for}$$

$$t = 1, 2, \ldots.$$

By repeated substitutions of this in the formula for $V(T)$, we obtain the *discounted-cash-flow formula*:

$$V(T) = \sum_{t=1}^{\infty} \frac{A(T + t - 1) - dNBV(T + t - 1)}{(1 + r)^t}.$$

The original Miller and Modigliani article (1961) can be consulted for the other two approaches they developed, the stream-of-earnings formula and the current-earnings-plus-future-investment-opportunities formula.

The Book-Plus-Profits Formula

The general approach of valuing a corporation at net book value plus the discounted present value of future economic profits is not a new approach. The value of a corporation has been analyzed (for example, Edey 1962) as the net book value plus the goodwill, where the goodwill is evaluated at the discounted present value of expected *super-profits*. We will first prove the book-plus-profits formula in the Miller-Modigliani framework used above, and then turn our attention to the underlying property rights – where the importance of the formula lies. Thus the *book-plus-profits formula:*

$$V(T) = NBV(T) + \sum_{t=1}^{\infty} \frac{\pi(T + t - 1)}{(1 + r)^t}.$$

To prove this formula, we first note that one dollar loaned out at interest yields an income stream of r dollars each year, so the present value of the income stream must be 1; that is:

$$\sum_{t=1}^{\infty} \frac{r}{(1 + r)^t} = 1.$$

For $t = 1, 2, \ldots$, the economic or pure profit is:

$$\pi(T + t - 1) = A(T + t - 1) - rNBV(T + t - 1).$$

For $t = 2, 3, \ldots$, the net book value $NBV(T + t - 1)$ can be expressed as the net book value $NBV(T)$ at time T plus the intervening changes:

$$NBV(T + t - 1) = NBV(T) + \sum_{j=0}^{t-2} dNBV(T + j).$$

Substituting in the expression for the economic profits yields:

$$\pi(T + t - 1) = A(T + t - 1) - rNBV(T) - r \sum_{j=0}^{t-2} dNBV(T + j).$$

Hence the present value of the future economic profits is:

$$\sum_{t=1}^{\infty} \frac{\pi(T + t - 1)}{(1 + r)^t} = \sum_{t=1}^{\infty} \frac{A(T + t - 1)}{(1 + r)^t} - NBV(T) \sum_{t=1}^{\infty} \frac{r}{(1 + r)^t}$$

$$- \sum_{t=2}^{\infty} \left\{ \frac{r}{(1 + r)^t} \sum_{j=0}^{t-2} dNBV(T + j) \right\}.$$

According to the previous observation that the income stream generated by one dollar loaned at interest must have a present value of one dollar, the middle term on the RHS of the above equation is just $NBV(T)$.

In the last term on the RHS, the double-summation term, we can collect all the occurances of $NBV(T)$ to get:

$$\frac{rdNBV(T)}{(1 + r)^2} + \frac{rdNBV(T)}{(1 + r)^3} + \cdots = \frac{dNBV(T)}{1 + r} \sum_{t = 1}^{\infty} \frac{r}{(1 + r)^t} = \frac{dNBV(T)}{(1 + r)}.$$

Collecting the occurances of $dNBV(T + 1)$ yields:

$$\frac{rdNBV(T + 1)}{(1 + r)^3} + \frac{rdNBV(T + 1)}{(1 + r)^4} + \cdots = \frac{dNBV(T + 1)}{(1 + r)^2} \sum_{t = 1}^{\infty} \frac{r}{(1 + r)^t} =$$

$$= \frac{rdNBV(T + 1)}{(1 + r)^2}$$

By similarly collecting occurences of the other $dNBV(T + t)$ terms, we can simplify the last RHS term as follows:

$$\sum_{t = 2}^{\infty} \left\{ \frac{r}{(1 + r)^t} \sum_{j = 0}^{t - 2} dNBV(T + j) \right\} = \sum_{t = 1}^{\infty} \frac{dNBV(T + t - 1)}{(1 + r)^t}.$$

Hence substituting back in the expression for the present value of the pure profits yields:

$$\sum_{t = 1}^{\infty} \frac{\pi(T + t - 1)}{(1 + r)^t} = \sum_{t = 1}^{\infty} \frac{A(T + t - 1)}{(1 + r)^t} - NBV(T)$$

$$- \sum_{t = 1}^{\infty} \frac{dNBV(T + t - 1)}{(1 + r)^t}.$$

Moving $NBV(T)$ to the other side shows the equivalence of the net-book-value-plus-future-pure-profits formula and the discounted-cash-flow-formula:

$$NBV(T) + \sum_{t = 1}^{\infty} \frac{\pi(T + t - 1)}{(1 + r)^t} = \sum_{t = 1}^{\infty} \frac{A(T + t - 1) - dNBV(T + t - 1)}{(1 + r)^t}$$

$$= V(T).$$

The book-plus-profit formula is thus proven by reducing it to the discounted-cash-flow formula.

Property Interpretation of the Book-Plus-Profits Formula

The book-plus-profits formula extends the capital-theoretic formula $V = C + V_0$ to a corporation as a capital asset. The book-plus-profits formula is important because it, unlike the other formulas used by Miller and Modigliani, allows one to discern the status of the property rights underlying the value of a corporation.

Our treatment of the book-plus-profits formula will illustrate a methodological principle used to derive property-theoretic results. One is ultimately interested in results that hold in the real world; that is, in a noncompetitive disequilibrium situation fraught with uncertainty. Yet the most highly developed models in economic theory are for competitive equilibrium. Indeed, there are no developed models in price theory for the noncompetitive disequilibrium marketplace. Yet the framework of property theory and property accounting is quite independent of any assumptions about competition, equilibrium, and uncertainty. For instance, the prices that occur in the realized valuations of property accounting could be from noncompetitive markets in disequilibrium. The functioning of the laissez faire property mechanism does not require the price mechanism to be in equilibrium. The property mechanism depends on contracts, and contracts are made even in markets that are in constant flux and disequilibrium.

It would be unconventional to directly formulate property-theoretic results for the general noncompetitive disequilibrium situation since conventional economic theory has no models of that generality. There would be no familiar context for the results. Hence we have taken a different expository approach: derive property-theoretic results in a familiar context (for example, a competitive model), and then generalize them by showing that they do not depend on any of the particular assumptions of the special case.

Value is the value of property. The book-plus-profits formula shows that the property whose value is the so-called value of the corporation is: (1) the property in the Total Assets and Liabilities T-account whose value is the net book value, and (2) the property in the future Whole Product T-accounts whose present value is the discounted sum of the future economic profits. The total assets and liabilities of the company are indeed existent property rights and obligations of the corporation. However, the future whole products must be appropriated so there is no present property right, held by the corporation or any other party, to those future bundles of rights and obligations. We have *assumed* that the corporation will make the required contracts to be in a position to appropriate the whole products. We could also make the contrary assumption and derive that the value of the corporation was only the value of the total assets and liabilities; that is, the net book value, since the whole products would then go elsewhere. The point is not whether the assumption is correct. The point is that it is a matter of the future contracts not of the present property rights.

The book-plus-profits formula, like the other valuation formulas considered by Miller and Modigliani, is based on the arbitrage equation, which was enforced by competitive arbitrage between loan and stock markets. In real markets, these formulas will tend to break down for a variety of reasons: noncompetitive market power, transaction costs, imperfect information, disequilibrium, uncertainty, and so forth. However, the property-theoretic results survive the breakdown of the idealized assumptions. The relaxation of the assumptions does not change the nature and structure of the property rights. A corporation still owns just its total assets and liabilities and may or may not appropriate the future whole products depending on its contracts.

The relaxation of the idealized assumptions certainly will effect the behavior of the market participants. Uncertainty about the future coupled with risk aversion may lead a party to avoid the role of the hiring party. Noncompetitive market power may help insure that another party can take on the contractual role of being the hiring party. But such market power is not a property right. If competition materializes that neutralizes the market power of a once dominant corporation, that does not violate a property right of the corporation. In the general noncompetitive disequilibrium situation, each corporation still owns only its total assets and liabilities. The whole product will be appropriated by the party who emerges as the hiring party from the market process; that is, the hiring conflict over who hires what or whom.

Accounting for Goodwill

Goodwill is traditionally defined as the difference between the market or capitalized value $V(T)$ of corporate assets and the net book value $NBV(T)$. By the book-plus-profits formula, the goodwill is the discounted present value of the future economic profits. The property whose value is the goodwill is the series of future whole products.

The nature and treatment of goodwill has been a perennial problem area in accounting—and for good reason. The peculiarities of *appropriation* emerge in accounting under the guise of goodwill. The property analysis allows us to see what goodwill is, what it is not, and how it should be treated in accounting.

Since the word *goodwill* is often used loosely, we must first be clear that our treatment will only deal with goodwill as the difference $V(T) - NBV(T)$ between the market and book value—and not with goodwill in some other sense. We will not be concerned with it in the sense of the consumer's favorable disposition since that does not represent a property right at all (so it could at best only be a reason for certain property rights having positive value). There might be situations where a corporation used a novel and patentable invention or idea in its production that, however, was never actually patented and shown as a balance-sheet item. If the corporate assets were hired out, then such inventions, ideas, or industrial secrets would probably be patented or otherwise secured and then entered on the balance sheet. We must assume that all such appropriable proprietory items have been duly claimed and reported on the balance sheet—so that the Total-Assets-and-Liabilities account accurately reflects the corporation's present property rights and obligations.

Goodwill is the present value of the future whole-product vectors. Since it is the present value of quite tangible but future whole products, it is not the value of some present mysterious intangible asset. Thus goodwill is not the additional value of the whole that isn't present in the parts, is not the additional value of the business as a going concern, is not the value of "business momentum," and so forth (see, for example, Zeff and Keller 1973, part 6). It is the value of the whole-product vectors that may be appropriated in the future. Since the whole products must be appropriated, there cannot exist any present property right to them. In other words, a corporation does not own what is called its goodwill.

In an important paper directed towards accountants, an economist, Professor Sidney S. Alexander, applied this mistaken capitalized-value-of-the-asset definitions of capital theory to a corporation itself (as did Miller and Modigliani).

> The Neverlose Manufacturing Company is engaged in the manufacture of gadgets. At the beginning of 19x5, it was expected that throughout all future time the company would manufacture a hundred thousand gadgets a year and sell them for $100,000 at a total cost of $90,000 including all charges, so affording an annual profit and an annual dividend of $10,000 indefinitely into the future. The current long-term interest rate is 5 percent, and so the value of the equity in the company is $200,000, the present value of $10,000 a year indefinitely into the future. (Alexander 1962, p. 140)

Professor Alexander goes on to argue that the income of the corporation should be measured by the changes in this capitalized value instead of the changes in the usual net book value. However, this argument misses a crucial point. Any notion of income should presumably be related to the changes in the value of the corporation's rights. Since the corporation has no present property right to the future whole products, their present value, the goodwill or going value, is not part of the value of the corporation's present rights. Hence changes in goodwill should not enter into income.

The point is *not* that the appropriation of future whole products is uncertain and thus the point is unchanged by assumptions about conditions of certainty. It is always instructive to compare the future stream of whole products with the future income stream attached to a bond. The payments on a bond are, of course, uncertain since the issuer might default and declare bankruptcy. The owner of the bond nevertheless has a legal right to the bond payments against the issuer—until bankruptcy. Hence there may be wishful thinking but there is no fallacy involved in valuing the bond at the present value of the bond payments. Future whole products must be appropriated, so there can be no present right to them. To present their discounted value, the goodwill, as part of the value of one's present rights is not just speculation in the face of uncertainty; it is a mistake. Goodwill is at best the value of the property that a party expects to *appropriate* in the future. The bondowner does not expect to appropriate the future bond payments since the owner already has the legal right to those payments. It is the actual delivery of the payments that the bondholder expects.

Accountants have quite rightly resisted the arguments, made by some economists, for recording changes in goodwill as income and for recording unpurchased goodwill as an asset. In neither case are there any present property rights to be accounted for. However, it is conventional to record, as an asset, any purchased goodwill. This is presumedly based on the realization principle, the purchase of the goodwill being a realized valuation. This is reminiscent of the story of the country bumpkin who goes to New York and is sold the Brooklyn Bridge. He could enter the Brooklyn Bridge as a purchased asset on his balance sheet since it was a realized valuation.

The point is that the seller of goodwill, like the seller of the Brooklyn Bridge, has no such property right to sell. Ordinarily, when goodwill is "purchased" the buyer is paying the seller to withdraw from the field and turn over his less than perfectly competitive market position to the buyer. The buyer is then in a position to appropriate the future whole products which have the goodwill as their present value. The buyer is not purchasing any enforceable present property right, tangible or intangible; otherwise there would be no reason to term it goodwill.

Capital expended to purchase a nonright should not be recorded as an asset; it should be recorded as a debit to equity. In the AICPA Accounting Research Study No. 10, *Accounting for Goodwill,* George Catlett and Norman Olson have (courageously) argued for this treatment of purchased goodwill.

> The amount assigned to purchased goodwill represents a disbursement of existing resources, or of proceeds of stock issued to effect the business combination, in anticipation of future earnings. The expenditure should be accounted for as a reduction of stockholders' equity. (1968, p. 106)

The debit to shareholders' equity would then be replenished if and when the anticipated future whole products were appropriated.

13 Appropriation in Neoclassical Price Theory

Appropriation in Theory of the Firm

Appropriation has also been neglected in the theory of the firm in economics. This oversight is in part because neoclassical economics has less of a theory of the firm and more of a theory of markets populated by "black boxes" that buy on input markets and sell on output markets. By detailing the stocks and flows of property rights and obligations in a productive enterprise, property theory and property accounting provide a basis for a nontrivial theory of the firm.

When the appropriation of the whole product is implicitly considered in conventional economics, the pattern, as in capital theory, is to construe the right to the whole product as being part of a preexistent property right. In its commonest form, this property right is called the *ownership of the firm*. The ownership of a firm is usually taken to mean the ownership of a corporation. But a corporation has no present property right to the future whole products that may be produced using its capital. Whether or not the corporation appropriates those whole products will depend on the contracts the corporation makes. If the corporation hires out its capital, then the whole product produced using that capital will be appropriated by the hiring party. If the corporation hires in labor and bears the costs of production, then it will appropriate the whole product produced using its capital. The appropriation is determined by who hires what or whom, not by the shareholders' ownership of the corporation. Thus the ownership of a corporation does *not* include any preexistent property right to the future whole products produced using the capital of the corporation.

If two inputs, A and B, are necessary for production, it is not determined prior to the input contracts whether the A-owner, the B-owner, or some third party will undertake production. The A-owner could hire B, the B-owner could hire A, or a third party could hire both A and B. The party who ends up as the hiring party will appropriate the whole product of production. It is important to understand the precontractual legal symmetry between the A-owner and the B-owner. For example, if the B-owner had traditionally been the hiring party and thus had appropriated the whole product, then it would be quite natural for the B-owner to begin to think that the right to the product was an intrinsic part of the ownership of *B*. Both capitalist and Marxist ideologies mistakenly hold that the right to the product is part of the ownership of *B* when *B* is the means of production or capital. The precontractual legal symmetry dispels that illusion. The *B*-owner appropriated the whole product because of his contractual role not because of his ownership of *B*. The ownership of *B* may, of course, have provided the bargaining power necessary to make the hiring contract in favor of the *B*-owner. If the hiring contracts were reversed, then the *A*-owner would have the contractual role to appropriate the whole product and would not need to buy the product from the *B*-owner.

Let us define the word *firm* to be the party who ends up appropriating the whole product:

Firm = Whole-Product Appropriator

The identity of the firm (in this technical sense of *whole-product appropriator*) is determined not by some preexistent property right, such as the so-called ownership of the firm, but by who hires what or whom. Firmhood is a contractual role not a property right.

Economists sometimes use a rather abstract version of the ownership of a firm. Technical production possibilities are represented by a production function, a production set, or some sort of "production-opportunity locus" (Hirshleifer 1970, p. 124), and then economists speak of the owners of these technical possibilities, for example, the "owners of the productive opportunity" (Hirshleifer 1970, p. 125). Neoclassical economics' lack of attention to property-theoretic details is illustrated by the postulation of this peculiar ownership of a mathematical description of technically possible production opportunities such as a production function or production set. If one wishes to use the metaphor of appropriating the whole product as trading with Nature (for example, Hirshleifer 1970, p. 20), then one should realize that there are no "owners" (Hirshleifer 1970, p. 20) of the production set of possible trades with Nature. There might be the ownership of certain specialized inputs, such as proprietory technical information, but that is only the ownership of inputs to the production opportunity not the ownership of the productive opportunity itself. There is no such property right as the ownership of a production function, a production set, or a productive opportunity.

The notion of ownership of a production set is probably intended as an abstract version of the ownership of a corporation. But, as we have seen, a corporation is an owner of certain inputs such as physical and financial capital. Whether or not that input owner or any input owner appropriates the whole product produced using those inputs depends on whether the input owner hires in a complementary set of inputs and bears the costs of production or whether the input is hired out. The ownership of any input does not include within it the ownership of the whole product produced using the input; the whole product must be appropriated. Thus the ownership of a corporation is not the ownership of the firm. There is no ownership of the firm. Being the firm is an activity (undertaking production) not a thing, a contractual role not a property right.

In double-entry property accounting, the whole product is a RHS T-account,

$$WP(T) = [NEGPROD(T) \, // \, POSPROD(T)].$$

Every T-account with nonnegative vectors, such as $NEGPROD(T)$ and $POSPROD(T)$, as entries decodes as a vector that, in general, will have positive and negative entries. The whole-product T-account decodes as a vector that will be called the *whole-product vector* and represented by the same symbol $WP(T)$—since context will sufficiently differentiate between the T-account and the corresponding vector. Thus the whole-product vector is:

$$WP(T) = POSPROD(T) - NEGPROD(T).$$

In the full model of property accounting, the whole-product vector is:

$$WP(T) = (- CASH(T), - FG(T), - RM(T), - 1, CASH(T), FG(T)$$
$$+ Q,RM(T) - X,1, - L,0),$$

and in the simplified model, the whole-product vector is:

$$WP^*(T) = (0,Q, - X, -1,1, - GBV(T), - L).$$

Whole-product vectors are not new in economic theory; they usually go by other names. In the modern mathematical treatment of production, inspired by the noncalculus mathematics of activity analysis (Koopmans 1951), the production opportunities are represented by a set of technically possible (whole-product) vectors. Such a feasible whole-product vector is called a *production-possibility vector* (Arrow and Debreu 1954, p. 267), an *activity vector* (Arrow and Hahn 1971, p. 59), a *production* (Debreu 1959, p. 38), or an *input-output vector* (Quirk and Saposnik 1968, p. 27). Economists represent the outputs as positive components and the inputs as negative components but without any interpretation in terms of accounting (assets and liabilities).

In the early models of perfectly competitive equilibrium, constant returns to scale in production were assumed. This assured zero economic profits in equilibrium, so from the viewpoint of value theory, it was immaterial who was the firm; that is, who appropriated the whole-product vector (since it had zero net value). According to Professor Samuelson:

> [I]t is precisely under strict constant returns to scale that the theory of the firm evaporates. (1967, p. 114; reprinted in Samuelson 1972, p. 27)

The Failure of the Arrow-Debreu Model

In 1954, Professors Kenneth Arrow and Gerard Debreu published a paper [Arrow and Debreu 1954] in which they claimed to show the existence of a competitive equilibrium under the general conditions of nonincreasing returns to scale; that is, decreasing or constant returns to scale. Under decreasing returns to scale, there would be positive economic or pure profits. Hence the Arrow-Debreu model alleges to show the existence of a perfectly competitive equilibrium with positive economic profits. In the following passage, Professor Arrow contrasts the Arrow-Debreu model with a model by Professor McKenzie (1959) that used constant returns to scale.

> The two models differ in their implications for income distribution. The Arrow-Debreu model creates a category of pure profits which are distributed to the owners of the firm; it is not assumed that the owners are necessarily the entrepreneurs or managers. . . .
>
> In the McKenzie model, on the other hand, the firm makes no pure profits (since it operates at constant returns); the equivalent of profits appears in the form of payments for the use of entrepreneurial resources, but there is no residual category of owners who receive profits without rendering either capital or entrepreneurial services. (Arrow 1971, p. 70)

Since the whole-product vectors can have a positive value in the Arrow-Debreu model, they had to face the question as to how these vectors got assigned to people. The Arrow-Debreu model answers the question by assuming that there is such a property right as the ownership of the production sets of technically feasible whole-product vectors. The train of reasoning is that production sets represent the production possibilities of firms and firms are identified with corporations, which of course are owned by their shareholders.

In a private-enterprise capitalist economy, there is no such property right as the ownership of production sets of feasible whole-product vectors. In the Arrow-Debreu model each consumer-resourceholder is endowed prior to any market exchanges with a certain set of resources and with shares in corporations. However, prior to any market activity, ownership of a corporation is only at best an indirect form of ownership of resources, the corporate resources. It is the subsequent contracts in input markets that will determine whether a corporation successfully exploits a production opportunity by purchasing the requisite inputs.

The Arrow-Debreu model mistakes the whole logic of appropriation. The question of who appropriates the whole product of a production opportunity is not settled by the inital endowment of property rights. It is settled only in the markets for inputs by who hires what or whom. In other words, the determination of who is to be the firm (the whole-product appropriator) is not exogenous to the marketplace; it is a market-endogenous determination. This perspective adds a whole new degree of freedom to the model, which can only be ignored in the special case of universal constant returns to scale when it doesn't matter (for income determination) who is the firm. As we have pointed out elsewhere (Ellerman 1980a), this new degree of freedom eliminates the possibility of a competitive equilibrium with positive economic profits, for example, with decreasing returns to scale in some production opportunity. General equilibrium theory for a competitive capitalist economy only works in the special case of universal constant returns to scale.

There is no mathematical error in the Arrow-Debreu model; it (contrary to their claim) simply does not model a perfectly competitive free-enterprise capitalist economy. By assuming that production possibilities are owned, the Arrow-Debreu model does not allow anyone but the owner to demand the requisite inputs. But in a free-enterprise capitalist economy, anyone can bid on the inputs necessary for some technically feasible production opportunity. In such an economy, production, the conversion of inputs into outputs, can be seen as a form of arbitrage, *production arbitrage,* between input markets and output markets. Traditionally, arbitrage is thought of as an exchange operation, for example, in currency markets. But if the price of Chicago wheat exceeds the price of Kansas City wheat plus the transportation costs, then the operation of buying inputs (Kansas City wheat plus transportation services) and selling the outputs (Chicago wheat) would still be called arbitrage. If the price of a good one period hence exceeds the current price plus storage costs, then:

> [A] sure profit could always be made by the time arbitrage, so to speak, of buying the commodity currently—borrowing, if necessary—and reselling one period later. (Fama and Miller 1972, p. 62)

But in general equilibrium models, where commodities are differentiated by spatial and temporal location, transportation and storage are examples of production. As more characteristics of the inputs, besides spatial and temporal location, change in the production process, there is no magic dividing

line that suddenly prevents the production arbitrage of buying all the requisite inputs and selling the outputs.

It is the concept of arbitrage applied to production itself, the concept of
production arbitrage, that kills the Arrow-Debreu model. When there is a
sufficient price differential between input and output markets to allow positive profits, a potential arbitrageur can attempt to reap those profits by purchasing the required inputs, bearing their costs as the inputs are consumed
in production, claiming the produced outputs, and then selling the outputs.
Naturally, such a grand arbitrage operation is difficult in the real-world
economy, but it is quite possible in an idealized textbook model of perfect
competition. Thus production profits can be viewed as arbitrage profits. A
competitive equilibrium is not possible when there are profitable arbitrage
opportunities; for example, profitable production opportunities. Production arbitrageurs (that is, entrepreneurs) would bid up input prices. Hence a
competitive equilibrium is not possible in the situation Professors Arrow
and Debreu attempt to model, a competitive capitalist economy with some
production opportunities exhibiting decreasing returns to scale.

For the last several decades, the Arrow-Debreu model has been received
doctrine in mathematical economics. Its failure is a major example of the
impact on economic theory of an appreciation of the nature and structure
of property appropriation. The reason for its failure, which was uncovered
by the analysis of appropriation, was the market-endogenous determination
of firmhood, of who is to appropriate the whole product and thus be the
firm. The whole product is assigned, by the laissez faire mechanism, to a
contractual role, not to a preexistent property right, and one's contractual
role is determined by the contracts one makes or does not make in the marketplace.

The extra degree of freedom, the market-endogenous determination of
firmhood, cuts much deeper into received doctrine than just the Arrow-
Debreu model. It changes the very conception of how competitive markets
operate, from an orderly process of equilibration to a game-theoretically
indeterminate struggle for positive profits. The conventional theory is that
there are two basic types of economic agents, consumer-resourceholders
and firms. The consumer-resourceholders supply inputs to the input markets and demand outputs on the output markets. The firms play the opposite role of demanding inputs on input markets and supplying outputs to
output markets. The flow of commodities from the consumers as resource
suppliers to the firms and the flow of products back to the consumers (with
the money flows in the opposite direction) are represented in the familiar
circular flow diagram (for example, Samuelson 1976, p. 46).

The conventional picture assumes that firmhood is determined prior to
market activity. The resource owners are lined up on one side and the firms
supposedly are lined up on the other side of the input markets. But this is

not the case in a free-enterprise capitalist economy. It is not legally predetermined that an input owner is a supplier of inputs rather than a demander of a complementary set of inputs. Prior to the market contracts, corporations are just other resourceholders. Any resource owner, corporate or otherwise, may aspire to be a firm in the technical sense of whole-product appropriator by attempting to purchase the complete set of inputs to a productive opportunity. Hence the customary analytical machinery of resource owners having input supply schedules and firms having input demand schedules prior to market activity breaks down. The identity of the firms (parties who will appropriate the whole products) is only determined at the end of the game-theoretically indeterminate market process, not at the beginning. This breakdown, under the impact of production arbitrage, of the conventional supply-and-demand analysis of input markets will not be further analyzed here.

Endgames in Low-Brow Price Theory

The neglect of appropriation is the major logical gap in neoclassical price theory. The property-theoretic discovery of appropriation has extensive implications for received doctrine in conventional economics. We have outlined a few negative results such as: (1) the imputation fallacies involved in capital theory and in some opportunity cost arguments, (2) the nonexistence of any ownership of production sets of feasible whole-product vectors (that is, the nonexistence of any ownership of the firm), and (3) the impossibility of a competitive equilibrium with positive economic profits in a free-enterprise capitalist economy. It is safe to assume that these results will not be gladly acknowledged by the guardians of the received truth. Hence one must play endgames.

Competitive general equilibrium in a free-enterprise capitalist economy is only possible under the assumption of universal constant returns to scale. A competitive equilibrium is not viable at a point of increasing returns to scale and negative profits—because no one wants to be the firm. A competitive equilibrium is also not possible at a point of decreasing returns to scale and positive profits—because everyone wants to be the firm. A competitive equilibrium is only possible under universal constant returns to scale where, by assumption, no one cares who is the firm.

The logical gap in neoclassical economics concerning the appropriation of the whole products is irrelevant in precisely the pinpoint special case of universal constant returns. Then the whole products have zero value so the legal mechanism of imputing the whole products to legal parties can, for price-theoretic purposes, be ignored. This stance may seem ostrichlike, but, in this instance, it is wise to restrict one's horizons. Out of respect for the power of competitive arbitrage or for other reasons, Professors Samuelson, MacKenzie, Koopmans, and many other neoclassical economists have not followed Professors Arrow and Debreu into the promised land of competitive equilibrium with positive pure profits. It seems ironic that the only viable model of free-enterprise capitalist competitive equilibrium is the constant-returns model where the capitalist firms and their profits both disappear.

The constant-returns model is often "justified" by an appeal to a metaphysical argument coupled with an application of Euler's Theorem in calculus. The metaphysical argument is that if one doubles all factors relevant to production, then the outputs will double. If the outputs do not double, then some relevant factor was not doubled. This metaphysical argument is irrefutable if not tautologous. It is then applied by arguing that if doubling the inputs in a production function doubles the outputs, then the production function exhibits constant returns to scale. By Euler's Theorem, there would be zero-profits in equilibrium.

The fallacy in this universal constant-returns argument is in the application of the metaphysical argument to the production function. The metaphysical argument says "doubling *everything* will double output" whereas the application to production functions says "doubling the *input variables* will double the outputs." The flaw is that the input variables do not represent *everything* that might be scarce but relevant to production. The input variables have market prices associated with them so they represent exclusively owned marketable commodities that may be bought and sold on input markets. Everything includes a myriad of other scarce factors affecting production such as: (1) commonly owned property or public goods (public roads, free parking, public parks, and such) and (2) unowned natural factors (air, river water, rainfall, sunlight, wind, oceans, and such). The proposition that doubling just the exclusively owned inputs will double outputs is a robustly empirical proposition and quite likely false. The presence of other scarce but not exclusively owned factors may introduce decreasing returns to scale in the marketable inputs. Indeed, Arrow and Debreu mention such a justification for decreasing returns in their original article (see the mention of *free-rationed goods* in Arrow and Debreu 1954, p. 267).

There are two models, a low-brow model and a high-brow model, in conventional economics that claim the existence of a competitive equilibrium under decreasing returns and positive profits. The *low-brow model* is the Marshallian short-run competitive equilibrium model used in the textbooks in microeconomic theory. The *high-brow model* is the Arrow-Debreu type model. Both models fail since a profitable capitalist competitive equilibrium is impossible.

We will investigate three sources of confusion and error in the low-brow textbook model: (1) the meaning of *fixed* factors, (2) the meaning of *free entry,* and (3) monopoly elements in *competitive* models. The emphasis here, as in the analysis of the high-brow model, is on logical problems in the theory not on empirical questions.

Capital equipment and plant size are conventionally considered to be factors fixed in the short run. The time required to install new capital equipment and to alter plant size projects such changes into the long run. Hence the fixed factors usually are left implicit in the shape of the production function and only variables representing *variable factors* are displayed. But the conventional treatment confuses short-term physical immobility with legal immobility. The physical fixity of the fixed factors hardly implies that the factors and their services are not marketable. After all, real estate is, by definition, physically immobile but there nevertheless exist markets for the purchase or leasing of land. The legal-use rights to short-run physically fixed production facilities can change hands in the short run, and it is precisely that rentability that permits production arbitrage to preclude a short-run competitive equilibrium with positive profits.

In a coherent model of a competitive capitalist economy, all resource owners would be modeled as offering their resource or the resource's services on the market at the market determined price. Those resources include the services of fixed physical production facilities. If a production-function notation does not display these marketable inputs, then the poor notation should be remedied. Any legal party could play the production arbitrageur's or entrepreneur's role by bidding on a complete set of exclusively owned inputs necessary for production. A person might play both roles of resource supplier and entrepreneur, in which case the model would assume that the person played each role consistently (for example, purchasing a resource from himself or herself at the going price).

Low-brow microeconomic theory asserts that there can be a competitive equilibrium with positive profits only in the short run. Profit-hungry entrepreneurs can gain free entry into profitable industries by constructing or converting production facilities, which postpones the competing away of the profits until the long run. But production arbitrageurs need not postpone their entry until the long run; instant free entry can be obtained in the short run by bidding away the existing resources. Consider any proposed set of market contracts at certain prices that allow positive profits in some production opportunity. The positive profit calculation would include as an expense the proposed rental accruing to the landlord of any short-run fixed physical facility. Clearly such a proposed set of contracts could not represent a competitive equilibrium because a production arbitrageur could intervene and bid away the resources by offering a higher rental and higher resource prices. Hence there cannot be a competitive equilibrium, short run or long run, with positive profits in the textbook model of low-brow microeconomic theory.

The device of leaving the services of fixed assets implicit in production functions is not based solely on the confusion between physical and legal mobility. It is also a gimmick that hides monopoly power in a so-called competitive model. In a free-market capitalist economy, the identity of the firm is determined by the outcome of the hiring conflict, the conflict over who hires what or whom. The winner is the hiring party, the party who hires the other inputs, appropriates the whole product (with its value being the profits), and controls the production process. The primary exercise of power in input markets is to determine the *direction,* not the terms, of the hiring contracts. The latter is only the negotiation of the terms of surrender for the losers in the hiring conflict.

The conventional concept of monopoly power applied to input markets is like justice defined by the victors; it only applies to the vanquished. The conventional theory holds that a resource owner is *monopolistic* if the owner can affect the selling price of the resource; for example, if the resource owner sells to a downward sloping demand curve. But it is only the losers in the hiring conflict who have to hire out their resources at all. The winning resource owner cannot be monopolistic. He does not manipulate the selling price of his resource since he does not sell his resource at all.

According to the conventional theory, if one-hundred workers join together in a labor union to hire themselves out at a higher price, that is a combination in constraint of trade, a market imperfection, a monopolistic lump in the competitive soup. But if a thousand times as many capital owners pool their resources together in a *capital union* called a *joint stock corporation,* then that is treated in conventional economic theory as a single producer. The combined capital owners are not being monopolistic because they have no designs to jack up the selling price of capital services. Indeed, their purpose is not to hire out their capital at all. The intended purpose of the capital union is to hire in labor and other complementary inputs, to undertake production, and to sell the outputs. All the input and output markets actually utilized in the model might be competitive. Thus large numbers of capital owners can join together in capital unions called corporations without there being any monopolistic market imperfections in the model. Each corporation is only a single producer participating in competitive markets for buying labor and selling the outputs. But a labor union would spoil the perfection of the competitive model. Given that "scientific" analysis of a competitive capitalist economy, who needs vulgar apologetics?

This digression on the treatment of monopolistic power and market imperfections in conventional theory is necessary to counter an endgame defense of a short-run competitive equilibrium in the low-brow model. The endgame attempts to thwart competitive production arbitrage by awarding each producer a local monopoly on certain fixed factors conveniently left implicit in the shape of the production function. The model is still called competitive since the markets explicitly used are assumed competitive. The monopoly power in input ownership is used behind the scenes to win the hiring conflict and thus to completely eliminate the markets in the monopolized factors. Such a model is hardly competitive, and it only appears so because the conventional notion of monopolistic market power is designed to apply only to the losers in the hiring conflict. In a genuinely competitive model, all resource owners supply their resources to the market at the going price.

Endgames in High-Brow Price Theory

Competitive equilibrium analysis in the case of universal constant returns to scale is one of the proudest achievements of modern mathematical economics (for example, the work of von Neumann, Leontief, Samuelson, Koopmans, MacKenzie, and many others). But the attempt to extend the competitive equilibrium analysis to the case of decreasing returns to scale and positive pure profits was an act of hubris that only provoked the demons of competitive arbitrage. They would not allow it. Once the defense about the ownership of production sets was penetrated, the Arrow-Debreu type models fell to a rather simple arbitrage argument that viewed production itself as arbitrage between input and output markets.

The failure of the Arrow-Debreu type models will not be easily recognized. Thus one must also explore endgames in high-brow price theory. Surely, it will be thought, there is some reinterpretation, some new assumption, some new mathematical technique, in short, some gimmick that will rescue the model. But the problem cannot be solved with new mathematical gimmickry. The problem is endemic to competitive capitalism.

Free-enterprise capitalism can be characterized by the fact that all input services are marketable. Humans may no longer be bought and sold, but human beings may be rented or hired; that is, human labor services may be bought and sold. The other exclusively or privately owned factors can be both bought and sold as well as rented. If all the factors necessary for production either are marketable commodities or are commonly owned or unowned factors, then there cannot be a competitive equilibrium with positive economic profits in any production opportunity (as noted in Ellerman 1980a). The possibility of profit would induce production arbitrageurs to bid up input prices precluding an equilibrium. If a model does not allow production arbitrageurs; that is entrepreneurs, to operate, then it does not model a free-enterprise capitalist economy. Rescue attempts that prevent production arbitrage only substitute another modeling error for the original Arrow-Debreu modeling error of assuming the ownership of sets of feasible whole-product vectors.

The principal endgame in high-brow price theory, as in low-brow price theory, is the assumption of *hidden factors* implicit in the shape of production sets. The assignment of the production set to specific legal parties is then justified by their ownership of the hidden factors. For instance, Professors Arrow and Hahn use the hidden factors device in their treatise on general competitive analysis.

> We will find it convenient to consider some commodities as being private to a firm or group of firms (e.g., managerial ability). (1971, p. 53)

> As already noted, not all inputs are, in fact, marketed. . . . For any vector y, let y^M and y^P be the vectors formed by considering only the marketed and private components, respectively. For the firm, assume that the private components are given: . . . From the viewpoint of the study of markets, only the vector y^M is relevant. (1971 p. 61)

Hence Arrow and Hahn restrict the whole-product or production vectors to their "marketed" components, and leave the "private" components implicit in the shape of the production sets.

The hidden-factors, or private-commodities, device requires several comments. First, it is a modeling error to assume any exclusively owned but nonmarketable input services in a model of a capitalist economy. There are none. Obviously the services of managers, like the services of fixed plant and equipment, are marketable in a capitalist economy. The possibility of production arbitrage does not disappear because model builders understandably "find it convenient" to leave certain marketable commodities implicit in their production-set formalism.

Second, Arrow and Hahn refer to the private commodities as not being *marketed* instead of as not being *marketable*. But the information as to what is ultimately marketed is hardly available *ex ante* when the production sets are being specified. Given a price vector, certain commodities in an initial endowment might be marketed while others might be retained for some reservation uses. At a different price vector, the split between the marketed and nonmarketed commodities might be different. In any case, it is *ex post* knowledge that assumes price information and is not available *ex ante* to be built into the specification of the production sets.

Perhaps Arrow and Hahn's intent is just to *assume* a priori that certain commodities are not marketed. Then the model is very likely inconsistent. As Burmeister points out:

> [A] formulation which *assumes* that certain markets do not exist is incomplete and, more importantly, it may be inconsistent with profit maximization. (1974, pp. 414–415)

At certain price vectors, profit or utility maximization might require marketing the private factors. Moreover, the assumption might vitiate the later theorems about competitive equilibria and pareto optimality. A *competitive equilibrium* might not be that, if the private factors were marketed. And, a *pareto efficient allocation* might be improved upon by a reallocation of the private factors. One cannot know if the theorems are meaningful or not since the nature and characteristics of the nonmarketed factors are hidden in the production sets.

The only way to "interpret" the Arrow-Debreu model as a consistent and meaningful theory is to use the hidden-factor device as a true gimmick by reinterpreting and conditionalizing the other assumptions in terms of the hidden-factor assumption. Each production set exhibiting decreasing returns to scale must be assumed to be jerry-rigged with an implicit factor that is exclusively owned but, by assumption, nonmarketable in order to block production arbitrage. Profit and utility maximization must be reinterpreted to mean *maximization unless it involves a reallocation of the hidden factors*. The concepts of competitive equilibrium and pareto optimality must be conditionalized by the imposed restriction on reallocating the implicit factors. Then the model works, and as Professor Koopmans points out, it has a limited usefulness.

> It follows that a postulate assigning production sets with decreasing returns to scale to a number of producers given in advance is tantamount to prescribing and freezing the assignment to various production processes of a certain number of indivisible commodities. Since these commodities are not introduced explicitly, but only implicitly through their influence on the shapes of the production sets, such a model cannot be used to explore possible gains in efficiency through reshuffling of these indivisible resources among producers. It is suitable, however, for tracing the effect of a given distribution of ownership or control of indivisible resources on the profits arising therefrom, which are perhaps more appropriately described as rents. (Koopmans 1957, p. 65)

Thus the Arrow-Debreu type models can be salvaged, but only at the cost of equipping each decreasing returns production set with a gimmick nonmarketable factor to ward off production arbitrageurs. The cost includes conditionalizing profit and utility maximization and all the theorems about competitive equilibrium and pareto optimality with the ad hoc hidden-resource assumptions.

The real cost is that the Arrow-Debreu type models cannot pretend any longer to model a competitive free-enterprise capitalist economy. Production arbitrageurs or entrepreneurs are excluded by being forbidden to bid on the profitable hidden factors. The models are even limited as a study of free markets, since they are founded on the assumed nonexistence of markets in the hidden factors. Moreover, since each decreasing production set is equipped with a perfect monopoly in a hidden resource, the models are only competitive in the Pickwickian sense of being competitive for the losers in the hiring conflict. Those fortunate enough to be endowed with a "special factor" can use their monopoly power to win the hiring conflict and thus to appropriate a whole-product vector from the production set associated with their hidden factor.

It is free enterprise based on outlawing entrepreneurs, it is free markets based on nonmarketable factors, and it is perfect competition based on perfect monopolies. The rehabilitation of the Arrow-Debreu type models using the hidden-factors gimmick is clearly a dubious victory. One way or another, competitive equilibrium theory must pay homage to the demons of arbitrage.

Appendix:
The Mathematical
Basis for Double-Entry
Bookkeeping

Introduction

This appendix presents an introductory treatment of the mathematical formulation of double-entry bookkeeping. The *algebra of T-accounts,* used informally in double-entry bookkeeping, is formalized and shown to be equivalent to the group of differences used in modern abstract algebra. This mathematical framework not only allows a rigorous formalization of the basic techniques of the double-entry method; it shows how the double-entry method can be generalized to accounting systems that work with multidimensional lists or vectors instead of just numbers. Thus the algebraic structure allows the generalization of traditional value accounting, which deals with numerical quantities representing economic values, to property accounting, which deals with vectors whose entries represent property rights.

In the following five sections, the intuitive double-entry algebra of T-accounts is formalized and generalized as the Pacioli-group construction, which is shown to be equivalent to the additive group of differences or multiplicative group of fractions. The mathematical development is relatively self-contained and elementary without sacrificing rigor.

Monoids and Groups

Given a set M, the *cartesian product $M \times M$* of M with itself is the set of all ordered pairs (m,m') where m and m' are elements of M. A *binary operation M* is a function $f: M \times M \longrightarrow M$, which associates with each element (m,m') in $M \times M$, some element $f(m,m')$ in M. For example, if M is the set of nonnegative real numbers $\dot{R}^+$ (that is, zero and the positive real numbers), then addition is a binary operation on R^+ that associates with each pair of nonnegative real numbers (r,r') their sum $r + r'$. A binary operation f on M is said to be *associative* if for any three elements m, m', and m'' of M, $f(f(m,m'),m'') = f(m,f(m',m''))$. For example, addition on the nonnegative reals is associative since for any r, r', and r'':

$$((r + r') + r'') = (r + (r' + r'')).$$

An element e in M is an *identity element* for the binary operation f if for any m in M, $f(m,e) = f(e,m) = m$. If f has an identity element, it is unique because if e and e' satisfied the definition of an identity element, then $e' = f(e,e') = f(e',e) = e$. For example, 0 is the identity element for the operation of addition on the nonnegative real numbers. Multiplication is an associative binary operation on the set of reals greater than or equal to 1 and 1 is its identity element.

A *monoid* is a set M with an associative binary operation f defined on M such that M contains an identity element e for the operation. The set of nonnegative real numbers R^+ under addition is an example of an additive monoid. The set Z^+ of whole numbers or integers greater than or equal to 1 under multiplication is an example of a multiplicative monoid. The nonnegative integers, also called *natural numbers,* form an additive monoid. A monoid is said to be *commutative* if for any m and m' in M, $f(m,m') = f(m',m)$. The monoids mentioned above are commutative, and all monoids considered henceforth are commutative.

Given an element m in the monoid M, an *inverse* to m is an element m' such that $f(m,m') = f(m',m) = e$. An inverse to m is unique if it exists since if m' and m'' were inverses to m, then:

$$m'' = f(e,m'') = f(f(m',m),m'') = f(m',f(m,m''))$$
$$= f(m',e) = m'.$$

A *group* is a monoid where every element has an inverse. The group is said to be *commutative* or *abelian* if the monoid is commutative. The identity element in a monoid is always its own inverse. Aside from zero, no element in the additive monoid (that is, monoid under addition) of nonnegative real numbers has an inverse. The set of all reals R, both negative and nonnegative, form an additive monoid that is also a group. The positive fractions or rational numbers form a multiplicative monoid, which is also a group, the multiplicative inverse of an element being its reciprocal.

For additional examples of monoids and groups, we introduce vectors of real numbers. For our purposes, a *vector* of real numbers is an ordered list of reals $X = (x,y, \ldots ,z)$, where each element $x, y, \ldots , z$ is called a *component* of the vector. The set of all vectors with n real components is the cartesian product of the reals R with itself n times:

$$R \times R \times \ldots \times R = R^n.$$

Addition is defined on R^n by adding the corresponding components of two vectors; that is:

$$X + X' = (x,y, \ldots ,z) + (x',y', \ldots ,z') = (x + x',y + y', \ldots ,z + z').$$

The zero vector, $(0,0, \ldots ,0)$, is the identity element and each vector in R^n has an additive inverse in R^n; that is, $-(x,y, \ldots ,z) = (-x,-y, \ldots ,-z)$. Thus R^n is a commutative group under addition.

A vector $(x,y, \ldots ,z)$ is *nonnegative* if each component is nonnegative. The set of nonnegative vectors in R^n is called the *nonnegative orthant* of R^n and it is denoted R^{n+}. The nonnegative orthant R^{n+} is a commutative monoid under addition, but is not a group.

A real number s in R is called a *scalar*, in contrast to the ordered lists of reals $(x,y, \ldots ,z)$ called vectors. Scalar multiplication is the operation of multiplying a scalar times a vector component-wise; that is, $sX = s(x,y, \ldots ,z) = (sx,sy, \ldots ,sz)$. Given two vectors $P = (p,q, \ldots ,r)$ and $X = (x,y, \ldots ,z)$ in R^n, their *scalar product* is the scalar:

$$PX = (p,q, \ldots ,r)(x,y, \ldots ,z) = px + qy + \ldots + rz.$$

Scalar products have a direct economic interpretation. If $(x,y, \ldots ,z)$ is a vector of different types of commodities, x units of the first good, y units of the second, and so forth, and if $(p,q, \ldots ,r)$ is a vector of unit prices, p the price per unit of the first good, q the unit price of the second good, and so forth, then the scalar product $px + qy + \ldots + rz$ is the total value of the market basket of commodities $(x,y, \ldots ,z)$.

The Pacioli Group of a Monoid

All monoids considered here are assumed to be commutative. Some of the monoids mentioned above, such as R^+ and R^{n+}, are not groups. However, R^+ and R^{n+} are a part of the larger monoids R and R^n, respectively, which are groups. The question arises of whether there is a standard procedure of constructing an extension of any given (commutative) monoid such that the extension is a group. There is such a standard construction in mathematics. Bourbaki calls it the *group of differences* of the monoid if the binary operation is written additively. If the operation is written multiplicatively, Bourbaki calls the standard construction, the *group of fractions* of the monoid (Bourbaki 1974, p. 20). It is customary, wherever possible, to write the binary operation of a commutative monoid as addition.

Given the additive monoids R^+ and R^{n+}, the corresponding groups of differences are R and R^n, respectively. For the multiplicative monoid Z^+ of integers (whole numbers) greater than or equal to 1, the group of fractions is the multiplicative group Q^+ of positive rationals (fractions). For the additive monoid of natural numbers (nonnegative integers), the group of differences is the group of integers Z.

Negative numbers do not appear in double-entry bookkeeping. The numbers that do appear are all drawn from the monoid of nonnegative real numbers R^+. One of the main results given below is that when the system of debits, credits, and algebraic operations on T-accounts is mathematically formulated, it is precisely equivalent to the standard construction of the group of differences of an additive monoid—when applied to the monoid of nonnegative real numbers R^+.

The double-entry system was developed by Italian merchants during the fourteenth and fifteenth centuries. It was first systematically expounded by the Italian mathematician Luca Pacioli in his famous work *Summa de Arithmetica, Geometria, Proporcioni et Proporcionalita* published in 1494. Pacioli does not claim to have invented the double-entry system, and, indeed, he points out that his "treatise will adopt the system used in Venice." Hence the double-entry system was originally known as the *Venetian method* or the *Italian method*.

We will first present the standard construction of the group of differences of an additive monoid. Then the system of debits, credits, and T-accounts will be algebraically formulated as the construction of a group from a given monoid. The Equivalence Theorem will show that the two constructions yield the same group. While we must leave the chronology of the development of the group-of-differences construction to historians of mathematics, the development of the double-entry method in the fourteenth and fifteenth centuries would seem to have precedence by a margin of centuries. Hence it would seem appropriate to name the group of differences of a commutative monoid M, the *Pacioli Group of M*.

The Construction of the Groups

Let M be a commutative monoid with the binary operation written as addition. The cartesian product $M \times M$ of M with itself is also a monoid, the *product monoid,* with addition defined component-wise on the ordered pairs in $M \times M$. The group of differences is constructed as a quotient of $M \times M$; that is, as the result of identifying together certain elements of the product monoid $M \times M$. Given elements d, d', c, and c' in M, the ordered pairs (d,c) and (d',c') in $M \times M$ are to be identified; that is, $(d,c) = (d',c')$, if there exists an element m in M such that:

$$d + c' + m = d' + c + m.$$

Definition: The *group of differences of an additive monoid M* is the quotient of the product monoid $M \times M$ obtained by identifying any ordered pairs (d,c) and (d',c') if there exists an element m in M such that: $d + c' + m = d' + c + m$ (for example, Bourbaki 1974, p. 17, where multiplicative notation is used).

This or related constructions can be found in Chevally (1956, p. 41), Kurosh (1963, p. 52), Lang (1965, p. 43), and MacLane and Birkhoff (1967, p. 45). Especially accessible treatments of special cases can be found in Dubisch (1965, p. 17) and Jacobson (1951, p. 10). The construction does indeed yield a group because given any pair (d,c), its additive inverse is (c,d). This is shown by noting that $(d,c) + (c,d) = (d + c, d + c)$ can be identified with the identity element $(0,0)$ by taking $m = 0$ in the above definition; that is,

$$(d + c) + 0 + 0 = 0 + (d + c) + 0.$$

This group of differences is an extension of M in two ways since the elements m of M can be equated with the elements of the form $(0, m)$ or the elements of the forms $(m, 0)$.

In normal double-entry bookkeeping, the numbers that appear are elements of the additive monoid of nonnegative real numbers R^+. As we algebraically formulate the machinery of double-entry bookkeeping, we will generalize it by allowing the elements to be from any additive monoid M. The elements of R^+ or, in general, M occur in what are usually called *T-accounts*. A T-account can be thought of as an ordered pair (d,c) of elements of M, the element on the left called a *debit* and the element on the right called a *credit*. Thus the set of T-accounts is the cartesian product $M \times M$ of M with itself; that is, the product monoid, which was also the initial datum in the group-of-differences construction.

Before proceeding with the algebraic manipulation of the T-accounts, we would like to introduce some new notation and terminology. The use of the parentheses in (d,c) can be confusing since when $M = R^{n+}$, the elements d and c are also vectors denoted by a list of components between parentheses. The use of an actual T symbol is too restrictive typographically. We propose, first, to use square brackets on the outside instead of parentheses. Second, instead of using a comma to separate the debit and credit, we will utilize a notational suggestion by Pacioli himself.

> At the beginning of each entry, we always provide *per*, because, first, the debtor must be given, and immediately after the creditor, the one separated from the other by two little slanting parallels (virgolette), thus, //. (Pacioli 1494, p. 43).

If we adopt Pacioli's double-slash suggestion then the T-account (d,c) would be written as $[d \mathbin{//} c]$. Furthermore, since the entities $[d \mathbin{//} c]$ will be used to represent not only the T-accounts but the debits and credits that can be added to a T-account, we will use the slightly more general terminology of *T-terms* or *T-elements* to refer to the entities $[d \mathbin{//} c]$, rather than calling them all T-accounts. A specific definition of T-accounts will be given in the text.

Thus the initial datum is the product monoid $M \times M$ whose elements are the T-terms of the form $[d // c]$. Addition of T-terms is defined by components; that is, debits add to debits and credits add to credits. For instance, if d, d', c, and c' are in M, then:

$$[d // c] + [d' // c'] = [d + d' // c + c].$$

If $M = R^+$ and a T-term $[d // c]$ intuitively represents a T-account such as Cash, then a debit of d' to the account would be algebraically represented as the addition of the T-term $[d' // 0]$; that is:

$$[d // c] + [d' // 0] = [d + d' // c].$$

A credit of c' to the account would be similarly represented as the addition of the T-term $[0 // c']$; that is:

$$[d // c] + [0 // c'] = [d // c + c'].$$

We have so far only considered operations on the T-terms in the product monoid $M \times M$ where $[d // c]$ does not equal $[d' // c']$ if d does not equal d' or c does not equal c'. We now must take a quotient of $M \times M$ by identifying certain T-terms together. This process of identifying T-terms is just an algebraic formulation and generalization of the accounting process of totaling a T-account to obtain a net credit balance or a net debit balance. Given a T-account $[d // c]$ where $M = R^+$, if the real number c is greater than or equal to the real number d, the T-account would be totaled to the account $[0 // c - d]$ with the net credit balance of $c - d$. In other words, the T-account $[d // c]$ is identified with the T-account $[0 // c - d]$ when c is greater than d. If d was greater than or equal to c, then $[d // c]$ is to be identified with the T-account $[d - c // 0]$, which has the debit balance of $d - c$.

The description of the identification of certain T-accounts in ordinary accounting is useful as intuitive motivation. However, it will not serve as a mathematical definition because it involves the ordering relation of *greater than or equal to* in the comparison of c and d, as well as the operation of *subtraction* (that is, addition of additive inverses) in the terms $c - d$ and $d - c$. Neither the ordering relation nor subtraction are available in an arbitrary additive monoid M so we must reformulate the mathematical definition of which T-terms are to be identified so that it only uses the operation of addition. For example, in $M = R^+$, instead of saying that c is greater than or equal to d and that $c - d$ is the nonnegative difference, it is equivalent to say simply that there is a nonnegative real c' (an element of R^+) such that $d + c' = c$. That reformulation does not explicitly involve the ordering relation or subtraction. Then we could say that the T-term $[d // c]$ is to be identified with the T-term $[0 // c']$ if there is an element m' in M such that $[d // c] = [m' // m'] + [0 // c']$ holds in $M \times M$ (for example, take $m' = d$).

Similarly, instead of saying that d is greater than or equal to c in R^+ and that the nonnegative difference is $d - c$, it is equivalent to say that there is an element d' in R^+ such that $d = c + d'$. Then $[d // c]$ is to be identified with $[d' // 0]$ if there is an element m' in M such that $[d // c] = [m' // m'] + [d' // 0]$ holds in $M \times M$ (for example, take $m' = c$).

Both cases are included if we identify $[d // c]$ with $[d' // c']$ whenever there is an element m' in M such that:

$$[d // c] = [m' // m'] + [d' // c'].$$

The only remaining deficiency in the definition of identification is its asymmetry; we must also allow a term $[m // m]$ on the other side. Hence the general algebraic definition is that any T-terms $[d // c]$ and $[d' // c']$ are to be identified if there are elements m and m' in M such that:

$$[d // c] + [m // m] = [m' // m'] + [d' // c'] \text{ holds in } M \times M;$$

that is, such that $d + m = m' + d'$ and $c + m = m' + c'$ hold in M.

Definition: The *Pacioli group* $P(M)$ *of a commutative monoid* M is the quotient of the product monoid $M \times M$ obtained by identifying any T-terms [d // c] and [d' // c'] if there are elements m and m' in M such that:

$$[d // c] + [m // m] = [m' // m'] + [d' // c'].$$

A T-term in $P(M)$ is actually an equivalence class of terms that are identified with one another. Distinct elements in an equivalence class are called distinct *representatives* of the T-term. For instance, in $P(R^+)$, $[5 // 9]$ and $[2 // 6]$ are distinct representative of the same T-term; that is $[5 // 9] = [2 // 6]$. It is a customary abuse of language in mathematics to refer to a representative as if it were the equivalence class; for example, to refer to a representative $[d // c]$ as a T-term in $P(M)$.

To prove that $P(M)$ is indeed a group, we must show that any T-term $[d // c]$ has an additive inverse. The obvious candidate is the reversed T-term $[c // d]$ so it must be shown that the T-term $[d // c] + [c // d]$ can be identified with $[0 // 0]$. But that is simple since taking $m = 0$ and $m' = d + c$, we have:

$$([d \mathbin{/\!/} c] + [c \mathbin{/\!/} d]) + [0 \mathbin{/\!/} 0] = [d + c \mathbin{/\!/} d + c] + [0 \mathbin{/\!/} 0].$$

Equivalence Theorem

Given any additive monoid M, the group of differences of M is the Pacioli group $P(M)$ of M.

Proof: Since both groups were defined as quotients of the product monoid $M \times M$, equivalence will follow from showing that the same identifications are made in the two cases. Thus we must prove that $[d \mathbin{/\!/} c] = [d' \mathbin{/\!/} c']$ in the Pacioli group $P(M)$ if and only if $(d,c) = (d',c')$ in the group of differences. If $[d \mathbin{/\!/} c] = [d' \mathbin{/\!/} c']$ in $P(M)$, then there are elements m and m' in M such that $d + m = m' + d'$ and $c + m = m' + c'$. By adding these equations, we have:

$$d + m = m' + d'$$
$$\underline{c' + m' = m + c}$$
$$d + c' + (m + m') = (m + m') + d' + c.$$

Hence $m + m'$ is an element m'' of M such that:

$$d + c' + m'' = m'' + d' + c$$

so $(d,c) = (d',c')$ in the group of differences. Conversely, if $(d,c) = (d',c')$ in the group of differences, then there is an element m'' of M such that $d + c' + m'' = m'' + d' + c$. Let $m = m'' + c'$ and let $m' = m'' + c$. Then we have:

$$
\begin{aligned}
[d \mathbin{/\!/} c] + [m \mathbin{/\!/} m] &= [d + m \mathbin{/\!/} m + c] \\
&= [d + c' + m'' \mathbin{/\!/} m'' + c + c'] \\
&= [d' + c + m'' \mathbin{/\!/} m' + c'] \\
&= [d' + m' \mathbin{/\!/} m' + c'] \\
&= [m' \mathbin{/\!/} m'] + [d' \mathbin{/\!/} c']
\end{aligned}
$$

all holding in $M \times M$ so $[d \mathbin{/\!/} c] = [d' \mathbin{/\!/} c']$ holds in $P(M)$. That completes the proof that the group of differences is the Pacioli group.

Properties of the Pacioli Group

Given two additive monoids M and N, a *monoid homomorphism* $f{:}M \longrightarrow N$ is a mapping from M to N that maps an element m in M to an element $f(m)$ of N in such a way that (1) $f(0) = 0$ and (2) $f(m + m') = f(m) + (m')$ for any m and m' in M. If distinct elements are always mapped to distinct elements (that is, $f(m) = f(m')$ implies $m = m'$) then the homomorphism is said to be *one-to-one* or *injective*. For example, there are two injective homomorphisms of the additive monoid R^+ into its Pacioli group $P(R^+)$, the one that maps any m to the credit of m, $[0 // m]$, and the one that maps m to the debit of m, $[m // 0]$.

If every element in N has some element of M mapped onto it (that is, if for every n in N, there is an m in M such that $f(m) = n$), then the homomorphism is said to be *onto* or *surjective*. A monoid homomorphism $f:M \longrightarrow N$ that is both one-to-one and onto is a *monoid isomorphism*. If $f:M \longrightarrow N$ is an isomorphism, then there is an inverse homomorphism $f^{(-1)}:N \longrightarrow M$ in the opposite direction that just reverses the effect of f. That is, for any m in M, $f^{(-1)}(f(m)) = m$. If there is an isomorphism between two monoids M and N, they are said to be *isomorphic*, written $M \cong N$. This means that, abstractly, M and N are the *same* monoid.

If M and N are additive groups, then a monoid homomorphism $f:M \longrightarrow N$ is said to be a *group homomorphism*. It will preserve additive inverses in the sense that $f(-m) = -f(m)$ because if $m + m' = 0$, then $0 = f(0) = f(m + m') = f(m) + f(m')$. Hence if $m' = -m$, then $f(m') = -f(m)$. A group homomorphism that is one-to-one and onto is a *group isomorphism*. If M and N are isomorphic groups, they are abstractly the *same* group.

Homomorphism can often be composed together to form new homomorphisms. If M, M' and M'' are monoids and if $f:M \longrightarrow M'$ and $g:M' \longrightarrow M''$ are monoid homomorphisms, then their *composition gf* is the homomorphism $gf:M \longrightarrow M''$ such that for any m in M, $gf(m) = g(f(m))$. If $h:M \longrightarrow M''$ is a monoid homomorphism, then the composition gf equals h, written $gf = h$, if for any m in M, $gf(m) = h(m)$. This is often said by saying that the mapping diagram as shown in figure A–1 *commutes*.

In mathematics, a standard construction can usually be uniquely characterized by a *universal mapping property*. The Pacioli group $P(M)$ of an additive monoid M (that is, the group of differences) is no exception. For any additive monoid M, there are two canonical homomorphism $M \longrightarrow P(M)$, the *debit map* that carries any m to $[m // 0]$ and the *credit*

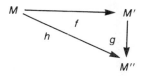

Figure A–1. A Commutative Diagram

map that carries m to $[0 \mathbin{/\!/} m]$. Let us arbitrarily choose one of them, say, the credit homomorphism and label it i. Then $i{:}M\longrightarrow P(M)$ has the following mapping property: it is a monoid homomorphism f from M to some additive monoid N such that for any m in M, $f(m)$ has an additive inverse $-f(m)$ in N. Clearly i has that property since when $f = i$ and $N = P(M)$, then $[m \mathbin{/\!/} 0]$ is the additive inverse of $i(m) = [0 \mathbin{/\!/} m]$. Moreover, i is the *universal map* with this property in the sense that if f is any other map with the property, then there is a unique monoid homomorphism $f'{:}P(M)\longrightarrow N$ such that $f'i = f$. Then f is said to *uniquely factor through i*.

Universal Mapping Property for the Pacioli Group $P(M)$

> If $f{:}M\longrightarrow N$ is any monoid homomorphism from M to an additive monoid N such that for any m in M, $f(M)$ has an additive inverse in N, then there is a unique monoid homomorphism $f'{:}P(M)\longrightarrow N$ such that $f'i = f$; that is, such that figure A-2 commutes.

Proofs of this property and related results can be found in Bourbaki (1974, p. 19), Lang (1965, p. 43), and Chevalley (1956, p. 41). The universal mapping property for $P(M)$ uniquely characterizes it in the sense that if any other monoid has the same universal mapping property, that monoid would be isomorphic to $P(M)$.

The universal mapping property for $P(M)$ can be used to prove that the Pacioli groups of the nonnegative reals R^+ and the nonnegative real vectors R^{n+} are R and R^n respectively. The following result is the basis for the equivalence of double-entry and single-entry bookkeeping. Double-entry bookkeeping computes in $P(R^+)$ and single-entry bookkeeping computes in R.

Corollary 1: $P(R^+) \cong R$

Proof: The injection $f{:}R^+\longrightarrow R$, which carries each nonnegative real to itself, factors uniquely through $i{:}R^+\longrightarrow P(R^+)$ by the monoid homomorphism $f'{:}P(R^+)\longrightarrow R$ such that $f'([s \mathbin{/\!/} r]) = r - s$. For any nonnegative real r, $f'([0 \mathbin{/\!/} r]) = r$ and $f'([r \mathbin{/\!/} 0]) = -r$. Since every real

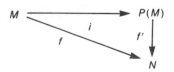

Figure A-2. Universal Mapping Property of $P(M)$

occurs as such an r or $-r$, f' is onto. To see that f' on one-to-one, suppose that for r, r', s, and s' in R^+, $f'([s // r]) = f'([s' // r'])$; that is, that $r - s = r' - s'$. But then $r + s' = s + r'$ so for $m = r'$ and $m' = r$, we have $[s // r] + [r' // r'] = [r // r] + [s' // r']$ holding in $R^+ \times R^+$ so $[s // r] = [s' // r']$ holds in $P(R^+)$. Hence f' is one-to-one, so $P(R^+)$ and R are isomorphic.

This result can be illustrated graphically. In figure A–3, the credits c are measured along the horizontal axis and the debits d are measured on the vertical axis. A representative $[d // c]$ is plotted at the point (c,d) with the horizontal coordinate c and vertical coordinate d. A 45-degree line is the locus of all points $[d // c]$ such that $c - d$ has the same value so each 45-degree line is an equivalence class in $P(R^+)$; that is, a T-term. The entire real line R is graphed at a northwest to southeast 45-degree slant through the origin. By continuing each 45-degree line until it hits the real line, each distinct T-term $[d // c]$ is associated with a distinct real number $c - d$ to illustrate the credit isomorphism $P(R^+) \cong R$. If each representative $[d // c]$ is considered as the vector or arrow from the origin to the point (c,d), then the sum:

$$[d // c] + [d' // c'] = [d + d' // c + c']$$

is graphed using the *parallelogram law of addition*. For example:

$$[3 // 0] + [0 // 2] = [3 // 2] = [1 // 0].$$

The additive inverse of any $[d // c]$ is represented by its mirror image $[c // d]$ on the other side of the 45-degree line through the origin. We are grateful to Professor Y. Ijiri for suggesting the use of this figure to illustrate corollary 1. Similar figures are used in MacLane and Birkhoff (1967, p. 45) and Jacobson (1951, p. 10) to illustrate the isomorphism between the group of differences of the natural numbers and the additive group of all integers Z.

Corollary 2: $P(R^{n+}) \cong R^n$.

Proof: If X is any vector in R^n, let $pos(X)$ be the vector in R^n that retains the nonnegative components of X but replaces all negative components by zero. Thus for any X in R^n, $pos(X)$ is in the nonnegative orthant R^{n+}. Let $neg(X) = pos(-X)$ so $neg(X)$ replaces all the negative components of X by their absolute value and replaces all the positive components of X by zero. Then for any X in R^n, both $pos(X)$ and $neg(X)$ are in R^{n+} and $X = pos(X) - neg(X)$. The injection $f:R^{n+} \longrightarrow R^n$, which carries each nonnegative vector to itself, factors uniquely through $i:R^{n+} \longrightarrow P(R^{n+})$ by the monoid homomorphism $f':P(R^{n+}) \longrightarrow R^n$ such that $f'([Y // X]) = X - Y$. For any vector X in R^n:

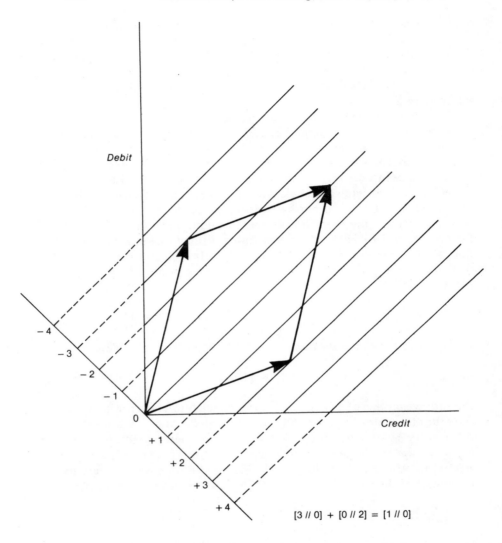

Figure A–3. Isomorphism of $P(R^+)$ and R

$$f'([neg(X) \,/\!/\, pos(X)]) = pos(X) - neg(X) = X$$

so f' is onto. To see that f' is one-to-one, suppose that for X, X', Y, and Y' in R^{n+}, $f'([Y \,/\!/\, X]) = f'([Y' \,/\!/\, X'])$; that is, $X - Y = X' - Y'$. But then $X + Y' = Y + X'$ so for $m = X'$ and $m' = X$, we have $[Y \,/\!/$

$X] + [X' // X'] = [X // X] + [Y' // X']$ holding in $R^{n+} \times R^{n+}$ so $[Y // X] = [Y' // X']$ holds in $P(R^{n+})$. Hence f' is also one-to-one, so $P(R^{n+})$ and R^n are isomorphic.

The Pacioli groups $P(R^+)$ and $P(R^{n+})$ are the principal ones relevant to accounting. However, to round out the picture, we will give a mathematical application of the Pacioli group to a multiplicative monoid, the monoid Z^+ of the positive whole numbers (excluding 0) under multiplication. The Pacioli group $P(Z^+)$ is then what is called the group of fractions of Z^+ and it will be shown that it is the multiplicative group Q^+ of positive rationals. In this multiplicative context, a T-term $[x // y]$ can be thought of as the fraction x/y. The identity element is $[1 // 1]$, and the monoid operation is written multiplicatively; that is, $[x // \dot{y}][x' // y'] = [xx' // yy']$. If the debit side in a T-term is construed as the numerator and the credit side as the denominator, then the universal mapping property should use the other canonical injection that takes x in Z^+ to the debit of x, $[x // 1]$.

Corollary 3: $P(Z^+) \cong Q^+$.

Proof: The injection $f:Z^+ \longrightarrow Q^+$, which carries each positive whole number x to the fraction $x/1$, factors uniquely through the *debit injection* $Z^+ \longrightarrow P(Z^+)$ by the monoid homomorphism $f':P(Z^+) \longrightarrow Q^+$ such that $f'([x // y]) = x/y$. Any positive rational in Q^+ can be expressed as the ratio x/y of some positive integers x and y, and $f'([x // y]) = x/y$ so f' is onto. To see that f' is one-to-one, suppose that for x, x', y, and y' in Z^+, $f'([x // y]) = f'([x' // y'])$; that is, $x/y = x'/y'$. But then $xy' = yx'$ so for $m = y'$ and $m' = y$:

$$[x // y][y' // y'] = [y // y][x' // y']$$

holds in $Z^+ \times Z^+$ and thus $[x // y] = [x' // y']$ holds in $P(Z^+)$. Hence f' is one-to-one, and $P(Z^+)$ and Q^+ are isomorphic.

Figure A–4 illustrates corollary 3. The points inside the positive quadrant with positive (nonzero) integer coordinates will be called *lattice points*. The positive rationals are in one-to-one correspondence with the lines through the origin and through a lattice point. If a lattice point has a horizontal coordinate of c and a vertical coordinate of d, then the line through that lattice point has a slope of d/c and the equation of the line is $y = (d/c)x$. Consider the vertical line over the horizontal coordinate of $x = 1$ as the positive real line. The rational numbers in Q^+ are situated along that line at precisely the intersections with the lines through the origin and the lattice points, since the vertical coordinates of the intersections are $y = (d/c)1 = d/c$. In figure A–3, each additive T-term was represented by a 45-degree line, and the southwest intersection of the line with either the ver-

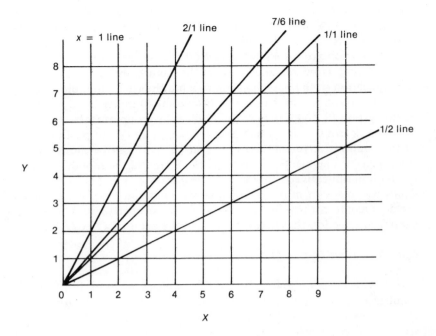

Figure A-4. Isomorphism of $P(Z^+)$ and Q^+

tical or horizontal axis represented the T-term in reduced form (chapter 5). In figure A-4, the most southwest lattice point on each rational line (the lattice point on the line closest to the origin) represents the fraction in lowest terms.

Accounting Monoids

Not all monoids M yield Pacioli groups $P(M)$ that are suitable for accounting. The following definition will single out the monoids that are appropriate.

> *Definition:* A commutative monoid M is said to be an *accounting monoid* if for any m and m' in M, $m = m'$ in M if and only if $[m \mathbin{//} m'] = [0 \mathbin{//} 0]$ in $P(M)$.

All the monoids considered so far are, in fact, accounting monoids. This will be evident from the next theorem, which gives a number of equivalent characterizations of accounting monoids.

Given a commutative monoid M (written additively), an element m is said to be *cancellable* (Bourbaki 1974, pp. 14–15) if for any m' and m'' in M, $m + m' = m + m''$ implies $m' = m''$. Intuitively, this means that information is not lost by adding m to elements m' and m'' because if the sums $m + m'$ and $m + m''$ are equal, then one can cancel m to obtain the equation $m' = m''$. All the elements in the additive monoids R^+ and R^{n+} are cancellable. For an example of an element that is not cancellable, consider the multiplicative monoid Z of all whole number or integers. Then zero is not cancellable because for any two distinct integers m' and m'', $0m' = 0 = 0m''$, but $m' = m''$ does not hold.

If all the elements of M are cancellable, then it is said that the *cancellation law holds* in M. Accounting monoids can now be characterized in several ways.

Characterization Theorem

Let M be an additive monoid. Then the following conditions are equivalent.

1. The cancellation law holds in M.
2. The credit (or debit) homomorphism $i{:}M$————$P(M)$ is one-to-one.
3. M is an accounting monoid.

Proof: The conditions can be proven equivalent by showing that (1) implies (2), that (2) implies (3), and that (3) implies (1).

To show that (1) implies (2), (1) is assumed. The credit homomorphism i, where $i(m) = [0 \mathbin{/\!/} m]$, is one-to-one or injective if for any m' and m'' in M, $[0 \mathbin{/\!/} m'] = [0 \mathbin{/\!/} m'']$ implies $m' = m''$. By the Equivalence Theorem, $[0 \mathbin{/\!/} m'] = [0 \mathbin{/\!/} m'']$ holds in $P(M)$ if and only if there is an m such that $m' + m = m'' + m$. Since any element m is cancellable by assumption, it follows that $m' = m''$ and thus that the credit homomorphism i is one-to-one. The analogous proof would show that the debit homomorphism is also one-to-one.

To show that (2) implies (3), (2) is assumed and it must be shown that M is an accounting monoid; that is, that $m = m'$ in M if and only if $[m \mathbin{/\!/} m'] = [0 \mathbin{/\!/} 0]$. If $m = m'$ then trivially $[m \mathbin{/\!/} m'] = [0 \mathbin{/\!/} 0]$ so it remains to prove the converse; that is, that $[m \mathbin{/\!/} m'] = [0 \mathbin{/\!/} 0]$ implies $m = m'$. If $[m \mathbin{/\!/} m'] = [0 \mathbin{/\!/} 0]$ in $P(M)$, then using $i(m) = [0 \mathbin{/\!/} m]$ and $i(m') = [0 \mathbin{/\!/} m']$:

$$[0 \mathbin{/\!/} 0] = [m \mathbin{/\!/} 0] + [0 \mathbin{/\!/} m'] = -i(m) + i(m'),$$

so $i(m) = i(m')$. But since i is one-to-one, it follows that $m = m'$.

To show that (3) implies (1), it is assumed that M is an accounting monoid; that is, that $m' = m''$ in M if and only if $[m' \mathbin{/\!/} m''] = [0 \mathbin{/\!/} 0]$ in

$P(M)$. For any m, let m' and m'' be elements of M such that $m + m' = m + m''$. Then, by the Equivalence Theorem, $[m' // m''] = [0 // 0]$ in $P(M)$ so $m' = m''$ holds in M. That completes the proof of the characterization theorem. For similar results, see Bourbaki (1974, p. 18), Chevalley (1956, p. 42) or Lang (1965, pp. 43–44).

Since zero is not a cancellable element in the multiplicative monoid Z of all integers, the multiplicative Z is not an accounting monoid. In $P(Z)$, $[m // n] = [m' // n']$ if there is an integer p such that $mn'p = nm'p$. But for $p = 0$, $mn'p = nm'p$ for any m, m', n, and n' so $P(Z)$ collapses to a single element, the identity element. In other words, the attempt to construct a nontrivial multiplicative group containing zero fails because "you can't divide by zero." In all the other monoids (aside for the multiplicative Z) considered above, such as R^+ and R^{n+}, the cancellation law holds so those monoids are all accounting monoids.

For accounting monoids M, the criterion for identifying T-terms has a simplified form:

$$[d // c] = [d' // c'] \text{ in } P(M) \text{ if and only if } d + c' = d' + c \text{ in } M.$$

Given two T-terms $[d // c]$ and $[d' // c']$, the sums of the debit entry in one with the credit entry in the other, namely $d + c'$ and $d' + c$, are called the *cross sums* of the T-terms. Hence in the Pacioli group of an accounting monoid, two T-terms are equal if and only if their cross sums are equal.

The Pacioli group $P(M)$ of an accounting monoid M is the precise formulation and generalization of the intuitive algebra of T-accounts used in traditional double-entry bookkeeping:

Algebra of T-accounts = Pacioli Group of an Accounting Monoid.

The double-entry method is a technique of using this algebraic machinery to perform valid additive algebraic operations on equations. The equivalence between equations $m = m'$ in M and T-terms $[m // m'] = [0 // 0]$, which characterizes accounting monoids, is the foundation of the double entry method. This use of the algebra of T-accounts in the double entry method is described in the body of the text (chapter 6).

The treatment of double-entry bookkeeping given herein is based on the observation that the algebra of T-accounts is equivalent to the group of differences constructed from the additive monoid of nonnegative reals. Although this observation is mathematically straightforward, it does not seem to appear in the literature (for example, DeMorgan 1869; Cayley 1894; Kemeny et al. 1962; Charnes, Cooper, and Ijiri 1963; Mattessich 1958, 1964; Williams and Griffin 1964; Ijiri and Jaedicke 1969; Ijiri 1967; Corcoran 1968; Shank 1972; Charnes, Colantoni, Cooper and Kortanek 1972; Ijiri 1979; and so forth).

Bibliography

Alexander, S.S. 1962. Income Measurement in a Dynamic Economy. In *Studies in Accounting Theory*. W.T. Baxter and S. Davison, eds., pp., 126–200. Homewood, Ill.: Irwin.

American Accounting Association. 1966. *A Statement of Basic Accounting Theory*. Evanston: American Accounting Association.

Anthony, R.N. 1970. *Management Accounting*. Homewood, Ill.: Irwin.

———. 1975. *Accounting for the Cost of Interest*. Lexington, Mass.: D.C. Heath.

———. 1978. Accounting for the Cost of Interest. In *Trends in Managerial and Financial Accounting*. Cees van Dam, ed., pp. 145–167. Leiden: Martinus Nijhoff.

Arrow, K.J. 1971. The Firm in General Equilibrium Theory. In *The Corporate Economy*. R. Marris and A. Woods, eds. Cambridge, Mass.: Harvard University Press.

Arrow, K.J., and Debreu, G. 1954. Existence of an Equilibrium for a Competitive Economy. *Econometrica* 22:265–290.

Arrow, K.J., and Hahn, F.H. 1971. *General Competitive Analysis*. San Francisco: Holden-Day.

Bierman, H., and Smidt, S. 1960. *The Capital Budgeting Decision*. New York: Macmillan.

Black, H. 1968. *Black's Law Dictionary*. St. Paul: West Publishing.

Boulding, K.E. 1962. Economics and Accounting: The Uncongenial Twins. In *Studies in Accounting Theory*. W.T. Baxter and S. Davidson, eds., pp. 44–55. Homewood, Ill.: Irwin.

Bourbaki, N. 1974. *Algebra I*. Reading, Mass.: Addison-Wesley.

Burmeister, E. 1974. Neo-Austrian and Alternative Approaches to Capital Theory. *Journal of Economic Literature* 12:413–456.

Burns, T., and Hendrickson, H. 1972. *The Accounting Primer*. New York: McGraw-Hill.

Canning, J.B. 1929. *The Economics of Accounting*. New York: Ronald Press.

Catlett, G., and Olson, N. 1968. *ARS No. 10: Accounting for Goodwill*. New York: American Institute of Certified Public Accountants.

Cayley, A. 1894. *The Principles of Book-keeping by Double Entry*. Cambridge: Cambridge University Press.

———. 1896. Presidential Address to the British Association for the Advancement of Science. *The Collected Mathematical Papers of Arthur Cayley* XI. Cambridge: Cambridge University Press.

Chambers, R.J. 1966. *Accounting, Evaluation, and Economic Behavior.* Englewood Cliffs, N.J.: Prentice-Hall.

Charnes, A.; Cooper, W.W.; and Ijiri, Y. 1963. Breakeven Budgeting and Programming to Goals. *Journal of Accounting Research* (Spring) pp. 16–41.

Charnes, A.; Colantoni, C.; Cooper, W.W.; and Kortanek, K.O. 1972. Economic Social and Enterprise Accounting and Mathematical Models. *Accounting Review* (January) pp. 85–108.

Charnes, A.; Colantoni, C.; and Cooper, W.W. 1976. A Futurological Justification for Historical Cost and Multi-Dimensional Accounting. *Accounting, Organizations and Society* 1, no. 4:315–337.

Chevalley, C. 1956. *Fundamental Concepts of Algebra.* New York: Academic Press.

Chung, K.L. 1975. *Elementary Probability Theory with Stochastic Processes.* New York: Springer-Verlag.

Corcoran, W. 1968. *Mathematical Applications in Accounting.* New York: Harcourt, Brace, and World.

Debreu, G. 1959. *Theory of Value.* New York: Wiley.

DeMorgan, A. 1869. On the Main Principle of Book-keeping. In *Elements of Arithmetic.* London: James Walton.

Dubisch, R. 1965. *Introduction to Abstract Algebra.* New York: Wiley.

Edey, H.C. 1962. Business Valuation, Goodwill, and the Super-Profit Method. In *Studies in Accounting Theory.* W.T. Baxter and S. Davidson, eds., pp. 201–217. Homewood, Ill.: Irwin.

Edwards, E., and Bell, P. 1970. *The Theory and Measurement of Business Income.* Berkeley: University of California Press.

Ellerman, D.P. 1980a. Property Theory and Orthodox Economics. In *Growth, Profits and Property: Essays in the Revival of Political Economy.* E.J. Nell, ed. Cambridge: Cambridge University Press.

————. 1980b. On Property Theory and Value Theory. *Economic Analysis and Workers' Management* 1, XIV:105–126.

————. 1981. Capital Theory and Property Theory. Unpublished paper. 33 pages.

Fama, E., and Miller, M.H. 1972. *The Theory of Finance.* New York: Holt, Rinehart, and Winston.

Furubotn, E., and Pejovich, S., eds. 1974. *The Economics of Property Rights.* Cambridge, MA: Ballinger.

Gale, D. 1973. On the Theory of Interest. *American Mathematical Monthly* (October) pp. 853–868.

Gomberg, L. 1927. *Eine Geometrische Darstellung der Buchhaltungsmethoden.* Berlin: Weiss.

Gordon, M., and Shillinglaw, G. 1969. *Accounting: A Managerial Approach.* Homewood, Ill.: Irwin.

Hirshleifer, J. 1970. *Investment, Interest, and Capital.* Englewood Cliffs, N.J.: Prentice-Hall.

Hendriksen, E.S. 1977. *Accounting Theory.* Homewood, Ill.: Irwin.

Ijiri, Y. 1965. *Management Goals and Accounting for Control.* Amsterdam: North-Holland.

————. 1966. Physical Measures and Multi-Dimensional Accounting. In *Research in Accounting Measurement.* R.K. Jaedicke, Y. Ijiri, and O. Nielsen, eds., pp. 150–164. New York: American Accounting Association.

————. 1967. *The Foundations of Accounting Measurement: A Mathematical, Economic, and Behavioral Inquiry* Englewood Cliffs, N.J.: Prentice-Hall.

————. 1979. A Structure of Multisector Accounting and Its Applications to National Accounting. In *Eric Louis Kohler: Accounting's Man of Principles,* W.W. Cooper and Y. Ijiri, eds., pp. 208–224. Reston, VA: Reston.

Ijiri, Y., and Jaedicke, R.K. 1969. Mathematics and Accounting. In *Contemporary Accounting and Its Environment* John W. Buckley, ed., pp. 315–336. Belmont, Calif.: Dickenson.

Jacobson, N. 1951. *Lectures in Abstract Algebra,* vol. 1. Princeton: Van Nostrand.

Kelso, L.O., and Adler, M.J. 1958. *The Capitalist Manifesto.* New York: Random House.

Kemeny, J.; Schleifer, A.; Snell, J.L.; and Thompson, G. 1962. *Finite Mathematics with Business Applications.* Englewood Cliffs, N.J.: Prentice-Hall.

Keynes, J.M. 1936. *The General Theory of Employment, Interest, and Money.* New York: Harcourt, Brace, and World.

Kohler, E. 1952. *A Dictionary for Accountants.* Englewood Cliffs, N.J.: Prentice-Hall.

Koopmans, T.C. 1957. *Three Essays on The State of Economic Science.* New York: McGraw-Hill.

Koopmans, T.C., ed. 1951. *Activity Analysis of Production and Allocation.* New York: Wiley.

Kurosh, A.G. 1963. *Lectures on General Algebra.* New York: Chelsea.

Lang, S. 1965. *Algebra.* Reading, Mass.: Addison-Wesley.

Leontief, W.W. 1951. *The Structure of the American Economy.* New York: Oxford University Press.

MacLane, S., and Birkhoff, G. 1967. *Algebra.* New York: Macmillan.

Mattessich, R. 1958. Mathematical Models in Business Accounting. *The Accounting Review* (July) pp. 472–481.

————. 1964. *Accounting and Analytical Methods.* Homewood, Ill.: Irwin.

McKenzie, L. 1954. On Equilbrium in Graham's Model of World Trade and Other Competitive Systems. *Econometrica* 22 (April) pp. 147–161.

————. 1959. On the Existence of a General Equilibrium in a Competitive Market. *Econometrica* 27:54–71.

Mill, J.S. 1848. *Principles of Political Economy.* Donald Winch, ed. Harmondsworth: Penguin Books.

Miller, M.H., and Modigliani, F. 1961. Dividend Policy, Growth, and the Valuation of Shares. *Journal of Business* 34, no. 4 (October) pp. 411–433.

Moore, C.L., and Jaedicke, R.K. 1967. *Managerial Accounting.* Cincinnati: South-Western Publishing.

Morishima, M. 1973. *Marx's Economics.* Cambridge: Cambridge University Press.

Pacioli, L. 1494. *Summa de Arithmetica, Geometrica, Proporcioni et Proporcionalita.* Trans. by J.B. Geijsbeek as *Ancient Double-Entry Bookkeeping.* Reprinted by Houston: Scholars.

Parker, R.H., and Harcourt, G.C., eds. 1969. *Readings in the Concept and Measurement of Income.* Cambridge: Cambridge University Press.

Quirk, J., and Saposnik, R. 1968. *Introduction to General Equilibrium Theory and Welfare Economics.* New York: McGraw-Hill.

Revsine, L. 1973. *Replacement Cost Accounting.* Englewood Cliffs, N.J.: Prentice-Hall.

Samuelson, P. 1937. Some Aspects of The Pure Theory of Capital. *Quarterly Journal of Economics* LI (May) pp. 469–496. Reprinted in Samuelson (1966), pp. 161–188.

————. 1957. Wages and Interest: A Modern Dissection of Marxian Economic Models. *The American Economic Review* 47, no. 6:884–912. Reprinted in Samuelson (1966), pp. 341–369.

————. 1961. The Evaluation of "Social Income": Capital Formation and Wealth. In *The Theory of Capital.* F.A. Lutz and D.C. Hague, eds., pp. 32–57. London: Macmillan. Reprinted in Samuelson (1966), pp. 299–318.

————. 1966. *The Collected Scientific Papers of Paul A. Samuelson Vol. I.* J. Stiglitz, ed. Cambridge, Mass.: MIT Press.

————. 1967. The Monopolistic Competition Revolution. In *Monopolistic Competition Theory: Studies in Impact.* R.E. Kuenne, ed., pp. 105–138. New York: Wiley. Reprinted in Samuelson (1972), pp. 18–51.

————. 1972. *The Collected Scientific Papers of Paul A. Samuelson Vol. III.* Robert C. Merton, ed. Cambridge, Mass.: MIT Press.

————. 1976. *Economics.* 10th ed. New York: McGraw-Hill.

Shank, J.K. 1972. *Matrix Methods in Accounting*. Reading, Mass.: Addison-Wesley.

Sprouse, R., and Moonitz, M. 1962. *ARS No. 3: A Tentative Set of Broad Accounting Principles for Business Enterprises*. New York: American Institute of Certified Public Accountants.

Sterling, Robert R. 1970. *Theory of the Measurement of Enterprise Income*. Houston: Scholars.

Stonier, A.W., and Hague, D.C. 1973. *A Textbook in Economic Theory*. 4th ed. New York: Wiley.

von Neumann, J. 1935. Über ein Ökonomisches Gleichungssystem und eine Verallgemeinerung des Brouwerschen Fixpundtsatzes. In *Ergebnisse eines Mathematischen Kolloquiums*. no. 8. Translated as A Model of General Equilibrium. *Review of Economic Studies* 13, no. 1:1–9.

Weston, J.F., and Brigham, E.F. 1971. *Essentials of Managerial Finance*. New York: Holt, Rinehart, and Winston.

Williams, T.H. and Griffin, C.H. 1964. *The Mathematical Dimension of Accountancy*. Cincinnati: South-Western.

Zeff, S.A., and Keller, T.F., eds. 1973. *Financial Accounting Theory I: Issues and Controversies*. New York: McGraw-Hill.

Index

About the Author

David P. Ellerman received the B.S. from Massachusetts Institute of Technology; the M.A. in philosophy of science and in economics, and the Ph.D. in mathematics from Boston University. He has taught both mathematics and economics in those departments at Boston University, and economics at the University of Massachusetts, Boston. Currently, he is teaching in the Accounting Department of the Boston College School of Management. He is also staff economist of the Industrial Cooperative Association, a non-profit consulting firm for worker cooperatives. He has published papers, or is currently conducting research, in a number of fields such as mathematics, economics, accounting, legal theory, political economy, and philosophy. The research themes include descriptive and normative property theory, democratic theory, the legal and capital structure for worker self-managed firms, the mathematics of arbitrage, accounting theory, and mathematical accounting.